Witchcraft and the Act of 1604

Studies in Medieval and Reformation Traditions

Edited by

Andrew Colin Gow

Edmonton, Alberta

In cooperation with

Thomas A. Brady, Jr., Berkeley, California
Sylvia Brown, Edmonton, Alberta
Berndt Hamm, Erlangen
Johannes Heil, Heidelberg
Susan C. Karant-Nunn, Tucson, Arizona
Martin Kaufhold, Augsburg
Jürgen Miethke, Heidelberg
M.E.H. Nicolette Mout, Leiden

Founded by

Heiko A. Oberman †

VOLUME 131

Witchcraft and the Act of 1604

Edited by

John Newton and Jo Bath

BRILL

LEIDEN • BOSTON
2008

On the cover: Woodcut from an eighteenth century chapbook edition of "The Witch of the Woodlands; or, the Cobler's New Translation", by LP, first published in 1655 (London, n.d.).

This book is printed on acid-free paper.

Library of Congress Cataloging-in-Publication Data

Witchcraft and the Act of 1604 / edited by John Newton and Jo Bath.
  p. cm. — (Studies in medieval and Reformation traditions; v. 131)
Based on a conference held in Mar. 2004 at St. John's College, Durham.
Includes bibliographical references and index.
ISBN 978-90-04-16528-1 (hardback: alk. paper) 1. Great Britain. Act against conjuration, witchcraft and dealing with evil and wicked spirits—Congresses. 2. Witchcraft—England—History—16th century—Congresses. 3. Witchcraft—England—History—17th century—Congresses. I. Newton, John. II. Bath, Jo.
  KD7852.W5W58 2008
  345.42'0288—dc22

                  2008004205

ISSN 1573-4188
ISBN 978 90 04 16528 1

CONTENTS

PART THREE

THE PASSING OF THE ACT

ACKNOWLEDGEMENTS

The original idea for a volume of essays based on the Witchcraft Act of 1604 grew out of a conference held at St. John's College, Durham, in March 2004, to mark the 500th anniversary of the legislation. About half of the essays in this collection have grown from papers presented at that time. With regards to the conference I must make special mention of Dr Richard Maber, who was at the time Director of the University of Durham's interdisciplinary Centre for Seventeenth-Century Studies, for letting me organise the event under the Centre's auspices. This volume reflects the tradition of inter-disciplinary enquiry which the Centre, and particularly Dr. Maber, fostered at Durham over many years. I would particularly like to thank the Society for Renaissance Studies who co-sponsored the event; and on a more practical note, Rosalind Webber, who did a splendid job with registration and administration.

A volume such as this is the sum of its parts. I must thank all the contributors who, in providing those parts, facilitated the smooth process of editing this volume; and also Dr. Guido Giglioni of the Warburg Institute who, when asked to look over my own translation of Canon 72, basically provided me with a new translation which was far superior to my own. I must also pour out my gratitude on my long suffering friend and co-editor, Jo Bath (although I'm sure she would much rather I poured out chocolate rather than gratitude). Without her the volume would have been poorer and not as much fun.

With all the things that went wrong at the last minute I must make grateful mention my mother, who kindly allowed me to use her computer when my own decided to stop working. My introduction for this book was on the hard disk at the time. Fortunately the rest of the book was on Jo's computer at that point. Finally, I must thank God who did seem to hear my prayers when I was in a tight corner, although not always in the way one might expect. *Ad Majoram Dei Gloriam.*

John Newton

NOTES ON CONTRIBUTORS

Jo Bath is a Research Associate in the Open University's Department of the History of Science, Technology and Medicine. She is also the Oral History Archivist at Beamish Museum in County Durham. Her published papers include "'In the Devill's Likenesse': Interpretation and Confusion in Popular Ghost Belief" in *Early Modern Ghosts* (Durham University, 2002), and "County Keeping, Corruption, and the Courts in the Early-Eighteenth-Century Borders: The Feud of William Charlton and William Lowes" in *Northern History* 40 (2003). Committed to widening access to history to a wider audience, she was commissioned to produce *Dancing with the Devil* (Tyne Bridge, 2003), a popular history of witchcraft in the region.

Jonathan Barry is Associate Professor of History and Head of the School of Humanities and Social Sciences at the University of Exeter. He has published extensively on society, culture and religion in early modern provincial towns, especially Bristol. He has co-edited two volumes on the history of witchcraft (*Witchcraft in Early Modern Europe* (Cambridge University Press, 1996) and *Palgrave Advances in Witchcraft Historiography* (Palgrave, 2007)) and is an editor of Palgrave's new 'Cultures of Magic' series. He is preparing a volume of his essays on witchcraft and demonology in south-western England *c.* 1640–1800.

Roy Booth is a Senior Lecturer in the English Department at Royal Holloway College, University of London. His research interests include sixteenth- and seventeenth-century poetry and drama, and he teaches an undergraduate course, 'Witchcraft and Drama 1576–1642'. His web presence includes 'Early Modern Whale', his academic blog at www.roy25booth.blogspot.com/.

Christopher Brooks is an Associate Professor of British Literature at Wichita State University. He has published articles about such figures as Samuel Johnson, Oliver Goldsmith, Samuel Richardson, as well as the gothic genre. He has presented papers on apparitions, ghosts, witches, and most recently on John Polidori's *The Vampyre*. He is currently engaged in a study of the monstrous and supernatural in early English literature and culture.

OWEN DAVIES is Reader in Social History at the University of Hertford-shire. He has published widely on the history of witchcraft and magic in eighteenth- and nineteenth-century England. He is the author of *Witchcraft, Magic and Culture 1736–1951* (Manchester University Press, 1999), *A People Bewitched* (1999) and *Cunning-Folk: Popular Magic in English History* (2003). His most recent book is *Murder, Magic, Madness: The Victorian Trials of Dove and the Wizard* (2005).

MALCOLM GASKILL is Reader in Early Modern History in the School of History, University of East Anglia. An authority on the history of witchcraft, crime and the law 1500–1800, he is the author of *Crime and Mentalities in Early Modern England* (2000), *Hellish Nell: Last of Britain's Witches* (2001), and *Witchfinders: A Seventeenth-Century English Tragedy* (2005). He is currently writing a *Very Short Introduction to Witchcraft* for Oxford University Press, while researching a book on mentalities in seventeenth-century English America.

MARION GIBSON is the programme leader in English at the University of Exeter's Tremough campus. Her research focuses on representations of witchcraft and magic in literature from the Renaissance to the Eight-eenth Century. Dr. Gibson's books include: *Reading Witchcraft* (Routledge, 1999), *Early Modern Witchcraft* (Routledge, 2000), *Witchcraft and Society in England and America 1550–1750* (Cornell University Press/Continuum, 2003), and *Possession, Puritanism and Print* (Pickering and Chatto, 2006). She also edited a facsimile edition of six key trial pamphlets, in the series *English Witchcraft 1558–1736* (Pickering and Chatto, 2003).

CLIVE HOLMES, having taught at Cambridge and Cornell Universities, is now a Fellow of Lady Margaret Hall, Oxford. He is the author of a number of books and articles on the Civil War, on administrative history in the seventeenth century, and on social history—including witchcraft—in the same period.

P.G. MAXWELL-STUART is a Lecturer in the Department of Modern History in the University of St Andrews. His particular field is the study of the occult sciences and witchcraft during the late Mediaeval and Early Modern periods. His most recent publications are *Witch Hunters, The Occult in Mediaeval Europe*, and an edited translation of the *Malleus Maleficarum*. He is currently engaged on a history of alchemy, and the third volume of his history of magic and witchcraft in Scotland.

JOHN NEWTON undertook post-graduate research at the universities of Durham and Oxford into supernatural beliefs in the sixteenth and seventeenth centuries. He was awarded his PhD from Durham in 2004. While doing his doctoral work he edited *Early Modern Ghosts* (2002). He has published various articles, most recently "'Sensible Proof of Spirits": Ghost Belief during the Later Seventeenth Century' (with Jo Bath) in *Folklore* 116 (2006).

TOM WEBSTER is a lecturer in early modern British history at the University of Edinburgh. He is the author of *Godly Clergy in Early Stuart England: the Caroline Puritan Movement, c. 1620–1643*, introduced and edited *The Diary of Samuel Rogers 1634–1638* for the Church of England Record Society (2004) and co-edited with Frank Bremer and contributed to an encyclopaedia, *Puritans and Puritanism in Europe and America* which was included in the Choice Outstanding Academic Titles list for 2006. His interests include religion in history, philosophy of history and he is currently working on an exploration of ways of understanding possession in early modern England.

INTRODUCTION

INTRODUCTION

WITCHCRAFT; WITCH CODES; WITCH ACT*

John Newton

A Witch is one who woorketh by the Devill, or by some develish or curious art, either hurting or healing, revealing thinges secrete, or foretelling
thinges to come, which the devil hath devised to entangle and snare mens
soules withal unto damnation.
George Gifford, *Concerning the Subtle Practises of Devils* (London, 1587),
sig. Bii.

A witch is a person that hath conference with the Devil to take counsel
or to do some act.
Edward Coke, *The Third Part of the Institutes of the Laws of England* (London, 1628), p. 44.

[A] Witch is one, who can do or seems to do strange things, beyond the
known power of Art and ordinary Nature, by vertue of a Confederacy
with Evil Spirits.
Joseph Glanvill, *Saducismus Triumphatus* (London, 1681), Part 2, p. 4.

Over the course of almost a century these three writers gave three fairly
consistent definitions of what a witch was and did. They shared certain
codes, certain interpretative practices, that allowed them to provide an
apparently fixed view of the nature of witchcraft. Yet 'witch' is a word,
a linguistic sign, and while it may appear to refer to something fixed and
definite this semantic stability is deceptive. The linguistic sign consists
of the signifier (the part one reads or hears) and the signified (what the
signifier means to us). The signifier is potentially capable of relating to
several different signifieds simultaneously, as well as meaning different
things to different people. Indeed the signifier is a nexus, diachronically
capable of connecting to an array of different images or concepts, and
synchronically evolving as the discourse of the culture develops.[1] As

---

* I would like to thank Jo Bath, Aaron Urbanzyk, and the readers at Brill for their
useful comments on earlier versions of this paper.
[1] At this point it is necessary to acknowledge Stuart Clark's pioneering use of semiotics as a way of approaching witchcraft. See *Thinking with Demons: The Idea of Witchcraft
in Early Modern Europe* (Oxford: Oxford University Press, 1997).

codes change so the relationship between signifier and signified shifts revealing new significations.

From the cultural discourse come codes that govern understanding. Out of these wider social codes we might isolate the specific codes that shape belief in witchcraft, and the Act of 1604 can be regarded as a refinement of certain key elements within these codes. The Act represented not the totality of those codes, so much as a matrix that fixed the meaning of certain elements which might otherwise have remained undetermined in the wider discourse. Significantly, this matrix was legitimated by the civil authorities; it provided a state sanctioned shorthand of the most important codes that circulated within society in 1604. Although the social energies which constitute the codes could not be restrained by the Act's limits, they were subsequently shaped by the elements it enshrined. The Act then represented the government's approbation of certain elements in the wider discourse. It is the loudest voice in a polyvocal exchange about the nature of witchcraft.

Monty Alexander identifies three sets of codes which operate within a culture: residual codes, which "are leftovers from an earlier set of cultural values and usages"; dominant codes, which are "the codes of the present day"; and emergent codes,

> [which] are not yet fully formed, so to speak, they are signposts to the future as it is now approaching over the cultural horizon [...] they are today still experimental, often tentative, sometimes outrageous when seen through 'dominant eyes'. But each of them is currently jockeying for a pole position and one of them is at least set to achieve dominance tomorrow.[2]

In 1603 there were, in addition to the established dominant codes, several emergent codes for witchcraft vying for approbation. The legal—and ecclesiastical—instruments of 1604 settled this struggle by legitimating or delegitimating the competing codes. Yet the structure of language is not hermeneutically sealed, it evolves as ideas are debated and refined, as the underlying paradigm gradually grows and shifts. After 1604 there were still nuances of interpretation, and different approaches to witchcraft were continuing to emerge, that would in turn vie for dominance.

---

[2] Monty Alexander, "Codes and Contexts: Practical Semiotics for the Qualitative Researcher" <www.semioticsolutions.ccm/ref.aspx/id=78> [Accessed 17/03/06].

The papers in this volume examine either the codes that led to the formulation of the 1604 legislation, or those that circulated after the Act until its repeal in 1736. Although the papers' authors would not employ this sort of terminology or approach, nevertheless, all of them explore different aspects of these shifts in the socio-cultural framework of the period, whether the influences on the Act, the influences the Act had, or the different ways in which it was used, engaged with, or even simply ignored by those who came into contact with what they labelled as 'witchcraft'. Many of the essays in this volume interlock or enter into dialogue with each other, complimenting, contrasting, and occasionally even conflicting with the points of view in other papers. My own introductory paper will touch on some of the ways that these individual essays dialogue with each other. However, I do not anticipate all the ways in which there arguments might mesh. I merely attempt to sketch a hypothetical framework in order to examine some aspects of how the codes concerning witchcraft shifted, with particular reference to the Acts, and also attempt to highlight how some of the research presented here elucidates aspects of these processes.

Significations of Witchcraft

The discourse of the early-modern England was saturated by the Bible, and the law of God provided a point of reference for the law of the land (the Witchcraft Act of 1563 had described the purposes of those who worked *maleficia* as "contrarye to the Lawes of Almighty God").[3] It was also the starting point from which writers would attempt to trace the "significations and etymologies" of witchcraft and its related terms.[4] Yet the Scriptures did not necessarily provide a straightforward guide to such phenomena. Henry Holland pointed out that the Bible used a variety of terms to describe different "sorts" of witches.[5] A number of different Hebrew terms were used in the Old Testament to denote

---

[3] This is a brief précis of the passage, for the actual text see Appendix I.

[4] King James uses this phrase in the chapter headings of the *Daemonologie* in Book 1, ch. 3 and Book 2, ch. 2.

[5] Eight different kinds of witches are described in the Hebrew according to Holland. See *A Treatise Against Witchcraft* (Cambridge, 1590), sig. B4–D4v. Facsimile of the same in *English Witchcraft, 1560–1736*, 6 vols, ed. by James Sharpe and Richard M. Golden (London: Pickering and Chatto, 2003), I: *Early English Demonological Works*, ed. by James Sharpe, pp. 17–33.

various magical practices, and since translators rendered these into English in different ways this was a complex matter. Even the King James Bible, which took a more consistent approach to rendering these terms into the vernacular than other versions, did not always use the same English word when translating the original text. So *kasaf*, which was usually given as "witch", became "sorcerer" in Exodus 7.11 and Malachi 3.5. This was almost certainly because of a conviction on the part of the translators that another term fitted better in context, but it demonstrates that words were potentially unstable, and their meanings open to dispute. Demonologists were acutely aware of the potential gap between what 'witch' signified in scripture, and what it might signify in early-modern England. Faced with this situation of hermeneutic indeterminacy Holland went so far as to deny that the common usage of 'witch' had any correlation to the practitioners of magic described in Scripture.[6] With a more pragmatic application in mind, the infamous Reginald Scot used it to argue that the crimes which were tried as witchcraft in England should not be seen as related,[7] and by extension that the Biblical call for the death of witches should not be applied to cases tried under English law.

Yet the relationship of 'witch' to cognate terms was open to debate. While before the Act (in 1548 and 1594 respectively) Thomas Elyot and William West tried to extricate 'magician' from the unlawful connotations of witchcraft (albeit for different reasons), after the Act William Perkins, John Barrett and Thomas Cooper regarded 'witch' and 'magician' as synonymous.[8] Cooper affirmed that a "Witch is a Magitician, who, either by open or secret league, wittingly and willingly, consenteth to use the aide of the devil in working of wonders." Feeling this needed further qualification he went on to add, "A *Magitian* I say, to signifie that she professeth and practiseth this Art, *Actes* 8.9. For that is the generall

---

[6] Holland, sig. A4. (*English Witchcraft, 1560–1736*, I, p. 10).

[7] Reginald Scot, *The Discoverie of Witchcraft*, ed. by Montague Summers (New York: Dover, 1972). From book six onwards (with the exceptions of eight and fourteen) Scot considers a different word in the first chapter of each book, and goes on to examine that type of witchcraft, or broadly related issues, in the rest of the book. The words considered are *Chassaph* (Book 6), *Ob* (7), *Onen* (10), *Nahas* (11), *Habar* (12), *Hartumim* (13), *Idoni* (15). Cf. Holland sig. B4–D4v, cited above.

[8] This may be related to the Authorised Version's use of 'magician' to translate one of the words otherwise rendered as 'witch' (*Idoni*) when it had not been used in previous translations. See David H. Darst with Steven L. Jeffers, 'Wizards and Magicians in the King James Old Testament' in *The Seventeenth Century*, 6 (1991), 1–10 (pp. 5–6).

name to all such as practise these unlawfull Arts".[9] Cooper believed
he had a biblical precedent for yoking together the two linguistic signs.
Given that the meaning of 'witch' was, to a certain extent, determined
by the way it was used there remained something undetermined about
the word. This can be seen in the ambivalence of terms such as 'white
witch' or 'good witch'. Among the common people this signified one
who worked beneficial magic, such as curing sick cattle, without recourse
to Satan. Other epithets were used in different localities, such as 'blessers'
or 'cunning folk', and this may reflect a desire to avoid any potential
connotation of witchcraft, or even a separation in terms of classification
between this class of practitioners and those who used *maleficium*.[10] For
many learned writers this was an artificial distinction and they would
have concurred with Cooper's assessment that all such practices resulted
from a "league with the devil".[11] This confounding of all magical terms
meant that in effect all such words were part of a nebulous set of terms
in which related signifiers were potentially interchangeable. It was all
too easy to fall foul of this sort of linguistic indeterminacy, as we can
see in the case of the cunning man Edmund Hartley.[12] Hartley had
successfully ministered to the children of the Starkey household, after
they suffered fits ascribed to possession. However, he was dismissed by
Nicholas Starkey, after demanding greater rewards for his successes, and
he then threatened that worse fits would resume. Having been initially
labelled as a cunning man Hartley was re-inscribed during subsequent
proceedings as a witch. He was accused of bewitching the children and
breathing the Devil into them. He was convicted of witchcraft and duly

---

[9] Thomas Cooper, *The Mystery of Witch-Craft* (London, 1617), p. 177. Cf. William
Perkins, *A Discourse of the Damned Art of Witchcraft* (Cambridge, 1608) pp. 167–68. Facsimile of the latter in *English Witchcraft, 1560–1736*, I, pp. 283–84.

[10] See Keith Thomas, *Religion and the Decline of Magic* (London: Penguin, 1991), pp.
517 ff; James Sharpe, *Instruments of Darkness: Witchcraft in England 1550–1750* (London:
Hamish Hamilton, 1996), pp. 70–71; and Owen Davies, *Cunning-Folk: Popular Magic in
English History* (London: Hambledon and London, 2003), pp. 29–35. It is also worth
noting that one of the epithets, 'charmer' (which is the term Perkins usually employs),
was covered by the Acts of 1563 and 1604. It is also found some versions of the Bible
(including the Authorised Version) to describe prohibited magical practices (Deuter-
onomy 18.11 and Isaiah 19.3).

[11] Cooper, p. 211. Italics removed. See also Holland, sig. F4; Perkins, pp. 174–78.
Facsimile of both in *English Witchcraft, 1560–1736*, I, pp. 49, 290–94.

[12] Tom Webster examines the case in some depth in his paper '(Re)possession of
Dispossession: John Darrell and Diabolical Discourse', in this volume, pp. 91–111.

hung.[13] Once one was associated with magical practices it was easy for the signifier attached to a cunning man or woman to shift to that of witch in certain circumstances. A cunning person might all too easily be relabelled with a far more dangerous signifier.[14]

There remained something inconclusive about the word 'witch'. For George Gifford, as for others, 'witch' was a catch-all category: "The conjuror, the enchanter, the sorcerer, the diviner, and whatsoever other sort there is, are in deede compassed within this circle."[15] For Scot it was an etymological nonsense, a distillation of certain historical categories (many of which he saw as trickery) which were anachronistically applied to contemporary beliefs. Yet even if there was something undetermined about the linguistic sign there was shared linguistic ground between Gifford and Scot. Both used the word witch, both shared its definition in common usage: it signified one who worked supernatural feats by satanic aid. The difference, as Stephen Greenblatt has noted, is that Scot ultimately attempted "to locate these beliefs not *in* but *as* the imagination."[16] Beyond any discussion about the roots of the various signifiers Scot refused to admit the potency of satanic power to achieve the feats attributed to it. Greenblatt makes a useful distinction when he characterises Scot's view of witchcraft as an illusion of fantasy in which one *believed* they possessed supernatural abilities. Nevertheless, we must note that despite Scot's view of all these phenomena as trickery or fantasy he shared the underlying assumption that in common parlance the word 'witch' signified one who could do all these things. That he saw them as feats of imagination instead of reality does not alter this. In trying to challenge such notions he affirmed the existence of a common set

---

[13] John Darrell, *A True Narration of the Strange and Grevous Vexation by the Devil, of 7. Persons in Lancashire, and William Somers of Nottingham* ([np], 1600), p. 1; George More, *A True Discourse concerning the Certaine Possession and Disposessio[n] of 7 persons in one familie in Lancashire* ([np], 1660), p. 14.

[14] Jo Bath equally points out that a reputation for cunning magic among marginal women in the North East could lead to accusations of *maleficia*. See 'The Treatment of Potential Witches in North-East England, *c.* 1649–1680' in this volume, pp. 131 ff.

[15] George Gifford, *Concerning the Subtle Practises of Devils* (London, 1587), sig. Bii.

[16] Stephen Greenblatt, 'Shakespeare Bewitched' in *New Historical Literary Study: Essays on Reproducing Texts, Representing History*, ed. by Jeffrey N. Cox and Larry J. Reynolds (Princeton: Princeton University Press, 1993), pp. 108–35 (p. 114). Italics mine. See extract from Scot, 'To the readers' in *Witchcraft and Society in England and America, 1550–1705*, ed. by Marion Gibson (London: Continuum, 2003), p. 81. Note this is lacking in the Dover edition of the *Discoverie*.

of significations. He affirmed that he shared the same essential codes for interpreting and understanding witchcraft as his opponents.

The Act of 1604 affirmed many of the dominant codes that were already shared within society. Indeed, it did more than that, in some cases it approbated codes which had been more marginal, essentially emergent in nature, and legitimated their role in the discourse of witchcraft. It functioned as a *point de caption*, where the meaning of the chain of signs is 'sealed', locking signifier and signified in a stable relationship. Perhaps with an eye to possible linguistic objections of the type Elyot or West had employed, it provided a list of synonyms for the crime, forbidding the use of "Witchcraft, Inchantment, Charme, or Sorcery". It certainly appears that, like Gifford, the Act was affirming a catch-all category, which encompassed all related practises.[17] However, this chain of words, which apparently tries to tie these signs together, was found in the Act of 1563, and had not prevented the debates outlined above, which are only a few illustrations of those published. Ambiguity could not be completely eliminated. Neither of the Acts could entirely fix the significations of witchcraft. Lacan suggests that the stability provided by a *point de caption* is illusory.[18] Certainly it is accurate to say that it only provides a momentary fixing before the shifting currents of the discourse potentially manoeuvre it into a redefinition. There remained something indeterminate about the words and terms used in the Act of 1604, which later writers exploited. Indeed Edward Coke's intriguing attempt to fix the meaning of "Witchcraft, Inchantment, Charme" and "Sorcery" in *The Institutes of the Laws of England* reads like an attempt to re-seal the accepted meanings, and reaffirm the accepted reading of the Act. Despite his very firm affirmation that such crimes have occurred he gives idiosyncratic definitions of the terms (which he turns into common nouns), the first two of which he associates with the devil, and the last of which he sees as receiving all the biblical references. He tries to settle the meanings of the words within the accepted sense, yet his definitions are ultimately provisional for all the authority both he and his text assume. Yet he does anchor the Act into a historic continuum whereby this is one expression, albeit the latest and most refined, of a consistent legislative approach to the crime of witchcraft.

---

[17] See Gifford, above.
[18] Jacques Lacan, *Écrits: A Selection*, trans. by Alan Sheridan (London: Tavistock Publications, 1977), p. 303 ff.

There are different ways of viewing the relationship between the Act
of 1604 and its immediate predecessor. Marion Gibson points out the
continuity with the Act of 1563, and the subtle nature of the changes
which were introduced in 1604. This analysis would have found favour
with the author of *An Advertisement to the Jury-Men of England*, who saw
it as the generally the same, "only the penalties have a little altered."[19]
This assessment is shared by Clive Holmes who describes it as a "slight
modification" of its predecessor.[20] Malcolm Gaskill on the other hand
refers to it as "significantly different [...because i]n theory, at least,
witchcraft was no longer just a sin of ill-will connected to misfortune,
but a blacker and more vivid crime of demonism, apostasy and conspiracy."[21] Sharpe similarly notes how the "1604 statute saw a shift
from *maleficium* as the main matter of witchcraft legislation". He cites
Wallace Notestein on the shift towards the familiar as the central form
of evidence in witchcraft trials: "one of the things which the framers of
the statute were attempting to accomplish [...] was to make the fact of
witchcraft as a felony depend chiefly upon a single form of evidence,
the testimony to the use of evil spirits".[22] While many of the codes we
find in the act of 1604 come directly from its predecessor of 1563,
others (such as the familiar) reflect English thought on the subject in
the years that preceded the new legislation. The answer to why certain
codes were included or excluded is one that lies in the genesis of the
statue's composition.

The Crucible of the Act

The role that King James VI & I played in the development of a new
Act is significant, but not the one he has traditionally been portrayed as
playing. Although earlier historians depicted him as imposing a statute
which reflected the harsher Scottish legislation, as part of a personal
campaign against witchcraft, there is no evidence for the King having a

---

[19] [Robert Filmer], *An Advertisement to the Jury-Men of England* (London, 1653), p. 2.
[20] Clive Holmes, 'Witchcraft and Possession at the Accession of James I: The Publication of Samuel Harsnett's *A Declaration of Egregious Popish Impostures*' in this volume,
p. 88.
[21] Malcolm Gaskill, 'Witchcraft, Emotion and Imagination in the English Civil War'
in this volume, p. 162.
[22] Sharpe, p. 91; Wallace Notestein, *A History of Witchcraft in England from 1558 to
1718*, cited in Sharpe, p. 91.

direct hand in the Act.[23] Indeed, the harsher aspect of Scots law (such as consulting a witch constituting a felony) are entirely lacking from the English statute.[24] More recent historians have come to the conclusion that this reputation as a witch hunter is ill-deserved, even though it continues to permeate popular narratives about the King.[25]

So, on one hand we must be cautious about directly ascribing the Act to James, lest we appear to be veering back to older notions of it as part of a determined campaign against witchcraft of the King's part. One the other hand, if we can take James's words about legislation at face value, then we have good reason to consider he saw all statutes—including this one—as his. In his speech of 21 March 1610 he stressed that kings, not lawyers, antiquity, or even parliaments made laws.[26] His theory of kingship placed him at the centre of the legislative machinery, and identified him as the sole arbiter of government whose signature alone could pass bills into law. However, rhetoric apart we lack evidence of James's direct involvement, other than his final approval when he signed it into law. Although, conversely, we have no evidence that he did not have some role, however indirect, either in the introduction of a new bill, or in its revision after it was introduced into the Lords. There may be lost conversations in palace corridors which firmly connect James with the substance of this law. However, we know of no such conversations, and to make any suggestion either way would be nothing more than speculation. P.G. Maxwell-Stuart sees it as "unlikely [...] that the drafting and passage of the 1604 Act owed anything in particular to James's direct request or intervention, although one can expect him to have taken an interest in it once the proposal for redrafting had actually been made."[27] What we can confidently

---

[23] For example, see R. Trevor Davies, *Four Centuries of Witch Beliefs* (London: Methuen, 1947), and (to some degree) Hugh Trevor-Roper, *The European Witch-Craze of the Sixteenth and Seventeenth Century* (London: Penguin, 1969).

[24] The 1563 Scots Act is given in *Witchcraft in Early Modern Scotland: James VI's Demonology and the North Berwick Witches*, ed. by Lawrence Normand and Gareth Roberts (Exeter: Exeter University Press, 2000), p. 89.

[25] See Sharpe, pp. 47–50.

[26] James VI & I, *Political Writings*, ed. by Johann P. Sommerville (Cambridge: Cambridge University Press, 1994), p. 183. Cited in Johann P. Sommerville, 'The Ancient Constitution Reassessed: The Common Law, the Court and the Languages of Politics in Early Modern England' in *The Stuart Court and Europe: Essays in Politics and Popular Culture*, ed. by R. Malcolm Smutts (Cambridge: Cambridge University Press, 1996), pp. 39–64 (p. 60).

[27] P.G. Maxwell-Stuart, 'King James's Experience of Witches, and the 1604 Witchcraft Act' in this volume, p. 40.

suggest is that the arrival of the new King raised interest in James's demonological writings making it an opportune time for a new bill on this theme to be raised. With his ascension came the usual interest in royal ephemera and related merchandise which we still see connected with major royal events today. Many of James's works were put to the press in 1603, as England became fascinated by the character of its new King,[28] and the *Daemonologie* went through two editions that year, presumably proving more interesting to readers than his treatises on kingship.[29] It is probable that James's writings engendered a climate in which certain codes (such as the Calvinist concept of a covenant with the devil as the central and defining feature of witchcraft) became acceptable, whereas previously they might have been seen as more marginal.[30]

Any interest in witchcraft that came with the coronation built on the fact that King James was already associated with *maleficia* in the minds of his English subjects. *Newes from Scotland* (1591) had chronicled the attempts of Doctor Fian and his coven to attempt to takes the King's life.[31] P.G. Maxwell-Stuart proposes that the pamphlet would have made a "particular impact" upon his English subjects.[32] No doubt the events at North Berwick must have been read as a challenge to established political and religious order in James's original kingdom. *Newes* depicts the gathering of the witches as a parody of a Presbyterian service, stressing the idea of an inverted, demonic covenant. As befitted an inversion of Christian rites the Devil adopted the role of the minister and, as preaching was central to Presbyterian worship, preached to

---

[28] See Jenny Wormald, 'James VI & I, *Basilikon Doron* and *The Trew Law of Free Monarchies*: The Scottish Context and the English Translation' in *The Mental World of the Jacobean Court*, ed. by Linda Levy Pack (Cambridge: Cambridge University Press, 1991), 36–54.

[29] Sharpe, p. 48. For more on the textual and printing history of the *Daemonologie* see *Witchcraft in Early Modern Scotland*, pp. 11 ff.

[30] Indeed, there was often negotiation between James and his subjects, whereby his written words would be quoted back to him in an attempt at political positioning. See James Doelman, '"A King of Thine Heart": The English Reception of King James VI and I's *Basilikon Doron*' in *The Seventeenth Century*, 9 (1994), 1–9 (pp. 3–5).

[31] For an introduction to the North Berwick trials see P. G. Maxwell-Stuart, 'The Fear of the King is Death: James VI and the Witches of East Lothian', in *Fear in Early Modern Society*, ed. by W. G. Naphy and Penny Roberts (Manchester: Manchester University Press, 1997) 209–25. For the most important recent interpretations of the North Berwick trials see the whole of Normand and Roberts, *Witchcraft in Early Modern Scotland*; and P. G. Maxwell-Stuart, *Satan's Conspiracy: Magic and Witchcraft in Sixteenth-Century Scotland* (East Lothian: Tuckwell Press, 2001), especially pp. 142–80.

[32] Maxwell-Stuart, in this volume p. 31.

his congregation from the pulpit.[33] Stressing the idea of a demonic covenant the author of *Newes* located the witches within what might be described as the characteristic scheme of Calvinist theology, predestination. In strictly predestinatory terms they are described as "vessels of God's wrath"—the reprobate, chosen by God for destruction.[34] Gibson argues that the covenant with the devil was one of the aspects which the godly stressed in their writings of witchcraft:

> Godly groups [...] felt themselves to be enacting a covenant with God. A blasphemous parody of that was what the Act [of 1604] represented as the central transgression of witches. It was perhaps unsurprising that covenant was specifically described in the legislation now, as a capital crime in its own right, by the new Scottish king—who was well acquainted with godly and especially Scottish Presbyterian conceptions of covenant, and under pressure from English godly to move closer to these in his ecclesiastical policy.[35]

However, this must be balanced against the observations of Clive Holmes who suggests that the new emphases in the Act "did not answer the concerns of those godly divines, like Gifford and Perkins, who thought the law too lenient".[36] It seems that while the Act may not have gone as far as many divines had wanted it did, nevertheless, go in a direction that they approved of. One might propose that the term could be accepted as respectable, even entering English law, because of its association with the King: even though the *Daemonologie* speaks of a "contract" instead of a "covenant" the idea is the same. Yet we should pause to consider that while the word "covenant" appears in the act it is not further defined. This left (potentially problematic) scope for speculation about its *significance*. Did it cover the witchmark, sometimes held to be an essential feature of the covenant? Questions of this nature remained open and would be the occasion for debate as the century progressed.

In the Act of 1604 the keeping of familiar spirits was made a felony for the first time. (Familiar spirits were mentioned, and examined at

---

[33] See *Daemonologie* in *Witchcraft in Early Modern Scotland*, 353–425 (p. 386).

[34] See *Newes from Scotland* in *Witchcraft in Early Modern Scotland*, 309–24 (p. 323). See also Romans 9.22. These ideas are found in other sources in the period, such as the sermon by William Perkins that became chapter eleven of his *Discourse of the Damned Art of Witchcraft*. Perkins, pp. 41 ff. Facsimile of the same in *English Witchcraft 1560–1736*, I, pp. 157 ff.

[35] Marion Gibson, 'Applying the Act of 1604' p. 118 of this volume.

[36] Holmes, p. 88.

some length, in the *Daemonologie*.)[37] However, it could be argued that this was not so much a case of learned ideas about witchcraft being distilled into the legislation, as one of the law incorporating certain assumptions that had been current in English thought for around half a century. James Sharpe suggests that the origin of the belief in familiar spirits lay in the image of a ritual magician being assisted by a demonic spirit in his occult operations,[38] while Emma Wilby suggests that fairy beliefs may have played a part in the emergence of the familiar from a complex web of elite and popular notions.[39] Whatever their origins, two of the earliest surviving witchcraft pamphlets, *The Examination and confession of certaine Wytches at Chensforde* and *The Examination of John Walsh* (both published forty years before the Act, in 1566) featured familiars as part of the narrative about the activities of the alleged witches. "As can be see with familiars, the demonic pact and the sabbat, what might have originated as an elite concept could be incorporated into popular thinking about witches, but was frequently changed in the process."[40] There a degree of acculturation and adaptation of these beliefs—almost certainly in part via a developing oral tradition—and they evolved to become one of the defining features of seventeenth-century witchcraft testimonies. The Act codified and legitimated these existing beliefs and gave them weight in law, making them punishable as offences in their own right. This gave writers further authority to affirm the presence of these phenomena as part of witchcraft and concretize them as a definite legal reality. Michael Dalton advised JPs that the two most important forms of proof in cases of alleged witchcraft were the witchmark and the familiar: "These [...] are [the] maine points to discover and convict these witches; for they prove fully that those witches have a familiar, and made a league with the devil."[41] In Dalton's mind the essence of the crime consisted of the two new additions to the law in 1604, and

---

[37] *Daemonologie* (I.vi) in *Witchcraft in Early Modern Scotland*, pp. 372–76.

[38] Sharpe, pp. 71–72. A similar picture can be found in *Daemonologie* where King James considers the contract (I.vi). See *ed. cit.*, pp. 372–73.

[39] Emma Wilby, 'The Witch's Familiar and the Fairy in Early Modern England and Scotland', *Folklore*, 111 (2000), 283–305. It should be noted that Sharpe also stresses the complex interaction of elite and popular ideas in the development of the tradition.

[40] Sharpe, p. 78.

[41] Michael Dalton, *The Country Justice* (1630), cited in ibid., p. 94.

the witches he advised JPs to look for were essentially the creatures defined by the Act.[42]

However, not all the codes circulating prior to the Act found themselves being sanctioned by it. Although the Act endorsed familiar spirits it was silent on the ability of a witch to send such a spirit to possess (or obsess) an individual. This was probably a politically sensitive idea, still bound up with the recent disputes surrounding the dispossessions of John Darrell. These controversies were pivotal to debates about witchcraft prior to James's accession to the throne. Controversy erupted during Darrell's attempts to dispossess William Somers in Mansfield in 1598. Somers claimed the ability to identify all the witches in the local area, and following his information Darrell had thirteen women arrested for witchcraft.[43] Following the arrests Somers wavered between claiming imposture under Darrell's tutelage, and relapsing into fits which he professed were genuine.[44] With Darrell's activities called into question he was hauled before the Bishop of London, and his chaplain Samuel Harsnett, and eventually convicted of fraud by the High Commission.

Finding himself in an awkward position Darrell (and his supporters) appealed to the public for vindication in a series of pamphlets, which were summarily answered by his opponents. This print war culminated in the publication of Harsnett's *A Declaration of Egregious Popish Impostures* in 1603. Although it was ostensibly targeted at a group of Catholic exorcists led by William Weston it was aimed at Darrell as much as it was at the priests.[45] Harsnett associated exorcism (and dispossession) with

---

[42] This is not to say that he does not go on to supplement his description of witchcraft with features not found in the legislation, such as the corpses of those supposedly killed by witchcraft bleeding if touched by the guilty party. However the very core of his definition is that provided by the Act.

[43] D.P. Walker, *Unclean Spirits: Possession and Exorcism in France and England in the Late Sixteenth and Early Seventeenth Centuries* (London: Scolar Press, 1981), p. 63.

[44] For a summary of these events see Walker, pp. 61–73. For a more recent consideration of these events see Marion Gibson, *Possession, Puritanism and Print: Darrell, Harsnett, Shakespeare and the Elizabethan Exorcism Controversy* (London: Pickering and Chatto, 2006), pp. 72–100. For Darrell's response to the charges see John Darrell, *An Apologie, or defence of the possession of William Sommers* ([np], [nd]), fol. 28. Facsimile of the same in *English Witchcraft 1560–1736*, II, p. 229.

[45] Darrell's supporters had, to some extent, provided a rod for their own backs by complaining that the authorities were against "those that desire reform [...] whom they persecute more eagerly than papists" (*The Triall of Maist. Dorell* ([np], 1599), p. 79). The decision to re-interview Weston and his associates, which led to the composition of *A Declaration* may have been a strategic response to such criticisms.

imposture and Catholicism, and in doing so effectively silenced Darrell and his supporters. In a passage of some rhetorical force Harsnett eloquently inculcates the Puritans in his invective against the Catholics. He says that the devil is:

> As ready to cry out at the mowing of an apish wench and the lowing or bellowing of a brainlesse empty fellow, *O the glory of God: O the power of prayer*, as the Romish guls [...] cry out at the conjuration of the Exorcist, *O the Catholic faith! O the power of the faith Catholique.*[46]

In Harsnett's rhetoric "Catholic Faith" and "[Puritan] Prayer" are paradigmatic elements in a syntagmatic chain: each expression is easily substitutable for the other depending on the context. Through linguistic manoeuvrings Harsnett established Darrell and Weston as essentially carrying out the same sort of practices, and if the Catholics are shamming, the Puritans must be too.[47] He argued that any differences between the two were interchangeable elements within their discourse, as at a structural level the discourse was the same. Of course, this may not have been true, but it is how Harsnett presented the situation. "Thus the Protestant dispossessors find themselves tarred with the same brush that has disfigured their Catholic enemies and opposites."[48] No further reply could be given by Darrell, without it appearing that he was equally justifying the exorcisms of the Romish priests.

Clive Holmes points out that during this exchange Darrell's circle "sought to recruit James VI as an ally to the anti-Bancroft position".[49] Darrell had already cited the *Daemonologie* in his *Apologie* for the Nottingham case.[50] The Puritan Dispossessor presumed that the Scots King was a fellow believer in such phenomena. Yet this was not necessarily

---

[46] Samuel Harsnett, *A Declaration of Egregious Popish Impostures* in F.W. Brownlow, *Shakespeare, Harsnett, and the Devils of Denham* (Newark: University of Delaware Press, 1993), pp. 191–413 (p. 331). Indeed the whole passage where this text is taken from sets up parallels between the two groups.

[47] In some ways More had opened the dispossessors to this critique when he asserted it as the sign of the true Church: "if the Church of England have this power to cast out devils, then the Church of Rome is a false church; for there can be but one true church, the principal mark whereof (as they say) is to work miracles, and of them this is the greatest, namely to cast out devils." George More. *A True Discourse concerning the Certaine Possession and Dispossessio[n] of 7 persons in one familie in lancashire* ([np], 1600), p. 5.

[48] Brownlow, p. 74.

[49] Holmes, p. 85.

[50] Darrell, *Apologie*, fol. 12. Facsimile of the same in *English Witchcraft 1560–1736*, II, p. 195. Gibson notes that Darrell makes "virtually *verbatim* quotation" from the *Daemonologie* (p. 163).

so: Holmes draws attention to the fact that James acknowledged that Catholic exorcisms could be counterfeited, potentially allowing him to have sympathies with Harsnett's arguments. The Puritans failed to notice James's nuanced reading of the phenomenon of possession. It is notable that he considered it in the third book of the *Daemonologie*, which dealt with spirits, and not the second that dealt with witch-craft. His arguments concerning possession were principally drawn from the texts of the New Testament, where there was no association with witchcraft. Rather James asserts that the spirits of the devil will trouble people where knowledge of the Gospel is lacking.[51] There was no support for any connection between possession and witchcraft in the royal demonological treatise, and no connection between the two was outlined in the Act. The matter of possession was dealt with the new code of canon law, also promulgated in 1604, which stated that ejecting and expelling demons and evil spirits was not to be attempted without permission of the diocesan bishop. No minister was to "try to eject and expel demons and evil spirits [...] under penalty of being charged with imposture".[52] Harsentt's accusations of deception lay in wait for any minister who claimed to dispossess or exorcise in future without due authorisation.

Enactment, Influence and Repeal

While certain codes made the transition into dominant codes by becoming part of the 1604 statute, others (such as the role of witches in possession) moved into a more residual position within the discourse. The Act provided a legitimated holding matrix into which certain codes were distilled and out of which they could be drawn in order to support particular positions. Some writers unreservedly embraced the composite image of witchcraft presented in the Act and further promulgated the same codes. We see this in the drama where the visual encoding of certain formal elements reinforced the literary encoding in the spoken

---

[51] *Daemonologie* (III.iv) in *ed. cit.*, p. 415 ff.

[52] For the full text see appendix III. It is worth noting that this canon also dealt with Prophesyings: Darrell's practices closely resembled these meetings, which had so troubled the Elizabethan Church. In this context one should note Charles Odingsell's sermon that considers the casting out of devils in the context of Prophesyings. See Charles Odingsell, *Prophecying, Casting Out Of Devils, And Miracles: Briefly Discussed In Two Sermons* (London, 1619).

text. A public that had been used to classical and quasi-historical depictions of witches, such as Medea in Senecan drama and Joan of Arc in
Henry IV Part 1, was treated to witches of a more contemporary hue
after 1604. For all of *Macbeth*'s points of contact with the demonological debates of the early 1600s the play was, as Roy Booth convincingly
argues, "[r]ather restrained in its witch activity".[53] Middleton's *The
Witch* offered a protagonist which displayed many of the traits and
tropes which had been legally associated with witchcraft in 1604, to
the extent that Chris Brooks considers whether the Act represented a
new era of belief for dramatists.[54] To some degree the answer is yes,
as from depictions of witches influenced by the statute we eventually
move to trial material being adapted for the stage. In 1621 *The Witch
of Edmonton* used the pamphlet account of Elizabeth Sawyer's trial as
its source material. Apparently very popular, it was performed at court
before King James.[55] The King whose work had provided an opening
for the statute saw the codes it contained reinforced and reaffirmed
when the *The Witch of Edmonton* came to court, and so such ideas were
disseminated and transmitted through society in dramatic form, thus
conveying them to for a wider audience. While Thomas Heywood and
Richard Brome's *The Late Lancashire Witches* largely depends on folkloric
motifs these are suggested by the trial accounts, and many characters
in the play are taken from the transcripts, although the central figures
were drawn from the dramatists' imaginations. The play was fiercely
topical, being produced just after the Lancaster Assizes, while four of
the accused were still imprisoned in the Fleet.[56] One can only specu-
late whether the codes present in the drama reflected back on general
belief to the extent that they influenced the trials, but there must have
been some circulation of social energy between the various contexts
in which witchcraft was encountered.

In many of the trials it is harder to find the same direct influence we
see in the drama (even though, as we have noted, some plays were based
on trial accounts). Marion Gibson infers "that the 1604 Witchcraft Act
had little or no effect on how witchcraft was presented by the courts or

[53] Roy Booth, 'Standing within the Prospect of Belief: *Macbeth*, King James, and
Witchcraft' in this volume, p. 47.
[54] Chris Brooks, 'Witchcraft and Stage Spectacle: Spectacular Witches after 1604'
in this volume, p. 147.
[55] Montague Summers, *The History of Witchcraft [and Demonology]* (London: Senate,
[1926] 1994), p. 290.
[56] Ibid., pp. 294–95.

reported from them."[57] Witchcraft prosecutions became scarcer as the middle of the century approached, and the events in areas such as East Anglia in the 1640s were exceptional, both in terms of prosecutions, and in the skill of the witch finders in bringing both the Act and other demonological texts to bear on the crime of witchcraft.[58] However, these were isolated incidents and well into the Restoration Jo Bath finds no direct correlation between legislation and local accusations in her examination of the North East. She notes that while "the range of crimes which people tried to take to court was clearly only a subset of the crimes of the Act [...] even when the activity was believed to be malefic, people chose their own response from a much wider range of options than those suggested by the Act."[59] While the legislation mirrored many of the perceptions which existed at local level, ordinary people were seemingly concerned with a very different set of phenomena when it came to levelling charges. Although the Act forbade charms and enchantments, individuals who provided 'magical' remedies in County Durham and its surrounding areas could generally practice their trade without fear of prosecution under the legislation. Even if disputes arose it does not seems that the Act was immediately seen as the appropriate piece of legislation to have recourse to. While they accepted the efficacy of charms and potions they did not necessarily equate the production of these with the witchcraft condemned by statute.[60]

Frederick Valletta's comment that "often the criteria necessary for convicting a suspected witch were laid down not by lawyers, but by writers of popular pamphlets"[61] has validity, although the division between lawyer and pamphleteer is not always as acute as this quotation might suggest. Many of the pamphlets were either written by those familiar with the law, or by those who borrowed heavily from the works of authors who were. Several demonological texts composed in the seventeenth century were specifically written as interventions in the legal process. They were intended to provide the judiciary and the jury

---

[57] Gibson, 'Applying the Act of 1604', in this vol., p. 127.
[58] For more on this see the remarks on Hopkins and Gaule below, and more importantly Malcolm Gaskill's paper in this volume. See also Malcolm Gaskill, *Witchfinders: A Seventeenth-Century English Tragedy* (London: John Murray, 2005) and *English Witchcraft 1560–1736*, III: The Matthew Hopkins Trials.
[59] Bath, in this volume, p. 145.
[60] Ibid., pp. 132–33.
[61] Frederick Valletta, *Witchcraft, Magic and Superstition in England 1640–1670* (Aldershot & Burlington: Ashgate, 2000), p. 218.

with an interpretative lens through which to read any alleged incident of witchcraft. This was by no means new: The *Discoverie of Witchcraft* had been composed with a similar aim in mind, and its re-issue in the 1650s may have been initiated by similar concerns in the wake of the East Anglia trials.[62] Certainly, the lawyer Thomas Ady was motivated to write by concern about the "wrongful killing of the innocent under the name of Witches".[63] Several tracts were composed in reaction to what their authors saw as the excesses of the trials in their local areas, but sometimes they were written to justify prosecutions in the face of more sceptical attitudes. (We might mention Richard Bernard who demanded to know from the more sceptically inclined, "If there were no witches, what neede these laws?")[64] However, there is not always a clear-cut division between the authors' beliefs. In many case the differences between them seem slight, even when they are arguing for diametrically opposite conclusions.

Select Cases of Conscience by Huntingdon cleric John Gaule was written against the activities of Hopkins and Stearne, conceivably in the hope of averting what he regarded as superstitious persecution from spreading to his parish. Yet Gaule was no sceptic in the matter of witches, and affirmed that "as God makes a Covenant of Grace with his: so doth the Devill with his a Covenant of Death." Indeed, in a passage reminiscent of the North Berwick dittays, we are told that the devil "preaches to them to be mindfull of their Covenant, and not to faile to revenge themselves upon their Enemies". The familiar is also present at this gathering, and we are informed that "oft times, he marries them ere they part, either to himselfe, or their Familiar, or to one another, and that by the Book of Common Prayer".[65] As Gaskill

---

[62] Equally it may have been reissued for commercial reasons, as it was a readily available text on a subject that readers were interested in due to recent events. Certainly, the 1666 reissue seems to fit this scenario, given the un-sceptical tone of the material added to that edition.

[63] Thomas Ady, *A Candle in the Dark* (London, 1655/56), sig. A3.

[64] Richard Bernard, *A Guide to Grand-Jury Men* (London, 1627), p. 88.

[65] John Gaule, *Select Cases of Conscience Touching Witches and Witchcrafts* (London, 1646), pp. 68–69, 63. He also considers the use of infants' bodies on p. 60. This was affirmed by the Act, but not always a significant feature of either the literature or trials. Thomas Potts, *The Wonderfull Discoverie of Witches in the Countie of Lancaster* (London 1613)—reprinted in *The Trial of the Lancaster Witches A.D. MDCXII*, ed. by G.B. Harrison (London: Barnes and Noble, 1971)—relates how in Salmesbury, Lancashire in 1612, three women accused of witchcraft were charged with having exhumed, cooked and eaten the body of a dead child. Sharpe attributes this to continental demonology,

points out in his notes to *Select Cases*: "Ironically, emphasis on the pact was also a central feature of the legal advice of Richard Bernard, the major influence on the opinions of the witchfinder John Stearne."[66] Indeed, all these writers accepted most of the novel features of the Jacobean statute, particularly the covenant and familiar, although their emphases varied.[67] Hopkins held a comprehensive view of the covenant, even arguing for the validity of ducking witches on covenantal grounds. Following the *Daemonologie* he proposed that since witches deny their baptism the waters will not receive them: a grossly materialistic view of the sacrament, but one which was genuinely held.[68] With a wide arsenal of tests for witchcraft at his disposal he was keen to prosecute for the crime. Conversely Gaule urged prudence, going so far as to say that if an accusation of witchcraft "remaynes so occult, as not to come within a legal conviction; it is a signe God hath reserved such for his owne iustice and Vengance".[69] Even in the matter of punishment Gaule was restrained, and advocated staying within the letter of "our owne Statute law in that behalf wherein (in my poor judgement) severall kindes and measures of penalties are well enacted against several kinds and degrees of Witches" and, perhaps with Hopkins in mind, calls for it to be "strictly observed".[70] While there were only subtle differences in their discourses, these differences are highly significant, to the extent that one might ponder to what degree they shared the same codes for interpreting witchcraft.

This demonstrates that while the text of the Act was highly influential in the discourse it did not necessarily favour any particular perspective, and those on all sides could safely draw on it in order to forward their own argument. One interesting approach comes in *An Advertisement to the Jury-Men of England Touching Witches* (which although published anonymously was probably written by Robert Filmer). It begins by giving an abridgement of the statute, which it somewhat misleadingly labels "1 Jacob. Cap. 17", suggesting that it is a transcription. According to the author although a witch is defined as one who practises the

---

since Grace Sowebutts, the fourteen year old who denounced the witches, had been schooled by a Catholic seminary priest (Sharpe, p. 77).

[66] *English Witchcraft 1560–1736*, III, p. 100.

[67] Matthew Hopkins, *The Discovery of Witches* (London, 1647), pp. 4–5.

[68] *Daemonologie* (III.vi), in *ed. cit.*, p. 424. For another consideration of the practice see John Cotta, *The Triall of Witch-Craft* (London, 1616), pp. 104–14.

[69] Gaule, p. 197.

[70] Ibid., p. 182.

activities describes in the Act there is still room for ambiguity as the signification of the words is not definitively fixed by the Act itself: "This Statute presupposeth that every one knows what a Conjurer, a Witch an Inchanter, a Charmer and sorcerer is, as being to be learned best of Divine; and therefore they have not described or distinguished betweene them".[71] So he sets out to find fixed signifieds for these linguistic signs. Like earlier authors searching for the meaning of these terms, he considers the etymology of the words and their possible significations. In doing so he contextualizes the Act in a wider demonological discourse, particularly relating it to the work of Perkins, the Jesuit Martin Delrio ("for both those of the reformed Churches, as well as those of the Roman in a manner, agree in their Definition of the sinne of Witch-craft") and King James.[72] By presenting his reader with an etymological investigation of the terms that presumes an *a priori* linguistic uncertainty about the words, he implies that the law itself may be uncertain. In doing so he challenges the established *point de caption*, un-sealing the accepted meanings of witchcraft contained in the Act. As we will see below he was challenging it by isolating elements, and removing them from their fixed context in the legal matrix in order to align them in a wider discourse, one he finds fault with at certain points.

Filmer's was not the only tract to contextualise the Act in this way. *The Laws Against Witchcraft* (1645) began by giving the Act in full and, having established the legal authority of the codes contained in it, proceeded to draw into the web of significations set up by the statute ancillary material on how to discover a witch. Like *An Advertisement* the pamphlet provided an expanded syntactic context, in which other codes were advanced as legitimate by their relationship to certain elements in the legal matrix. Some of these, such as the witchmark, were merely contingent readings of codes such as the 'covenant'; others, such as the idea of dead bodies bleeding if witches touch them, augment the codes of the Act.[73] Moving by steps from the statute, via a guide for identifying witches, it finishes with the confession of Mother Lakeland of Ipswich, who confessed to having killed by means of the "three Imps, two little dogs and a Mole" Satan had given her. The end result

---

[71] *An Advertisement to the Jury-Men of England*, p. 2.
[72] Ibid., p. 3.
[73] These supplementary codes came from Dalton's *Country Justice*. Malcolm Gaskill points out that the ultimate sources of this material are Bernard's *Guide to Grand-Jury Men* and Thomas Pott's *Wonderful Discovery of Witches* (London, 1613).

of all the foregoing material is brought home by the conclusion that, "for all which she was by Law condemned to die, and in particular to be burned to death, because she was the death of her husband, as she confessed; which death she suffered accordingly."[74] The pamphlet begins with the linguistic codes of the law and ends with the death of an individual condemned under those same codes. As Peter Rushton remarked, "Words were [...] powerful in law and witchcraft alike, they could, in the right framework [...] kill their victims".[75]

The Laws Against Witchcraft could not have been more different from *An Advertisement*, which raised questions about the very possibility of prosecuting for witchcraft. One central difficulty, according to Filmer, lies in semantically proving that *witch*craft has occurred, for "the art must be the Witches Art, and not the Devills, otherwise it is no Witch-craft, but Devils-craft".[76] This is a radical challenge to the fundamental presumption of the Act that the witch is the guilty party. Instead he argues that the witch is ultimately no more than a counsellor to the Devil who does the real harm:

> Now the difficulty will be how the *accesary* can be *duely and lawfully convicted and attained* according as our Statute requires, unless the Devill who is the Principall be first convicted, or at least outlawed, which cannot be, because the Devil can never be lawfully summoned according to the rules of our Common-law.[77]

Most demonologists begun with the assumption that the divine law was transgressed in the crime of witchcraft. Filmer sidesteps this, and by setting aside the context of the law of God (which implicitly underlies witchcraft as an offence) shows that there are logical absurdities in trying witchcraft purely in the context of English law. Indeed, by treating the devil as any other party he heightens the sense of incongruity about cases of witchcraft. He then pushes his cases home with regards to the difficulty of the law of the land in dealing with the supernatural:

> If the devil appear to a grand Jury, in the likenesse of some known Man, and offer to take his Oath, that the person in question is a Witch should

---

[74] *The Laws Against Witches* (London, 1645), pp. 7–8. Facsimile in *English Witchcraft 1560–1636*, III, pp. 65–66.

[75] Peter Rushton, 'Texts of Authority: Witchcraft Accusations and the Demonstration of Truth in Early Modern England' in *Languages of Witchcraft*, ed. by Stuart Clark (Basingstoke, Hampshire: Macmillan, 2001), pp. 21–39 (p. 35).

[76] *An Advertisement to the Jury-Men of England*, pp. 6–7.

[77] Ibid., p. 7.

the Enquest receive his Oath, or accusation to condemne the party? He
[Perkins] answers, surely No; and yet that is as much as the testimony of
another Witch, who only by the helpe of the Devill revealeth the Witch:
if this should be taken for a sufficient proofe, the devil would not leave
one good man alive in this World.[78]

The law relies on the credibility of the witnesses, and he establishes, with
a dash of wit, that witnesses might not be as reliable as the law assumes
in cases of witchcraft. He never dismisses the existence of witchcraft,
but rather on linguistic and logical grounds shows that it is intrinsically
problematic to prove that witchcraft has occurred. This position does not
seem to have been widely shared, and Joseph Glanvill, writing fifteen
years later, re-asserted the reliability of legal procedure.

In a letter to the Somerset JP Robert Hunt, Glanvill concludes a long
list of evident proofs for the existence of witchcraft with an appeal to
the legal situation:

Laws in many Nations have been enacted against those vile practises;
those among the *Jews* and our *own* are *notorious*; such cases have been
often determined near us, by wise and *reverend Judges*, upon clear and
convictive Evidence: and thousands in our own Nation have *suffered death*
for their *vile compacts* with *apostate spirits*.[79]

Like earlier authors he invokes the Bible's authority,[80] but here the appeal
to the scriptural prohibitions is in the context of legal codes ("Laws
[…] among the Jews"). The two systems of law, the biblical and the
national, are assumed to be part of the reader's culture. Both serve to
reinforce the existence of witchcraft as an inductive fact, and Glanvill
re-emphasises this point by showing that these laws have been enacted
under rigorous legal standards of evidence—thus proving the reality
of witchcraft. Of course this stood in contrast to Filmer's views. These
rejections of trial evidence as empirical scientific data undercut the
whole notion of judicial proof (indeed the idea of the reliable witness
providing accurate empirical observation was key to Glanvill's idea about
the verification of ostensibly supernatural phenomena). Clark notes that

---

[78] Ibid., p. 12. Italics inverted.
[79] Joseph Glanvill, *Saducismus Triumphatus* (London, 1681), Part 1 Sect. 2 ('Some
Considerations About Witchcraft'), pp. 4–5. It should be noted that the pagination is
somewhat complicated. It restarts twice in the first part, each time being preceded by
several unnumbered pages of prefatory material.
[80] Indeed, like earlier works, there is a consideration of the various terms in the
Saducismus Triumphatus provided by Henry More (in response to John Webster's criticisms
of Glanvill's earlier works), see Part 1 ('The Postscript'), pp. 19–57.

"it was precisely the way that judicial proofs in witchcraft trials (like scientific findings in general) were arrived at that guaranteed social order" and to question these "implied social chaos".[81] Given that he was defending his worldview it is no surprise that Glanvill railed against the sceptic who must (he argued) believe the "Laws are built upon *Chimera's* [*sic*]; That the *gravest* and *wisest Judges* have been *Murderers*".[82]

The tension between these two worldviews was to continue as the eighteenth century approached, and ultimately it was something closer to the reductive scepticism of Filmer, rather than the philosophical scepticism of Glanvill, that was to triumph. Sharpe draws attention to a London broadside of 1682 that records how the accused was acquitted:

> The jury having been some time out, returned and gave in their verdict that she was not guilty, to the amazement of some who thought the evidence sufficient to have found her guilty; yet others who consider the great difficulty of proving a witch, thought the jury could do no less than acquit her.[83]

Both worldviews were found among the spectators: those who accepted the scientific view of trial evidence, and those who regarded such cases as too difficult to prove beyond reasonable doubt. Neither denied witchcraft, both worked within the legislation of 1604, but there was increasing unease about convicting those accused of witchcraft. Despite Glanvill's keen argument, the empirical observation of witnesses was increasingly insufficient to convict someone accused of witchcraft. One JP at the Surrey quarter sessions in the 1690s asserted the existence of the crime, and reminded jurors it was punishable both by divine law and the 1604 statute, before pressing on them caution because witchcraft was "so hard a matter to have full proof brought of it".[84]

While Sir Francis North bemoaned the difficulties of trying witchcraft when faced with different views about the nature of evidence, Judge John Holt was openly sceptical in court, raising the "suspicion of fraud and [using] sarcasm about the evidence to undermine the possibility of prosecution."[85] In tandem with a reluctance to convict there was a shift in the codes used to interpret witchcraft among some of the

---

[81] Clark, *Thinking with Demons*, p. 176.
[82] Glanvill, Part 1 Sect. 2 ('Some Considerations About Witchcraft'), p. 5.
[83] Sharpe, p. 227.
[84] Kitteridge, *Witchcraft in Old and New England*, p. 596. Cited in ibid., p. 227.
[85] Jonathan Barry, 'The Politics of *Pandemonium*', in this volume, p. 185.

judiciary. Views similar to Holt's began to gain ground. Yet, it is worth
noting that such codes are not necessarily the inheritance of Scot, Ady,
Filmer, or even Harsnett, although they strongly associated imposture
and claims of supernatural power.[86] In the institutes of the *Laws of
England*, Coke had introduced the idea of imposture in connection with
the prohibitions against activities such as finding treasure or procuring love, commenting that "The mischiefs before this part of the Act
was: That divers Imposters, Men and Women, would take upon them
to tell, or doe, these Five things here specified, in great deceipt of the
people, and cheating and cousening them of their money and other
goods."[87] Although the general thrust of the commentary reaffirmed
traditional views of witchcraft the codes for cozenage could be found
in the standard seventeenth-century manual for reading the law. Owen
Davies describes how witchcraft was increasingly spoken of in terms
of imposture as the seventeenth century passed into the eighteenth.
He also relates how the same period saw vigorous attacks against cunning folk and fortune tellers, usually not on the grounds of diabolism
(although such charges did continue) but rather on the grounds of
imposture. Following Malcolm Gaskill, Davies points out that in the
early eighteenth century "the term 'witchcraft' was increasingly redefined in publications to denote the fraudulent activities of conjurers,
fortune tellers, jugglers and other 'pretenders', rather than the diabolic
activities of witches."[88] The rhetoric of disbelief was part and parcel
of the changing codes of the wider culture, which was beginning to
emphasise rationalistic approaches to supernatural phenomena.[89] Con-

---

[86] It is must be noted that after the Restoration rhetoric linking imposture and
witchcraft was employed by both John Wagstaffe, *The Question of Witchcraft Debated* (London, 1669) and John Webster, *The Displaying of Supposed Witchcraft* (London, 1677). It is
interesting that the former does this in the context of an examination of the meaning
of the Hebrew words of the Old Testament. It may be that this approach was regarded
as saleable, hence the title of John Brinley's *A Discovery Of The Impostures Of Witches
And Astrologers* (London, 1680). While it advanced that natural phenomena needed to
be divided from supernatural it did not particularly link witchcraft with legerdemain,
and the title under which it was re-issued in 1686 (*A Discourse Proving By Scripture &
Reason And the Best Authours, Ancient and Modern, that there are Witches*) is probably a more
apt description of the tome.

[87] Coke, *The Third Part of the Institutes of the Laws of England*, p. 46.

[88] Owen Davies, 'Criminalising the Witch: The Origin of and Response to the 1736
Witchcraft Act', in this volume, p. 220.

[89] This is not the same thing as saying society was becoming more rationalistic
about the supernatural. With reference to the wider European situation P. G. Maxwell-
Stuart points out that the royal edict of Louis XIV of France in 1682, which similarly
reclassified various magical practices as superstitious, may have involved an attempt to

victions were in decline, and the shifting politics of England eventually engendered a situation where a new bill could be framed that reflected the dominance of these codes among the intelligentsia, and granted them legal approbation.[90]

Conclusion

On 29 September 1604, the Jacobean statute passed into law, declaring that witches were indeed creatures of the devil, workers of arcane arts who trafficked with Satan. The meaning of the word 'witch' was sealed in relationship to the other words in the document. It became part of a syntagmatic chain that stopped the shifting of signifiers and provided a *point de caption*, a hard and fast definition. As Rushton rightly observed words were powerful. Words conjured devils. Words lamed horses. Words sent spirits to torment children. Words stopped cows milking. More fundamentally words fixed the meaning of exactly what a witch was and could do.

On 24 June 1736, 'witchcraft' was legally stripped of its previous significations. Just as in 1604 the meaning of the word 'witch' was sealed in relationship to the other words in the document so it was to be now. But these were different words to those that had sealed its meaning over a century before. These words associated witchcraft with pretence, delusion, and fraud. For the time being the idea of a witch as someone who could 'do strange things' was a residual code, an understanding from a previous time that had now passed. Now 'witch' signified a cozener. The supernatural power of witches had been repealed by an Act of Parliament.

---

emotionally distance himself from the magical plots of *l'affaire des poisons*, rather than reflecting increasing acceptance of rationalistic approaches to witchcraft. See P.G. Maxwell-Stuart, *Witchcraft: A History* (Stroud: Tempus, 2004), p. 155 ff. Maxwell-Stuart's remarks in relation to the Act of 1736 are also note worthy. See ibid., p. 159 ff.

[90] There is a wider context to the general 'decline' of witchcraft beliefs than I can relevantly describe here. I would refer the reader to Brian Levack, 'The End of the Witch Trials' in *The Witchcraft Reader*, ed. by Darren Oldridge (London & New York: Routledge, 2002), pp. 373–86; Ian Bostridge, *Witchcraft and its Transformations, c. 1650–c. 1750* (Oxford, 1997); and Owen Davies, 'Urbanization and the Decline of Witchcraft: An Examination of London', *Journal of Social History*, 30 (1997), 597–617.

PART ONE

THE NEW KING AND THE CRUCIBLE OF THE ACT

KING JAMES'S EXPERIENCE OF WITCHES, AND THE 1604 ENGLISH WITCHCRAFT ACT

P.G. Maxwell-Stuart

When James VI succeeded Elizabeth Tudor as sovereign of England and stepped over the border in early April 1603, he came into a foreign country of which he had no direct experience until that point; whose language was familiar, but not his own; whose legal system was quite different from that he was accustomed to administer; and whose religious establishment presented to the eye what may have been a misleading picture of unity. The King's expectations were great, as were those of his new subjects, and of all the stories the English may have heard about their new monarch, the one which is likely to have made a particular impact is that James had had a very frightening personal brush with hostile magic. It was an experience which had sunk deep into his psyche—not too deep to be eradicated, or at least mitigated, as time would tell, but deep enough to have left him acutely aware of how real and how active was the malice of Satan against humankind in general, and the righteous in particular.

The 1563 Scottish Witchcraft Act, which remained in force until its repeal in 1736, was devised at a time when a relatively new Protestant regime was concerned and busied by somewhat inchoate ideas about ungodly behaviour among the common people, although its understanding of popular magical beliefs and practices tended to be vague and penetrated by the notion that Catholicism, if not quite a system of magic in itself, certainly encouraged the use of magic unless it could be stopped.[1] It was aimed at both practitioners of magic—"witchcrafts, sorceries and necromancy"—at belief or claims of belief in their efficacy (designated as abuse of the people), and at anyone who consulted such magical operators, and imposed the death penalty on both magician and client. Two years earlier in England, the Bishop of London, Edmund Grindal, was demanding a new English Act to replace that of

---

[1] See further J. Goodare: 'The Scottish Witchcraft Act', *Church History*, 74 (2005), 39–67.

1541/2, which aimed at the practice of magic as both a fraud and a felony, and thereby built into itself an ambiguity. Was the basis of the crime of practising magic real or imaginary? Grindal had learned at least some of their animus from religious exiles in Germany, and their wishes for more severe penalties and a more serious view of the crime were reflected in the English Witchcraft Act of 1563. This assumed that the basis of the offences it designated were real, and called for the death penalty in cases of causing another's death by magic and conjuring evil spirits, and of other repeated acts of divination. It was an Act riding on the back not only of very highly-placed lobbying, but also on specific incidents of hostile magic in Chelmsford, which had seen precisely the kind of actions condemned by the new law.

The two national Acts of 1563 had one interesting point in common. The Scottish Act was drafted by a Protestant minister, we do not know who, as part of a Protestant programme under a Catholic Queen, while the English Act sprang essentially from mounting concern in ecclesiastical circles that there were insufficient secular powers to deal with the problem of witchcraft. In both cases, the driving force was Calvinist religious sensibility. One might expect, therefore, that James VI would react to the immense fright he received in 1590 from the treasonable plots to kill him through magical means by introducing and pursuing a pogrom of magical operators throughout Scotland and by revising the already severe legislation to enable him to do so more effectively. Neither pogrom nor revision, however, took place.

The recorded instances of Scottish magic designated 'witchcraft' by the secular courts, which were taking place during James's minority, were concerned largely with the invocation or appearance of spirits whose peculiar qualities were those of preternatural assistants enabling the practitioner to look into the future or prescribe cures for a client's illness, or more specifically of fairies performing those same tasks for the operator. Thus, in 1568, Sir William Stewart, Lyon King of Arms, was charged with conspiring to take the Regent's life by sorcery and necromancy, although the details of his case suggest that he had used the shears and riddle—devices of 'popular' magic—to divine the future, consulted witches, and invoked a spirit called *Obirion* with the intention of asking him about the immediate future of the realm. This latter consultation caused Stewart to prophesy that the Regent would die by violence before 17 November 1567, and gave him (it was claimed) foreknowledge of King Henry's death in March that same year. Twisting this into a conscious conspiracy to effect treasonous murder was not difficult, but the evidence had to be reinterpreted to produce such an outcome, as it would not of itself lead directly to this conclusion. In 1572, when King James was six, Janet Boyman was tried for curiously similar offences—she divined, she cured, she had dealings with fairies and an apparition she had conjured—but since her enquiries were not directed towards the King or his ministers the elements of treason did not enter her case and she was tried as any other witch. Four years later, when James was ten, the case of Elizabeth Dunlop repeated many of these distinctive features: a spirit or fairy who claimed to be someone nearly thirty years dead, divination (largely for lost or stolen articles), and magical cures. Elizabeth was even summoned on one occasion by the Archbishop of St Andrews himself to counter an illness he feared had been caused by magic, and it was this which, more than anything else, made her case celebrated.

The colour of Scottish magic at this time seems, therefore, to have been a mixture of largely beneficent practices such as could be found all over Europe and the evocation of spirits who were more closely allied to fairies or the dead than to the demons which clergymen feared and which received intensive scrutiny in learned disquisitions by non-Scottish authors. Indeed, there is the curious fact that the trial of Tibbie Smart in 1586 accused her of some of just those elements most closely connected with the learned Continental view of hostile magic, especially shape-changing of the witch herself; and yet Tibbie Smart was not executed but sentenced to perpetual banishment and branding on the cheek.[2] As far as King James was concerned, then, witchcraft (or indeed magic of any kind) was widespread in his kingdom, but not especially rife, and was adequately tried and punished by the statute passed during his mother's reign. Detection depended principally on the efficiency of the kirk and presbytery sessions which were being set up to govern and reform the people's morals and behaviour, and in as far as these chose to interpret the charges of magic brought before them—slander between neighbours, misguided but correctable lapses, serious moral offences which had divagated into the territory of prosecutable crime—the problem of magical practitioners could be controlled without the need to worry either Crown or Kirk unduly.

---

[2] For these cases, see further P.G. Maxwell-Stuart, *Satan's Conspiracy: Magic and Witchcraft in Sixteenth-Century Scotland* (East Linton: Tuckwell Press, 2001), pp. 57–107.

In 1590, however, the situation changed. The so-called 'North Berwick' affair involved the King directly and opened to his horrified eyes
a world of magic quite unlike that either he or many of his ministers
had thought existed. The general outline of the incident is as follows.[3] In November 1590, as a result of severe maltreatment by her
employer and a number of other men, a servant-girl, Geillis Duncan,
confessed she was a witch and named others as witches with whom she
was acquainted and who used to meet together. One of these, Agnes
Sampson, revealed under interrogation that the previous All Hallows'
Eve, while King James had been furth of Scotland, intending to marry
Anne of Denmark and bring her back home with him, a meeting of
witches, both male and female, had taken place in a church at North
Berwick. Satan too had come to this meeting, wearing a black gown
and a black hat, and had called the roll of those present, just as though
he were a schoolmaster, after which two graves were opened and
plundered for certain body-parts used in hostile magic. This meeting,
however, betrayed few of the characteristics of a conventional Sabbat.
The witches danced to the sound of a Jew's harp played by Geillis
Duncan; but none of them came to the meeting by flying through the
air—Agnes, for example, travelled on horseback—no one changed
shape, the Devil appeared as a man, not as an animal, there was no
feasting, nor were lights doused to provide darkness for a sexual orgy.
To be sure, the participants honoured Satan with the *osculum infame*,
otherwise the convocation was more like a shareholders' meeting at
which progress and deficit were noted, and the chairman of the board
urged everyone to make further effort.

As interrogations of the arrested multiplied, however, there came
to light four separate plots to injure or kill the King by magic. One
was to raise a storm while he was still at sea on his way to Denmark;
a second involved the magical consecration of a picture of the King;
a third centred on a wax image of James, consecrated after a similar
fashion; and the fourth involved expressing venom from a toad, mixing it with other noxious substances, and placing it over or under a
doorway through which the King was sure to pass quite frequently. All
four plots depended on magic for their efficacy; all were centred upon

---

[3] See *Witchcraft in Early Modern Scotland*, ed. by Lawrence Normand and Gareth
Roberts (Exeter: Exeter University Press, 2000), Part 2, The Texts. Maxwell-Stuart,
Satan's Conspiracy, pp. 142–80.

King James; and all involved more or less the same group of magical operators, among whom the most notable was Richard Graham, a magician known (and known to be such) by some very important people including the Chancellor, the Earl of Bothwell (who was credited with being the fount and origin of the conspiracy as a whole), and William Schaw, Master of the King's Works.

Whether all, or any part, or none of these plots was real does not concern us here. They were real, or potentially real enough, as far as James himself was concerned,[4] and he took an active part in the interrogation of some of those involved. His interest in the proceedings is scarcely surprising, since he himself had been the object of the witches' apparently murderous intentions and there is no reason to suppose he did not take these revelations seriously, since no one, least of all the Scottish Calvinist establishment, doubted the reality of Satan or Satan's plans to overthrow humanity, or his ability to work through human agents. James had given no prior indication of scepticism on these points, and although he had not shown any particular interest in the subject heretofore, he had not been personally involved before, either. So when witches and magicians came into his presence, as they now did between 1590 and 1591, his reaction seems to have been a mixture of the curious—as though he were being confronted by the denizens of a strange, exotic bourn—and the judicial. Thus, Geillis Duncan played her Jew's harp for him, "who, in respect of the strangeness of these matters, took great delight to be present at [the witches'] examinations"; and John Fian was twice examined by the King, on the first occasion giving "a great screech [...] sometime bending himself, and sometime capering so directly up that his head did touch the ceiling of the chamber, to the great admiration [*astonishment*] of his Majesty and the others then present".[5]

That James was frightened as well as intrigued can be gauged from his reaction to the verdict brought by an assize in the trial of Barbara Napier, another accused of witchcraft and conspiracy to murder.[6]

---

[4] Probably with at least some degree of reason, because surviving documents from Richard Graham and Barbara Napier, another of the accused, strongly suggest a plot of some kind, if only to inculpate the Earl of Bothwell to his detriment. See further Maxwell-Stuart, *Satan's Conspiracy*, pp. 155–56.

[5] *Newes From Scotland* in Normand & Roberts, *Witchcraft in Early Modern Scotland*, pp. 318–319.

[6] She was also part of a sub-plot which had nothing to do with the King, and everything to do with a piece of disputed property. See L. Yeoman, 'Hunting the Rich

Guilty of consultation with witches but not of treason, said the assizers; whereupon the King flew into a fury and threatened to put the assize itself on trial for wilful error unless the assizers retracted their finding. His anger seems to have been stimulated by his growing conviction that the witches were telling the truth and that the Earl of Bothwell had indeed been trying to get rid of him with their help. The hesitation he had displayed at the beginning of the process was thus giving way to a belief in and acceptance of the reality of the peril he had escaped by the grace of God. It was an impression which left its mark on his psyche for some time to come.

One result of this experience was James's decision to write a short treatise based on what he had discovered and upon a small amount of reading undertaken, one presumes, in the spirit of scholarship. The *Daemonologie* took shape in some form perhaps as early as 1591 while James was in the midst of interrogations and the uncertainty and growing fearfulness generated by these magical plots against his life. Its form and general observations are entirely conventional, its tone that of a Protestant pastor rather than that of a monarch, a tone which may reflect the source or sources who were feeding the King his scholarly material.[7] Cast into three books, the *Daemonologie* deals with magic, witchcraft, and spirits, with the passages most reminiscent of the 1590–91 examinations appearing in Book Two, an agglomeration which makes one ask whether James did not conceive and make notes for this second Book first, before deciding to turn his jottings into a publishable work by adding the usual history and explanation of magic to begin with, and discussion of various kinds of spirits and their operations last. Given the oddity of Book Three—its chapters deal with ghosts, obsession and possession, incubi and succubi, exorcism (from an anti-Catholic perspective), fairies, and tack the trial and

Witch in Scotland: High-Status Witchcraft Suspects and their Persecutors, 1590–1650', in *The Scottish Witch-Hunt in Context*, ed. by Julian Goodare (Manchester: Manchester University Press, 2002).

   [7] It is noteworthy, for example, that the Calvinist Andrew Melville included among questions for debate in the University of St Andrews three relating to witches and their activities. The first asks why should not witches and those who consult them be executed? The second suggests that trial by 'swimming', or the discovery of the Devil's mark, should be accounted sufficient proof of a person's being a witch. The third deals with transvection and shape-changing. See his *Scholastica diatriba de rebus divinis* (Edinburgh, 1599), questions 18–20. They are entirely conventional questions and clearly indicate that the responder should be acquainted with the kind of treatises James cites in the preface to his *Daemonologie*.

punishment of witches on to the end—it is interesting that this should have given a title to the work as a whole, a small indication, perhaps, of the source of his deepest fears. Attempted assassination by knife or bullet or poison was one thing, and although frightening enough in themselves, represented the kind of hazard to which monarchs were often liable by the nature of their office, and which James experienced more than once. Murder by magic, however, which involved the invocation and assistance of powers greater than human was quite another matter and, considering the gravity of the offence, we should perhaps congratulate James on his courage in facing the apparent conspiracy without recourse to any kind of pogrom.

Personal experience of witchcraft for James was thus intimately connected with politics, and while it is notable that the years immediately following the so-called North Berwick episode did not produce any particular increase in the number of witch-prosecutions in Scotland, in spite of the fact that it was a neurotic time, dominated by apparent threats of Catholic invasion from without and armed rebellion within the kingdom, the later 1590s did see an increase in a struggle. Politics again, of course, and therefore the King must had found it gratifying that in February 1597 the General Assembly of the Kirk reluctantly granted him extended powers in such affairs. These powers most clearly bore fruit in July. The King was in St Andrews where he not only examined "informations exhibited against sundry principal officers and preachers in the university there and for the trial and punishment of witches",[8] but also deprived of the rectorship of the university Andrew Melville, (a Calvinist minister who had been endeavouring for some time to have the Kirk remoulded along stricter Presbyterian lines). In the autumn, the King at last published his *Daemonologie* whose pastoral-judicial tone fitted well the role he was now aspiring to play in matters which, until that year, had strictly speaking, belonged to the Kirk rather than the state. A couple of noteworthy outbreaks of witch-prosecution also occurred at this same time, one of which involved James. It burst out in Fife and was carried over to Glasgow before the woman responsible for it was brought back to Fife for trial. She had been claiming to be able to identify people as witches merely by looking at their eyes, and when it was suspected she was a fraud, James was obliged

---

[8] Report by Robert Bowes to Lord Burghley, *Calendar of State Papers, Scotland*, 13.56.

to recall the commissions he had signed and issued against those she had accused, and discharge them until further consideration had been made by the Estates.

After 1597–98, however, the number of such prosecutions in Scotland dropped away sharply, and it can be said that while James's experience of witchcraft in Scotland had been at one stage highly personal, and that during the 1590s witchcraft seems to have been a component in the power struggle between James and the Kirk for dominance in Scotland, there is no evidence that the King stimulated any prosecution of witches there, or pursued them from personal motives of fear or revenge, or indeed saw them as a major branch of the criminal fraternity. These, then, were the fairly straightforward views of witches and witchcraft which James brought with him to England.

At least one case had recently come to a conclusion just before he arrived, that of Mary Glover who had alleged, the previous year, that one Elizabeth Jackson had bewitched her and caused her to have fits, and to suffer periods of blindness and inability to speak. Elizabeth, however, was fortunate enough to have someone to address the court in her defence, a physician, Edward Jorden, who maintained that Mary was not suffering from any magically-induced affliction, but from a type of hysteria, and was neither bewitched nor fraudulent, but genuinely ill. The case attracted widespread attention and resulted in Jorden's writing a medical treatise, *Briefe Discourse of a Disease called the Suffocation of the Mother*, published in 1603, and if we cannot be sure that the King was acquainted with the details, it is perfectly possible he heard the general outline before he had been long in London; and indeed there is the claim, made by John Swan, writing in 1603, that an account of Mary Glover's case by a highly-placed clergyman, Samuel Harsnett, had been presented to James.

During the first year of James's residence in London, from May 1603 to June 1604, there was a flurry of interest in witchcraft in the English capital, almost certainly stimulated by the accession of a monarch known to have been personally attacked by witches. There were two English editions of his *Daemonologie*, for example, the first of which was entered on the Stationers' Register on 3 April 1603, in flattering time for the King's arrival in London on 7 May; and on 4 June James was petitioned by John Dee who wanted to clear his name of the imputation of sorcery by means of a public trial, "if by any due, true, and just meanes, the said name of Conjurer, or Caller, or Invocator of

Divels, or damned Spirites, can be proved";[9] and there is a tradition
(not attested by contemporary evidence) that in that same year James
ordered copies of Reginald Scot's *Discoverie of Witchcraft*, whose opinions
he had hoped to refute by his own publication, burnt by the hands of
the public hangman. In 1604, the King granted a pardon to Thomas
Weech's wife on charges of witchcraft; George Gifford's *Dialogue Concerning Witches and Witchcraftes*, a work originally published in 1593 arguing
that witches were credited with too much power and that anyone suffering apparent bewitchment should bear it patiently as a trial from
God, was reprinted in 1603, one must presume because the publishers
calculated there would be a ready market for it. The A text of Marlowe's
Dr Faustus was published; an anonymous play, *The Merry Devil of Edmonton*
which, like *Faustus*, dramatises the exploits of a real magician, in this
case Peter Fabel, was being performed as early as 1604; and Thomas
Heywood's *Wise Woman of Hogsdon*, centred upon the activities of a
cunning woman, was probably written in this year, too. So perhaps it
is not surprising to find that the day after Dee's petition to James, the
Calendar of State Papers, Domestic, notes that "amendments [were] to be
made in the Act against Conjuration, Witchcraft, etc."—a reference to
the English Act of 1563—amendments which would produce a fresh
Act, more stringent than that of Elizabeth Tudor's Parliament, but less
so than that of 1541/42 which had prescribed the death penalty for
each and every one of the offences designated therein.

In view of James's known interest in the subject matter, and London's apparent eagerness to seek royal favour by republishing books
and putting on theatrical performances dealing with just such topics,
it is therefore interesting to ask whether the 1604 Witchcraft Act was
merely another attempt to flatter the King by refreshing legislation
along lines it might be thought would please him, or whether James
himself had a hand in stimulating Parliament to promulgate a new
law to combat the activities of a dangerous set of people. The first
thing to note, perhaps, is that James did not walk into a situation of
intense witch-prosecution in England in April–May 1603. Indeed, it
is remarkable that the numbers of such prosecutions, in the Home
Counties at least, fell spectacularly from the moment his English reign

---

[9] Quoted in P.J. French, *John Dee: The World of an Elizabethan Magus* (London: Routledge & Kegan Paul, 1972), p. 10.

began, nearly halving in the decade 1600–1609, and maintaining the same kind of momentum thereafter.[10] So James did not arrive with a preconceived agendum to prosecute witches in his new kingdom, and indeed it was not until 1605 that two cases came to his attention. The first happened in January while the King was in Huntingdon. There had been a rash of prophecies that England would suffer fire and sword because of disagreements over religion, and a man called Butler who was described as a witch and had a local reputation for being able to work extraordinary cures was sent to London for closer examination by the Lord Chief Justice. As James wrote to Robert Cecil, "I have been out of privy intelligence with you since my last parting for having been ever kept so busy with hunting of witches, prophets, Puritans, dead cats, and hares".[11] Then in May, two young women, allegedly suffering from an ailment suggesting bewitchment, were held in Cambridge for further trial. The suspected originators of their suffering were a Franciscan and a Puritan clergyman, so it may have been this which caused James to take a brief interest in the case rather than the actual witchcraft, just as his interest in Butler is likely to have been stimulated by the political aspects of his prophesying rather than his status as a local witch and healer.

It seems unlikely, then, that the drafting and passage of the 1604 Act owed anything in particular to James's direct request or intervention, although one can expect him to have taken an interest in it once the proposal for redrafting had actually been made. Nor do the specific terms of the new Act seem to mirror James's personal experiences. It provides the death penalty for those who conjure or consult evil spirits, (a provision which does not appear to imply ghosts and therefore technically should not have included necromancers or their clients, whose aim was to raise the spirits of the dead in order to obtain answers to questions largely about the future). Death was also prescribed for those who used whole corpses or parts of dead bodies for magical purposes, a provision not contained in either the 1541/42 Act or in that of 1563, and thus seemingly new. But although the North Berwick witches had raided graves for body parts during their All Hallows' Eve convention in 1589, one cannot assume that this new provision necessarily came from

---

[10] See James Sharpe, *Instruments of Darkness: Witchcraft in England 1550–1750* (London: Penguin, 1997), pp. 108–10.

[11] *Letters of King James VI & I*, ed. by G.V. Akrigg (Berkeley: University of California Press, 1984), p. 250.

James since the use of body parts by witches in manufacturing a deadly ointment is chronicled by several earlier European experts—Paolo Grillando in *Tractatus de sortilegiis* (1536), Johann Wier in *De praestigiis daemonum* (1583), and Sebastien Michäelis in *Pneumologie* (1587), for example—and the information could equally well have come from them. But, the practice was not unknown in England well before James's time, for Sir Edward Coke noted that "a man was taken in Southwark with a head and a face of a dead man, and a book of sorcery in his male [bag], and was brought into the King's Bench before Sir John Knevett, then Chief Justice", and this dates the incident to the later 1360s.[12] It is true, however, that the practice turns up with increasing frequency in stage plays after 1604. The pilot's thumb, Jew's liver, Turk's nose, Tartar's lips, and birth-strangled baby's finger of *Macbeth* (*c.* 1606) will come to mind, along with "three ounces of the red-haired girl I killed last night" from Thomas Middleton's *The Witch* (1613–15); and some twenty-four years after the passing of the Act, matters had reached such a pass that Coke was able to observe that mere intention to use dead bodies for the purpose of witchcraft constituted a felony in itself.[13] But these could just as well have stemmed from the Act as from anything James or others may have remembered from North Berwick fourteen years previously.

The Act also prescribed death for anyone who sought successfully to harm or kill another human being by means of magic—a straightforward condemnation of malefice, which cannot be narrowed down to James's experience. Using magic for the purposes of divination, or to provoke love, to harm a person's possessions, or to seek unsuccessfully to harm or kill a human being, carried the penalty of a year's imprisonment and a stipulated period in the pillory, a reaffirmation of the provisions of the 1563 Act. A repetition of any of these offences, however, carried an increased punishment, life imprisonment in 1563, changed to the death penalty in 1604. It can be said, therefore, that the Act of 1604 did not go as far as that of 1541/42 in designating any use of magic a felony with the death penalty attached, (and dealt with a somewhat different range of magical operations, too), but did draw specific attention to the magical use of body parts, and make the

[12] *Third Part of the Institutes of the Laws of England* (London, 1797), p. 44.
[13] *Op. cit.* supra, p. 45.

penalty for several acts of hostile magic a good deal more severe than
that in Elizabeth Tudor's legislation.

Nevertheless, it did not go as far as the Scottish Witchcraft Act of
1563, the one with which James must have been familiar. The provisions
of the Scottish Act were simple. No one was to use acts of witchcraft,
sorcery, or necromancy; or to claim knowledge of how to employ such
acts, because this amounted to tricking and deceiving people; and no
one was to consult such magical practitioners, either. The penalty in
all instances was death. It is worth noting that the reference to "abus-
ing the people" does not necessarily imply scepticism on the part of
the drafter of the law. Magical acts might very well be effective in
themselves, but there were persons who chose to pretend that they
were genuine magical practitioners, and it was these frauds at whom
this section of the Act was aimed. Where a more general scepticism
about the efficacy of magic can be seen in the Act is its initial phrase
about "credence given in times past" to acts of witchcraft, sorcery,
and necromancy, a reference stemming, as Julian Goodare points out,
from the legislators' evident opinion that witchcraft was a remnant of
Catholic belief. The Scottish Act, therefore, represented a draconian
attempt by largely Calvinist clergy and lawyers to eradicate Catholic
practices and magical operations, (which they regarded as scarcely
different in essence), from among the Scottish people as a whole, not
just the commons—hence the distinct provision that the Act applied to
"person or persons of whatsoever estate, degree, or condition". It was
thus an Act heavily redolent of the precise time and exact conditions
under which it was drawn up.[14]

If the Scottish Act did not provide a model, or even a source of
suggestion, for the new English Act, neither, it must be said, did James's
Daemonologie. His text bears clear marks of the influence of the North
Berwick episode, its overall intention was to inculcate correct Protestant
beliefs concerning witchcraft and its practitioners, and it recommends
the death penalty for both magical operators and their clients, on the
grounds that the latter are as guilty as the former. This is entirely
consistent with the Scottish Act, but not with either the English Act
of 1563 or that of 1604, both of which concentrate their fire on the
operators, although it must be said that the 1604 provision against

---

[14] See further Maxwell-Stuart, *Satan's Conspiracy*, pp. 35–45; Goodare, 'The Scottish
Witchcraft Act', pp. 51–59; *Witchcraft in Early Modern Scotland*, ed. by Normand and
Roberts, pp. 90–91.

operators, "aiders, abettors, and counsellors", could be interpreted so as to include their clients. In practice, however, this does not seem to have happened. Similar in many ways to the 1563 English Act, that of 1604 quite notably treats as real, not imaginary, the magical offences it condemns and substantially increases the severity brought to bear against workers of magic. Treating the offences as real it inherited from 1563, so although King James could have assured the drafting committee on this point from his own experience, this attitude does not depend on the King's personal recollections.

The extra judicial rigour, on the other hand, strikes one as perhaps owing not a little to the opinions or prejudices of one individual in particular—not King James, but Sir Edmund Anderson, an elderly member of the committee which drafted the Act and Chief Justice of the Court of Common Pleas, a post to which he had been appointed by Elizabeth Tudor and in which he was confirmed by James on 11 April 1603. Anderson was someone of Anglican conservatism, equally hostile to Catholics and to Puritans, an able lawyer and a man of limited intellectual interests, with a sharp temper and intemperate behaviour. He had been active on the bench during the 1580s and 1590s when prosecutions for witchcraft in the Home Counties had been very high, and this may have coloured his outlook when it came to the Mary Glover case of 1602. "The land is full of witches; they abound in all places", he said to her jury. "I have hanged five or six and twenty of them. There is no man here can speak more of them than myself [...] Their malice is great, their practices devilish, and if we shall not convict them without their own confession or direct proofs, where the presumptions are so great and the circumstances so apparent, they will in a short time over-run the whole land". He was openly rebutting the evidence of Edward Jorden, a physician, who had argued that Mary was not the victim of bewitchment but was suffering from a kind of hysteria, and Lord Chief Justice Anderson was having none of it. "Divines, physicians, I know they are learned and wise", he said to the professional witnesses in court, "but to say this natural, and tell me neither the cause nor the cure of it—I care not for your judgement. Give me a natural reason and a natural remedy, or a rush for your physic!"[15]

---

[15] Stephen Bradwell, 'Mary Glover's Late Woeful Case', in *Witchcraft and Hysteria in Elizabethan London*, ed. by Michael MacDonald (London: Routledge, 1991), pp. 28–29 (separately paginated).

Anderson was not necessarily a bigot. He was perfectly capable of suspecting fraud when he saw it, as he did in the case of John Darrell, a Puritan minister who specialised in exorcising individuals possessed by evil spirits, and William Somers, a boy who played up to him by acting out possession; and he also accepted a "not guilty" verdict in the case of Alice Freeman accused of bewitching Somers's sister, even though it was the third time she had been tried and the two previous juries had found her guilty.[16] But he was clearly convinced of the reality of witchcraft and when, during the case of Anne Kerke, tried for witchcraft in November 1599, the Bishop of London who was on the bench remarked that "he saw nothing that might not be counterfeited" and was therefore unwilling to press for a conviction, Anderson and the other judges "thought it necessary for the satisfying of the jury to urge the Scriptures for proof that there is witchcraft", and to let the jurors know some of their own experiences of the reality of possession.[17] Cases such as these produced a rash of sermons on the subject of demoniacs, preached at St Paul's Cross in 1602–03. So the atmosphere in London which James found upon his arrival in May 1603 was one of feverish interest in the demonic possession of individuals, caused by bewitchment, and an apparent eagerness to pander to what people perceived or assumed was James's personal preoccupation with the hostile activities of witches; and it was in such an atmosphere that Lord Chief Justice Anderson sat down with six earls, twelve bishops, and Sir Edward Coke, to draft a new Witchcraft Act in 1603–04.[18]

How far this atmosphere stirred fear or nervousness in James, reviving memories now over a decade old, and thus pushed him into requiring a review of existing English witchcraft legislation, or how far Anderson, with specific and hostile opinions on the subject of witches, took advantage of James's arrival to press for change in accordance with an agendum of his own, is open to debate. To be sure, it took only eight

---

[16] Freeman case (1598), see D.P. Walker: *Unclean Spirits: Possession and Exorcism in France and England in the Sixteenth and Seventeenth Centuries* (London: Scolar Press, 1981), p. 63. Darrell & Somers (1599), see *Witchcraft in England 1558–1618*, ed. by Barbara Rosen, 2nd edn (Amherst: University of Massachusetts Press, 1991), pp. 298–99.

[17] See Walker: *op. cit.* supra, p. 72.

[18] Coke does not seem to have had as great an animus against witches as did Anderson. His section on witchcraft in the *Third Part of the Institutes of the Laws of England* sticks largely to a few historical observations and legal definitions and comments on the 1604 statute. The nearest he comes to emotion is the sentence, "It had been a great defect in government if so great an abomination had passed with impunity", but this is in the context of a comment upon Saul and his consultation of the witch of Endor.

days for James's first Parliament to set in motion steps to revise the 1563 Act, and we are told by Edward Fairfax in the preface to his *Discourse of Witchcraft* (1621) that the King "found a defect in the statutes [...] by which none died for witchcraft but they only who by that means killed, so that such were executed rather as murderers than as witches". But there is no necessary reason to suppose that it must have been James himself who drew attention to any defect in the existing Act. Indeed, Fairfax's remark, made seventeen years after the event, makes little sense in the light of the 1604 Act since by the Act's provisions witches still did not die as witches but as felons, and the difference between that and "murderers" is difficult to see, especially as in fact the 1563 legislation executed witches as felons, too. Fairfax therefore throws no light on the matter, and his observation seems to be little more than a small piece of flattery aimed at pleasing the King. We have seen, too, that even in the midst of the magical conspiracy against him in 1590–91, James did not embark on a vengeful pogrom against witches, so it seems somewhat unlikely that he would set in motion the apparatus to do so in England when there was no immediate (or even distant) threat to him there from a similar source.

As for the effect of the new Act on James himself, it appears to have done nothing to stimulate him into pressing for more prosecutions or intensified rooting out of witches. Indeed, we can actually see the King leaning towards the opinion that several of the cases brought into court were impostures rather than genuine instances of witchcraft. Two Cambridge women (1605), Anne Gunter (1606), a boy called Smith (1616), and the boy from Bilston (1620), for example, were cases of possession in which the King took an interest and decided that they were, in one way or another, fraudulent. Hence Thomas Fuller's observation that "the frequency of such forged possessions wrought such an alteration upon the judgement of King James that he, receding from what he had written in his *Daemonologie*, grew first diffident of, and then flatly to deny the workings of witches and devils, as but falsehoods and delusions".[19]

---

[19] *The Church History of Britain from the Birth of Jesus Christ to the Year MDCXLVIII*, 6 vols (Oxford: Oxford University Press, 1845), *Witchcraft in England 1558–1618*, ed. by Barbara Rosen, 2nd edn (Amherst: University of Massachusetts Press, 1991), V, pp. 451–52. Cf. ibid., p. 450 for other cases. Indirect flattery of the King for his perspicacity in recognising and exposing such cases can be detected in Ben Jonson's comedy, *The Divell is an Asse*, performed by the King's Players in mid autumn 1616. See P. Happé's comments in his edition of the play (Manchester: Manchester University Press, 1994), p. 14.

Doubts about possession and doubts about the efficacy of hostile magic, however, are two different things, and if James did have reservations anent the former, they did not necessarily transfer themselves to the latter. Witches therefore continued to be prosecuted under the new Act, to be found guilty, and executed, in accordance with its declared intention of "better restraining" and "more severe punishing" of conjurations, enchantments, and individual acts of witchcraft. But to suggest that James arrived in England armed with hostility, legislated against magical operators, and then changed his mind under the pressure of several cases, is a gross over-simplification of the evidence which seems rather to point to others undertaking a review of legislation more or less independently, on the assumption that James would not object and would indeed be pleased by endeavours which flattered both his presumed interest and his perceptive judgement.

STANDING WITHIN THE PROSPECT OF BELIEF
MACBETH, KING JAMES, AND WITCHCRAFT

Roy Booth

Macbeth is one of the most iconic of Shakespeare's plays.[1] An image search on the Internet will display Ellen Terry as Lady Macbeth, versions of Macbeth and the dagger, Banquo's ghost, Lady Macbeth wringing her hands. But in production photographs, theatre posters, artistic interpretations and visual quotations, it is the witches who recur, doubly redoubled. *Macbeth* without the witches seems as remote from imaginative feasibility as *Hamlet* without the prince. The Cheek by Jowl company did once reduce them to voices, but that has to be a very rare directorial gambit. Whatever the extent of their influence over the protagonist amounts to, the collective mental picture seems to have made the weird sisters imaginatively inseparable from the play. Parts of their rhyming enchantments are in the common repertoire of Shakespearean tags. The economy with which Shakespeare cast this spell is remarkable. The witches are not large roles for the performers, nor was their part in the action developed into anything approaching a sub-plot. They have no narrative that is told through to its conclusion, but are always enigmatic, "imperfect speakers" for an audience that will also always want to know more. They simply (and characteristically) vanish at IV.1.132.

If the Macbeth narrative is re-read in the source texts, however, then the play might actually be seen as rather restrained in its witch activity. After the first "strange and uncouth woonder" of meeting what "common opinion" subsequently took to be either the "weird sisters, that is (as ye would say) the goddesses of destinie" or else "some nymphs or feiries, indued with knowledge of prophesie by their necromanticall science", Holinshed's Mackbeth acquired an entourage of supernatural advisers:

[1] All quotations taken from *Macbeth*, ed. by Kenneth Muir, The Arden Shakespeare (London: Methuen, 1962). The title adapts the lines "to be King / Stands not within the prospect of belief" (I.3.73–74).

he had learned of certeine wizzards, in whose words he put great confidence [...] that he ought to take heed of Makduffe, who in time to come
should seeke to destroie him.

   And suerlie hereupon had he put Makduffe to death, but that a certeine
witch, whom hee had in great trust, had told that he should never be
slaine with man borne of anie woman.[2]

This Macbeth, a tyrant like the emperor Tiberius, anxious to ascertain
more of the future from mutually contradictory soothsayers, might have
been something Shakespeare considered and discarded. Similarly, in
developing the murder of Duncan from Holinshed's account of the
murder of King Duff by Donwald, an elaborate earlier attempt by
witchcraft on Duff's life disappears from view (though the insomnia
suffered by Duff whilst his wax image was being slowly roasted probably was remembered).[3] By limiting the number of "instruments of
Darkness" (I.3.124) to the Weird Sisters, Shakespeare obviously gave
focus to his compact tragedy, and prepared for a hero who will "keep
alone" (III.2.8). But it also is apparent that Thomas Middleton seems
to have thought that Shakespeare had been too restrained, and so
added in Hecate, three extra witches, song and flight. It could have
been worse: from the source, he might have retrieved witch or wizard
assistants to Macbeth.

   If we can see *Macbeth* as restrained (and part of doing this involves
mentally subtracting the Hecate material from the text, especially as
augmented by recent editors who import extra lines from *The Witch*),
then the question that follows is why Shakespeare did not make more
of the witchcraft. He had a monarch who was willing to believe that
black magic had been practiced against him. The accused in the East
Berwick witch trials were able to see that James liked to hear of his
divine imperviousness to the charms that had been raised against him.[4]
Shakespeare might have developed scenes, from Holinshed's account of
King Duff, of a less blessed king under an initial supernatural assault.

---

   [2] *Ed. cit.*, Appendix A, pp. 177–78; 182.
   [3] Insomnia induced by witchcraft will be one of the afflictions visited on the "master
o' th' *Tiger*" (I.3.7; 19–23), introducing a motif for the whole play.
   [4] Janet Kennedy, deposing in the presence of the King (June, 1591), gave an account
of the wax image of the King being miraculously resistant to melting, despite Bothwell
urging the witches to make the fire more intense. "Whereupon Agnes Sampson said
that all was in vain they assayed against the king for nothing of their craft could do
at him." In *Witchcraft in Early Modern Scotland*, ed. by Lawrence Normand and Gareth
Roberts (Exeter: University of Exeter Press, 2000), p. 185.

A contemporary, asked to comment on the way that Macbeth has a doctor treating his wife, rather than consulting the witches about her, might have seen an opportunity spurned (theatrically speaking), and the weird sisters as offering a more suitable choice of therapist anyway. Even the doctor feels out of place (V.1.71). Judging from the revision of the text by Middleton, and all questions of "state or tenet of witches" set aside, it is clear that the acting company wanted more exploitation of the performance possibilities of witchcraft.[5] Davenant's version of *Macbeth* (*c.* 1664) added further witch material, including two more songs, and a set of ambiguous prophecies elicited by Macduff.

Consideration of what *Macbeth* might have been leads on to the emergence of this Scottish play in the repertory of the King's Men. The company seems to have set off in their new status with every reason for confidence. Lawrence Fletcher was the man-in-place. He had—to the horror of the Kirk—led English actors to Scotland, and had seen his troupe richly rewarded.[6] He reappears in England when his name heads the list of the King's Men in their royal patent of May 1603. As far as the limited evidence available shows, it seems that Fletcher might have established with James a relationship something like that the court jester Archibald Armstrong enjoyed. The opposition of the Kirk made them allies: the King, not on his moral dignity, roguishly condescended to make jokes about Fletcher, pretending to be angry at a report that Fletcher had been hanged. In reciprocation (at least according to the Kirk), Fletcher's English actors made jokes about the King.[7] In subsequent years in England, boy players would mock the King so directly that scholarship has had to cast around for explanations of the tolerance extended to them. But perhaps James had from the start encouraged players to believe that they would be indulged. Their very presence in his country was a moral affront to some: maybe this impelled the actors to play up on their impudence. James was not always a sober man, and could at times indulge in horseplay and bawdy jesting. In England, Thomas Kyd testified that, shortly before his death,

---

[5] I take the phrase cited from Nathaniel Tompkins' disappointed reaction to *The Witches of Lancashire*, quoted in Andrew Gurr, *Playgoing in Shakespeare's London*, 2nd ed. (Cambridge: Cambridge University Press, 1996), p. 113.

[6] In 1594 and 1599 they were given £333.6s. 8d in pounds Scots (worth a twelfth of an English pound), in 1601, £400. See E.K. Chambers, *The Elizabethan Stage*, 4 vols (Oxford: Clarendon Press, 1923), II, pp. 265–70.

[7] "The comedians, in their playes, checked your royall person with secreit and indirect taunts and checkes" (quoted by Chambers, p. 268).

Christopher Marlowe had envisaged trying his chances in Scotland.[8] Perhaps the theatre companies had some impression that, for one reason or another, the Scottish King might be especially indulgent. And perhaps, when everybody was in England, Lawrence Fletcher had some part in persuading the King's Men that they could base a play on the Gowrie conspiracy.[9] Scottish subject matter would clearly be interesting to an audience with a new Scottish King, and, as far as the company's patron was concerned, it was potentially a form of flattering attention. In a way, it is half surprising that there weren't more such plays; the rapid evolution of anti-Scottish satire probably took over. But, with such a subject as Gowrie, the company must have thought they could operate far outside normal constraints, the familiar restrictions Ben Jonson had so over-confidently infringed at the end of *Every Man Out of his Humour*.[10] Despite past experience, the King's Men were prepared to bring the new monarch on stage, in a play as nearly topical as the last scenes of Marlowe's *Massacre at Paris* had been.

The play put on by the King's men gave offence, as far as it is recorded, to certain unspecified members of the Privy Council, for doing just that: representing a living monarch.[11] Either the company had been overcome by a fit of neo-Marlovian daring, or they had believed they could operate with unprecedented latitude. As for the King, rather than burying the memory of an embarrassing episode, James continued throughout his reign to celebrate the anniversaries of his deliverance from what had been a widely disbelieved 'conspiracy'. Among the first acts of his reign in England had been proclamations for the arrest of

---

[8] Quoted in Charles Nicholl, *The Reckoning* (London: Jonathan Cape, 1992), p. 260.

[9] Fletcher is recorded as being in Scotland in 1595, 1599 and 1601. The conspiracy was played out on 5th August, 1600. John, 3rd Earl of Gowrie, and his brother Alexander, Master of Ruthven either intended to abduct the King, or kill him, or, as was widely believed at the time, James paid a surprise visit with the aim of setting on his servants to eliminate the brothers. There is a gathering of early documents at <www.home1.gte.net/loganfalls/Gowrie.htm> [Accessed 01/07/05]. The 'Gowry' play was performed on 18th December, 1604.

[10] See *Ben Jonson* ed. by C.H. Herford and Percy Simpson (Oxford: Clarendon Press, 1927), III, Appendix A, p. 602, for Jonson defiantly asserting that his initial intention to represent the Queen on stage "was not so great a part of the Heaven awry, as they would make it."

[11] "Whether the matter or the manner be not well handled, or that it be thought unfit that Princes should be played on the stage in their lifetime, I hear that some great councellors are much displeased with it, and so 'tis thought shall be forbidden" (Winwood, cited in Chambers, *The Elizabethan Stage*, I, p. 328).

the two surviving Gowrie brothers.[12] Like Bothwell before them, they were warned not to approach within ten miles of his person. The theatre company had, in a way, responded to the prominence which the King himself gave to the case.[13]

To summarize, as a subject for the King's Men, the Gowrie conspiracy seems so inherently risky that the possibility that someone had thought that James might condone such a theme has to be considered. Lawrence Fletcher, or anyone who had been in Scotland at the time, would have known of the Kirk's incredulity about the King's claims about the Ruthven brothers. It is even conceivable that the English actors in Scotland, allies of the King against the Kirk, might have evolved some Gowrie conspiracy material as part of the considerable propaganda aimed at discrediting the late brothers (who had been strong favourites of the Kirk). But if such material had been performed in Scotland, the unsuitability of a fully-formed Gowrie play was quickly asserted in England. This lost text probably featured witchcraft, as the allegations about the Earl of Gowrie, made to support James's strange story, had predictably ramified into accusations of witchcraft.[14] A spotless prince pitched into such a murky episode required opponents who were in league with nothing less than the forces of evil. Such an aspect might have been mentioned incidentally or dramatised in the lost play, to fill out the character of Gowrie himself.

Any notion that the actors were entertaining that the new reign would have allowed them a latitude to put on plays of a contemporaneity and daring not seen since Marlowe must have been reassessed when their play triggered an old basis of offence. Had they got away with it, holding up a flattering mirror of James's slightly younger self, unassailable, heaven-guarded and pure, it is easy to imagine that a play

---

[12] See *Stuart Royal Proclamations*, ed. by James F. Larkin and Paul L. Hughes (Oxford: Clarendon Press, 1973), I, p. 9 (Proclamation 5, 27 April 1603).

[13] The two younger Ruthven brothers had, like Malcolm, fled to England. William escaped abroad when James VI became James I, but Patrick was imprisoned in the Tower of London for nineteen years.

[14] The Earl of Gowrie was a cabbalist and student of astrology; his family seems to have had a history of consulting wizards. A notebook interpreted as containing magic was found on his body after he had been killed in the affray: "Much effort was made to demonstrate from this that Gowrie was a sorcerer and necromancer" <www.home1. gte.net/loganfalls/Gowrie.html>. The bones of Sir Robert Logan were exhumed for trial for his alleged complicity in the conspiracy (in 1609). This attempt to do things to the dead would hardly seem very distinct from a necromantic attempt to do things with the dead.

based on the Earl of Bothwell would have been the next play of Scottish conspiracy and witchcraft. Bothwell had been a far more serious threat than anything James had either fancied about or faced from the Ruthven brothers. Always turbulent, and too powerful to bring down by military force, he had even accomplished what the Ruthvens might have been attempting, making James his abducted captive. Bothwell had finally been brought down, in part, by the insistent charge that he had recourse to witchcraft against the King.[15] One way to see *Macbeth* would be as the considered offering by the senior dramatist of the company of a Scottish tragedy in place of a Bothwell play. That Macbeth was Duncan's cousin, as Bothwell was James's, passes so quickly by that it might register (if at all) as the unspecific use of the word cousin that was typical of the time ("O worthiest cousin" (I.4.14)). Like Massinger revising his *Believe As You List*, after the over-risky venture of *Gowry*, and instead of any other Scottish play of recent conspiracy, witchcraft and attempted usurpation, Shakespeare switched his Scottish history into the deep past.

A witchcraft charge was "a standard Scottish political weapon".[16] From English history, Shakespeare was accustomed to allegations of witchcraft being in part a political charge. He had depicted Humphrey, Duke of Gloucester, brought down by entrapment of his credulous wife Eleanor; his Richard III used the claim with audacious perfunctoriness as an excuse to quarrel with and eliminate Hastings.[17] Behind the Witchcraft Act of 1604 was a political instinct that King James would have developed from his own experience. Witchcraft had been a main charge against Bothwell, and had played some role in the haggling about the late Earl of Gowrie. James was adept at discovering who was a witch, or an exploiter of witchcraft. He never had to face his real purpose, nobody charged him with cynicism. Latent political utility hardly appeared when Lord Chief Justice Coke's draft act of such a

---

[15] See discussion in Lawrence Normand and Gareth Roberts, *Witchcraft in Early Modern Scotland*, pp. 39–49 and the associated texts numbered by the editors 24, 25, and 26. Denounced by the Scottish privy council as "ower altogidder in the handis of Sathan" in June 1591 (*ed. cit.* p. 42), Bothwell escaped trial in that year, and had himself duly acquitted of those charges in 1593 in a trial staged after his successful coup of July 1593. His reluctance to eliminate the King led to him rapidly losing all his power, and he fled into exile abroad in 1595.

[16] Arthur H. Williamson, quoted in Normand and Roberts, *Witchcraft in Early Modern Scotland*, p. 51, note 80.

[17] *Henry VI, Part 2*, I.4 and *Richard III*, III.4.61–81.

morally imperative piece of legislation was referred on to a committee of Bishops. But any strengthened act against witchcraft strengthened the royal hand against aristocratic conspirators, and James certainly expected to find conspirators in England (the Main and Bye plots were the first local candidates). An absence of plots was just about unthinkable, and establishing the guiltiness of treasonous conspirators was (like the guilt of witches) a process where suspicion was tantamount to proof. As James sagely wrote, heaven would not allow the innocent to be accused. Of course, as early as 1605, he was involved in exposing the village witchcraft allegations of Anne Gunter as fraudulent. But that was hardly a year to convince James that diabolical conspiracies against his own person were imaginary.

Somebody in Shakespeare's company knew enough recent Scottish history to have written a play based on the murky Gowrie incident. If Lawrence Fletcher or one of his company hadn't picked up on what was said in Scotland about the Gowrie case, the genuinely desperate struggle against Bothwell might have conveyed the same message: James was willing to use personal charges which some people found incredible to discredit and help eliminate opponents. Though it has been considered by some to have been in essence a royal command performance, *Macbeth* is a wary play, that might be thought to be operating its own form of mental reservation, even to be equivocating with the King.[18] It treats witchcraft with a restraint that is unexpected (considering the King as its potential audience and as a potentially exploitable source of witch-related material), and neither gratified the King's prejudices with a fully demonological exposure of the nature of the "weird sisters", nor showed their apprehension. It offers a model for royal miraculousness that is firmly located in an English holy king, who looms over the two morally doubtful Scots of royal or aristocratic blood who sought political asylum at his court. We learn that Edward the Confessor (who is too awesomely holy to be seen in person or even named) solicits heaven to cure sick people, a thaumaturgy James had shown himself unwilling to utilise, and would always disavow fully crediting as *his* act. Edward's

---

[18] The argument made in H.N. Paul's *The Royal Play of Macbeth* (New York: Macmillan, 1950). Nicholas Brooke (*Macbeth*, The Oxford Shakespeare, 1990, Introduction, pp. 73–76) is sceptical about the notion that *Macbeth* involves flattery of the King. Though the present article speculates about the relationship between King James and English actors, *Macbeth* is neither seen as a calculated attempt to play up to his interests, nor to present Macbeth and Lady Macbeth as witches, the emphasis of Garry Wills's *Witches and Jesuits: Shakespeare's Macbeth* (Oxford: Oxford University Press, 1995).

"heavenly gift of prophecy" (IV.3.157) is recounted to one man who has lost a father, another who has lost all his family: men without any claim to foresight. It would be interesting to know just how well James knew his Stuart ancestry (as it was then accepted): whether it was thorough enough for him to register and appreciate (if he ever saw the play) the coolly deployed lie about Mackbeth's co-conspirator Banquho which the play delivers, alongside the elimination of Mackbeth's relatively just and relatively lengthy reign.[19] That the Stuart royal line, presented by an ancestral ghost summoned up by black magic, seems to have depended on the good fortune of having a youthful ancestor capable of running away quickly enough makes a strange basis for regal pride.[20] A play for a Scottish king in which such kingship is presented as precarious and desperate, however authentic the King's own earlier life, or that of his much-murdered Stuart ancestors made it, indirectly stresses the sovereign balm of English kingship.

Judging by what they let Middleton add in to the play, it is hard not to think that the King's Men must have considered that their senior dramatist had left them with some splendid, but under-exploited, witchcraft material. Shakespeare could have scripted more in the way of external, extroverted witchcraft, and this is what Middleton generally enhanced. If the king thinks that witches can fly, let them be seen flying.[21] But perhaps Middleton's only distinctive intellectual contribution to the text was one that seems to distance Macbeth from the inverted worship of witchcraft.[22] Hecate is made to complain that Macbeth is merely a "wayward son, / Spiteful, and wrathful; who, as others do, / Loves for his own ends, not for you" (III.5.11–13), and is not therefore a proper recipient of the sisters' efforts. This seems like a moment of

---

[19] James probably possessed a manuscript of William Stewart's vast poem, *The Buik of the Chronicles of Scotland* (Brooke, *ed. cit.*, p. 68), alongside more accessible genealogical charts. Banquo was not a historical personage, but part of an invented lineage the Stuarts had adopted.

[20] Shakespeare might have noted, in relation to Banquo appearing in IV.1, that James insisted in *Daemonologie* that the spirit of Samuel being summoned up by the Witch of Endor did not mean that Samuel had himself been a witch.

[21] James, in one of those canny personal deductions that characterise *Daemonologie*, thinks that witches can indeed transvect, but only as long as they can hold their breath. He apparently believed that anyone passing through the air fast enough would be asphyxiated.

[22] Introducing Hecate, Middleton develops a hierarchy among "Night's black agents". Shakespeare's weird sisters are so akin to the Fates, that it is a surprise to hear them refer to "our masters" (IV.1.63).

sensitivity about making even Macbeth sound like a thoroughgoing servant of the devil. In doing this, Middleton aligned himself with Shakespeare's apparently instinctual tact—Macbeth may have tried to extinguish the Stuart line, but he was still a Scottish king. A diabolic pact, and final descent into hell, soliloquising like Faustus, might (in a putative court performance) have gratified the King as demonologist, but still have had an element of *lesae-majestatis*.

But women were, James said, more susceptible to the "gross snares" of the devil.[23] Lady Macbeth seems very close to pact-witchcraft. Developed from Donwald's malevolent wife, Lady Macbeth would be diminished in interest for us if she were seen employing an embodied spirit. But any view that her chilling invocation of "Spirits / That tend on mortal thoughts" (I.5.40–41) is self-evidently superior to a staged manifestation of their actual appearance wouldn't necessarily have been so obvious to contemporaries. In *The Witch of Edmonton*, the dramatists had the witch's familiar stray from the witch who has summoned him up, to play a role in a murder, without the murderer ever registering his presence: Tom very apparently "tends" on Frank Thorney's "mortal thoughts". A Lady Macbeth with a visible familiar, one that independently spurred Macbeth in his murders, might have been quite acceptable, inoffensive to a King who believed women more susceptible to diabolic pacts than men.

The main argument thus far is that the play's witchcraft is relatively restrained in its dramatic presentation, while the directions a more demonological *Macbeth* might have taken have been indicated. But if Shakespeare eschewed both theatrically extrovert and fully demonological witchcraft, he was more fully responsive to its imaginative possibilities at the level of style and dramatic language than editorial and critical scholarship has yet fully highlighted.

Criticism has given an insightful and detailed focus on the language of doubled senses in *Macbeth*, and there is no intention to duplicate work on equivocation here.[24] But inventing suitably ambiguous words for the father of lies was not a task that everybody could do with facility.[25] John Fian, a schoolmaster, did have Satan "making a sermon of doubtsome

---

[23] *Daemonologie*, ed. by G.B. Harrison (London: John Lane, 1924), p. 44.
[24] See, for example, Russ McDonald, *Shakespeare and the Arts of Language* (Oxford: Oxford University Press, 2001), ch. 7.
[25] York reads "the devil's writ" delivered in *Henry VI, Part 2*, and cites classical precedent for its simple ambiguity (I.4.58–62).

speeches", and claiming that his servants "should never want and should ail nothing so long as their hair was on." Fian probably knew that all body hair was shaven off during a search for the devil's mark—what sounds reassuring actually predicates the witches' doom.[26] Tom in *The Witch of Edmonton* simply lies to Elizabeth Sawyer, and threatens her for equivocating with him (II.1.130–45). Facing her fate, she complains of the devil as a "damned deceiver", but Dekker tends to stress not the devil's cleverness, but the human malignancy which leads people into his clutches. Barnabe Barnes' devil-worshipping Pope is victim of a cheap lawyer's trick by the devil.[27] In practice, the language imputed to witchcraft was less a record of *Seven Types of* (Diabolic) *Ambiguity*, than the rhyming charm, a mode that was within reach of the least sophisticated of inventors. The unusual prevalence of rhymed lines in *Macbeth* merits investigation against this context.

> Commer go ye before, commer go ye;
> If ye will not goe before, commer let me

sang the witches on their way to the church at North Berwick, according to the author of *Newes from Scotland*.[28] In Agnes Sampson's court indictment, her "dittay", a more responsible reporter produces her rhyming prayers, which she used, as a 'wise woman', in curing the sick. Couplets like this are the operative parts of the charm, after invocation of supernatural aid:

> Forth of the flesh and of the bone
> And in the earth and in the stone[29]

---

[26] Normand and Roberts, *Witchcraft in Early Modern Scotland*, p. 227.

[27] *The Devil's Charter*, ed. by R.B. McKerrow (Louvain: A. Uystpruyst, 1904), ll. 3100–17. McKerrow's footnote elucidates the passage. Barnes's play was performed at court by the King's Men in 1606.

[28] Normand and Roberts, *Witchcraft in Early Modern Scotland*, p. 316. 'Commer' means (the editors point out) "gossip or female friend".

[29] Ibid., p. 241. Agnes Sampson is conjuring the ailment out of the body and into the ground. In other cases she would take the illness on herself as a half-way house in casting it out, or transferring it to another person. Her rhyming prayers were otherwise impeccably Catholic:
And all your hallowaris [saints] loved be
To pray to them to pray to me
And keep me from the felon fee
And from the sin that soul would slay...(p. 237).

Isabel Gowdie, during the Scheherazade spell in which she staved off execution by spinning her tale of marvels, recited the simple metrics of her charm for self-transformation:

> I sall goe intill ane haire
> With sorrow, and sych, and meikle caire.[30]

John Lyly's Mother Bombie, the Wise Woman of Rochester, speaks her soothsayings in an odd rhyming prose: a character comments in the play, "These doggrel rimes and obscure words coming out of the mouth of such a weather-beaten witch are thought divinations of some holy spirit" (III.1).[31] Heywood's Wise-Woman of Hogsden is another prose-speaker who can, on occasion, rise to a couplet if she has a suitable client.[32] Dekker's Elizabeth Sawyer is taught a rhyming charm by Tom, a short inverted prayer to him as devil, which will cause him to appear to his follower:

> If thou to death or shame pursue'em,
> *Sanctibicetur nomen tuum.*[33]

The charms chanted by the witches in Ben Jonson's *Masque of Queenes* are predominantly couplets, increasingly frenzied:

> Black goe in, and blacker come out;
> At thy going downe, We giue thee a shout:
> Hoo![34]

In *All's Well That Ends Well*, when Helena is about to cure the King, she switches into a rhyme for incantatory effect: she has to convince him to try what she can do. Russell Fraser's editorial note tendentiously glosses this switch as capturing the moment when divine power invests

---

[30] In *Early Modern Women Poets*, ed. by Jane Stevenson and Peter Davidson (Oxford: Oxford University Press, 2001), p. 399.

[31] For instance, "You shall be married to morrow hand in hand, and by the Lawes of God, nature and the Land" (III.1). *The Plays of John Lyly*, ed. by Carter A. Daniel (Lewisburg: Bucknell University Press, 1988), p. 260.

[32] She tells the gentleman Senser, "A bargain, strike me luck, cease your sorrow, / Fair *Luce* shall be your Bride betimes to morrow" (II.1.75–76).

[33] In *Three Jacobean Witchcraft Plays*, ed. by Peter Corbin and Douglas Sedge (Manchester: Manchester University Press, 1986), II.1.175–76. Again, the charm is quasi-catholic, as it incorporates Latin. Dekker makes a joke against the ignorant witch, when she permutates it into "*Contaminetur nomen tuum*" (II.1.181).

[34] C.H. Herford and P. Simpson, *Ben Jonson*, VII (Oxford: Clarendon Press, 1941), p. 299 (lines 316–18). It does not appear to have been noticed that T.S. Eliot took the "Hoo Har Hoo" at the end of *Sweeney Agonistes* from this masque.

itself in the heroine. Her 'supernatural' success needs careful placing in the play, for a contemporary audience might have seen it as more equivocal.[35]

In writing *Macbeth*, Shakespeare wanted a language that would combine succinctness (King James did not like long plays), a quasi-magical forcefulness, and an acoustically loud presence. This latter quality is important in a play full of sound effects, hallucinatory noise, and alterations of pitch. Macbeth is a hero whose fate has been foretold to him in a series of charms. These magical distichs he repeats, and re-formulates. To be fully attentive to the detail of the matter, not all of these words of power are full heroic couplets; a prominent variant consists of a rhymed line and a half, so that the rhyme occurs in a briefer syntactic unit. Rhyme begins to acquire a nightmare hold. Indeed, Macbeth can sometimes reformulate a charm in a way that loses the rhyme of the distich he had heard pronounced. Reciting the spell, he breaks the spell, as though it is no longer quite so strong for him. Or in place of the rhymes he has heard, Macbeth pronounces his own semi-oracular utterances about his condition.

Simon Palfrey has suggested in his excellent study, *Doing Shakespeare*, that there is an obvious issue of agency in couplets like those given to Macbeth: "Is the rhyme controlling the speaker, or the speaker controlling the rhyme?"[36] Palfrey, with many texts to discuss, does not, however, relate this general observation to the rhyming charms of supernatural agency, as a language characteristic of witchcraft. But when couplets resemble oracular distichs, the question of whether Macbeth is in charge of the couplets, or the couplets in charge of him, becomes acute. Examined together, the couplets given to Macbeth enact a particularly noticeable *agon* between self-determination and being externally

---

[35] Russell Fraser, ed., *All's Well that Ends Well* (Cambridge: Cambridge University Press, 1985), II.1.126–206. Helena switches the King's dismissive, interview-closing couplets into a heightened style at l.130 ff. 'Supernatural' as a word appears in only this play and *Macbeth*. The other resemblances between the two texts are (first) that Bertram's fate seems to be so much in the hands of three inescapable women: his mother, Helena, and Diana. The idea of being deceived as though by "a double-meaning prophesier" also appears (IV.3.94–95). The comedy looks like the lesser by-product of the imaginative labour that had produced *Macbeth*.

[36] Simon Palfrey, *Doing Shakespeare* (London: Thomson Learning, 2005), p. 97. Palfrey is talking about the couplets recited by Iago, but he goes on to quote *Macbeth*, V.5.47–52, commenting "these rhymes are absolutely Macbeth's: because so grimly *chosen* by him, because spoken as though with a choking grip upon rising hysteria. But then they are not his at all, because so suggestive of overdetermined impotence" (ibid.).

determined. A witch's charm is always, in its nature, a language which exerts power over others, but bought at the cost of self-surrender to a power greater than the witch's.

Macbeth is a hero haunted by rhyme. In a tragedy where rhymed couplets feature so noticeably, the always-imminent rhyme is that on his name: "Go pronounce his present death/And with his former title greet Macbeth" (I.2.66–67). If the sanguinary narrative given by the "bloody man" hadn't already fixed the idea, the Macbeth/death association is triggered by this early couplet from Duncan. Rosse replies to Duncan's command to "pronounce" with a curt "I'll see it done", an assent which hasn't enough loud finality for Duncan, who makes these words part of another lop-sided couplet (as though he wants to "*hear* it done'): "What he hath lost, noble Macbeth hath won."

In scene three, directly following this exchange, the witches begin, rather like New Historicists, with a prose anecdote about a sailor's wife. For their active malice, they switch into the heptasyllabic couplets Shakespeare used for special recitations.[37] Macbeth's arrival is heralded by that mysterious drum, which excites the third witch to a couplet of four syllable lines (I.3.31–32). They then wind up a charm which either settles the fate of the shipman or prepares for the moral shipwreck of Macbeth. He enters, as all readers notice, with an unknowing reformulation from one of their couplets ("Fair is foul, and foul is fair" (I.1.11) and "So foul and fair a day I have not seen" (I.3.38)). In the encounter that follows, Banquo is initially more loquacious, despite the witches' gesture of silence to him. Macbeth emerges from his "rapt" state to demand to know more. The internal rhymes of "more/Cawdor" "Stay/say/way" "whence/intelligence" (between I.3.70 and 76) capture his agitation, his way of tumbling words over to make scarcely comprehensible sounds into sense. The witches vanish, and Rosse arrives with his recapitulation of how Duncan received accounts of Macbeth's preternatural successes in battle, which he tells back to the doer. In them, Macbeth seems to materialise in "the stout Norweyan ranks" as if he had got there by transvection from the other scene of slaughter. Once there, he is "nothing afeard of what thyself didst make, / Strange images of death" (I.3.95; 96–97). "Strange" is one of the key words of the play: Rosse's account makes Macbeth's fighting sound like the practice of malefic image-witchcraft. "As thick

---

[37] Other examples are in *Measure for Measure* and *The Tempest*.

as hail" (97) seems to be the right editorial reading: the restored word "hail" echoes the witches' much repeated word, and prefigures Rosse's own formal "hail" at line 106. One might deduce that Duncan meant to manage the ambitions of his dangerously effective cousin with a tantalising suggestion of a "greater honour" to follow his becoming Thane of Cawdor (104). But as we have not heard Duncan say any such thing, Rosse's implication of incremental honours, especially when Macbeth has just heard Angus talk only of some deferred recognition (I.3.100–03), might seem to confirm both the abnormal speed and the effectiveness of invisible incitements. Like others in the play, Rosse has become semi-oracular, an unconscious conduit for prophecy.[38]

The critical attention here is to relatively minor suggestions in the text: Macbeth's exchange aside to Banquo, and his rapt soliloquy, are explicit discussions of whether the Devil can "speak true" (107). But, pursuing couplets, Macbeth ends with a rhyming tag that attempts to settle himself to an acceptance of a future that cannot be determined, only endured:

> Come what come may,
> Time and the hour runs through the roughest day. (I.3.147–48)

This rather anodyne motto, intended to soothe himself into passivity, contrasts strongly with the fiery couplets triggered when Macbeth hears that he may have to act (I.4.48–53). He later stiffens his resolve prior to the murder itself with curtly sententious half-line and line couplets (II.1.60–61; 63–64). This control disappears after the murder has been committed: reporting the various cries and blessings he heard on his way to the crime, Macbeth hysterically repeats what he has heard, despite his wife's warning about such obsessiveness, until he arrives at a rhyming charm pronounced against him:

> Glamis hath murther'd Sleep, and therefore Cawdor
> Shall sleep no more, Macbeth shall sleep no more! (II.2.41–42).

---

[38] Other persons or objects that become prophetic include Lady Macbeth ("I feel now / The future in the instant." (I.5.57–58)), those who talk in their sleep at II.2.41–42, the "obscure bird" "prophesying with accents terrible" (II.3.60; 58), the trumpets that are "clamorous harbingers" (V.6.10) and other odder glimpses of futurity, like Macduff imagining Banquo rising from death like a sprite "To countenance this horror" (II.3.81). Macbeth, like Tarquin before him, knows what his crime will really do to him even before he commits it.

Plotting Banquo's death, Macbeth can still do a variant on his couplet about Duncan's exit (II.1.63–64 and III.1.140–41). What sounded callous before now sounds worse, as Macbeth approaches a grimly parodic repetition of himself. His wife is already muttering broken couplets of utter loss (III.2.4–7).

In III.3, Macbeth produces a successful piece of verbal charming, invoking "seeling Night" (46), and, within four lines, heralding the success with which he has summoned up darkness ("Light thickens…"). Self-aligned in temporary confidence with the rest of "Night's black agents", he chants an exultant couplet, while his wife "marvels". He concludes here, strongly in control, with an icy Senecan rhyming tag. After the ghost of Banquo has appeared, Macbeth's speech of juddering terror might be read as monorhymed on "blood" (III.4.121–25). The horrific transition he makes into initiating the death of Macduff apparently indicates that Macduff's blood will be offered to Banquo's ghost. Macbeth speaks of his secret sources of knowledge, and then turns to a better source still, the Weird Sisters. He seems to know where to find them, is confident that he can compel them: and he switches into couplets which fight for determination (134–39; 141–42).

The cauldron scene (IV.1) is of course the climax and culmination of the play's supernatural business. Among the mainly heptasyllabic couplets, Middleton seems to have liked the repeated "Double, double toil and trouble" longer-lined couplet (IV.1.10–11; 19–20; 35–36), and his additional passage has a chant of "Round, around, around, about about / All ill come running in, all good keep out!" The tumbling rhymes "Open, locks, / Whoever knocks" perhaps prompted Middleton's short-lined song for Hecate; a charm to open a locked door is standard piece of the magical repertoire.[39]

Consultation of a divineress would have recalled Saul with the Witch of Endor. Saul indemnifies the witch, who is reluctant to make prophecies using such illicit means as divination by summoning up the dead. As in the Bible, so in the play, the prophecy is made without subsequent punishment of the seer. In 1563 Scottish law had made consultation with a witch a capital offence; James had the jurors who acquitted Barbara Napier rather than see her condemned on that basis charged with wilful error.[40] This part of the Scottish Act was of naked

---

[39] See Normand and Roberts, *Witchcraft in Early Modern Scotland*, p. 229.
[40] Ibid., p. 91.

political utility: who else would consult a witch about the succession but
an interested and ill-intentioned party? The difficulty James had faced
in securing a conviction when the penalty was so draconian perhaps
helped prevent such a clause being insinuated into the English 1604
Witchcraft Act. As Keith Thomas points out, a "striking" novelty in
the 1604 Act was that it made it a felony to "consult, covenant with,
entertain, employ, feed, or reward any evil and wicked spirit to or for
any intent or purpose".[41] These may be the actions of the witch, not
her client, but the person commissioning the consultation might have
been said to be consulting the evil spirit.

   Shakespeare's scene was powerful enough for the Caroline courtier-
dramatist Lodowyck Carlell to imitate it closely for some melodramatic
court politics in *Argalus and Parthenia*.[42] Macbeth receives from the apparitions three rhymed pronouncements; a preliminary warning and two
false reassurances. He reacts in echoic rhymes, and will go on repeating
these mantras. At V.3.1–10 his repetitions are unrhymed, chaotic, until
he staggers into a couplet that tries to express resolution:

> The mind I sway by, and the heart I bear,
> Shall never sag with doubt, nor shake with fear.

"Fear", so defiantly denied here, obsesses Macbeth ("I cannot taint
with fear"; "those linen cheeks of thine / Are counsellors to fear";
"Hang those that talk of fear"—3; 17; 36).[43] His exit couplet in his
best resolute style:

> I will not be afraid of death and bane,
> Till Birnam forest come to Dunsinane. (V.3.59–60)

But this does not close the scene, being undercut by the bathos of the
Doctor's near-parodic couplet about his own terror. Macbeth continues
to deny fear (V.5.9–15). He responds to the news that the wood is actually on the move with a set of three couplets that stop and resume as
if in a losing struggle against an immense inertia (V.5.47–52). In the

---

[41] Keith Thomas, *Religion and the Decline of Magic* (London: Weidenfeld and Nicolson,
1971), p. 443.
[42] Carlell's play (1639) is close enough to *Macbeth* to reveal how he understood
Shakespeare's play. The courtier Adrastus consults a witch about the succession, and
the fate of the King (Part I, Act V). Told that he will himself murder the King, he
promptly does so. Carlell's take on *Macbeth* stresses the hero's fate as absolutely determined for him by the prophecy he hears.
[43] The word appears more times than in any other Shakespeare play.

dead finality of these lines, a type of utterance that Macbeth repeated against despair has become the authentic voice of it. Once in battle, Macbeth is brisker ("What's he, / That was not born of woman? Such a one / Am I to fear, or none"), though his formulation here singles out and anticipates the "one" that he is so soon to meet. His last full repetition of his charm is after he has killed young Siward (V.7.12–13), he repeats its essential message to Macduff after telling him "I bear a charmed life", before being stunned by Macduff's decisive refutation in "Despair thy charm".

As an aside, it may not be obvious, but one of the hazards faced in early modern soldiering was that of coming up against charmed opponents. Sir John Harrington gloomily accounts for the failure of his men to detain Rory Oge, who had walked through their ranks in full confidence of his magical invulnerability, as stemming from the way they had decided that they could do nothing against him.[44] Enemy soldiers believed to have used occult means of self-protection were liable to summary execution: "The enchaunted men were all condemned to be hanged [...] because against the law of Arms they had used unchristian means to [...] shed Christian blood", Thomas Churchyard ineffably complained about soldiers of the Duke of Alva.[45] It is an effect conferred by witchcraft: the witch who astonished Parliamentary soldiers by surfing on a plank across the River Kennet at Newbury in 1643 caught and derisively chewed the musket balls fired at her.[46] That Macbeth believes in his charmed life would not have seemed unusual.[47]

Macbeth is not, of course, the only character given couplets to speak in the play. They occur throughout the text. At their worst, they suggest that peculiar absence of real creative involvement with Macbeth's opponents which marks this text (IV.3.239–40; V.4.17–18; V.6.7–10). But

---

[44] "The idle faith which possesses the Irishry concerning magic and witchcraft seized our men and lost the victory...this belief doth much daunt our soldiers...he effected all by dint of witchery, and had by magic compelled them not to touch him". Quoted in E.M. Tenison, *Elizabethan England*, 14 vols (Leamington Spa: privately printed, 1956), X, pp. 132–33.

[45] Thomas Churchyard, *True Discourse* (1602) in Tenison, *Elizabethan England* (1933), II, p. 16.

[46] *A Most Certain, Strange, and true Discovery of a VVITCH* ([np], 1643), p. 6.

[47] The Earl of Gowrie's belief in magic extended to carrying "a little close parchment bag full of magical characters and words of enchantment, wherein he seemed that he had put his confidence". The unplanned, near impromptu nature of his coup (if that is what it was) was perhaps a product of over-confidence that he knew the future. Cited from <www.home1.gte.net/loganfalls/Gowrie.html>.

stray rhymes can have unexpected pathos ("The Thane of Fife had a wife", Lady Macbeth says, as if starting a nursery rhyme—the desolate and premature end follows—"where is she now?" (V.1.41–42)). *Macbeth* is the story of a man doomed to hasty repetition, murder after murder, to a series of "dread exploits". The rapid return of rhyme sounds suits that story: "Macbeth / Death"—"Macduff / enough".

Harry Berger suggests that it might be inferred from the play that Scotland is doomed to repetition, that the condition of its kings will always be precarious, the cycle of murder will only begin again.[48] Malcolm indulges a strange urge to confess to crimes that he hasn't committed, and seems to find his legitimacy only by attaining belief in the integrity of Macduff, which he only finds credible when he has made Macduff give up all hope in him. His attempt to "unspeak mine own detraction" (IV.3.123) leaves Macduff silent (137). Despite prompting, Macduff doesn't seem to see a cancellation, but is fixed at "Such welcome and unwelcome things at once", a mixture of fair and foul, good and evil entangled, not distinguished. Devilish Macbeth has tainted imaginations throughout his kingdom: the self-division Menteth diagnoses in Macbeth (V.2.22–25) seems endemic.

So the text contains a hero who is not a witch (as Garry Wills tried to argue), but one who is given a characteristic form of utterance whose effect suggests witchcraft's mixture of dominance and subordination. A witch can curse effectually, but cannot escape the fate accepted to purchase that power. Macbeth's language (to this extent) mimes witchcraft, the simultaneous fate-dealing and the fatedness of "night's black agents".

Serena in *Mother Bombie* complained of "doggrell rimes" and "obscure words" as the typical utterances of a witch. Editors of *Macbeth* have given some attention to what the late Jeremy Maule referred to as Macbeth "fathering new linguistic children—new words for the new tasks ahead of him": neologisms in the play (or at least, the words entering literary language for the first recorded time).[49] The on-line version of the *OED* allows a far more thorough investigation of *Macbeth* citations.[50] An

---

[48] Harry Berger, Jr., *Making Trifles of Terrors* (Stanford: Stanford University Press, 1997), pp. 92–93.

[49] In an unpublished lecture entitled 'Second Sight and Second Sight' at Royal Holloway College, 1992.

[50] To avoid an intricate and lengthy footnote, verbal innovativeness in the listed words can be verified by checking entries for these words in the *OED*, which will also give an act and scene reference to the occurrence in the play.

expanded list of first occurrences, or of newly formed adjectives out of nouns, or new figurative senses by transfer, revives the once-strange language of *Macbeth*, a poet's response to the problem of "deeds without a name". "*Aroint*", "*incarnadine*", and "*assassination*" are well known, as is the outrageous-sounding insult "*rump-fed runnion*", where both the noun and its bizarre compound adjective are previously unrecorded. The "*choppy*" fingers of the witches throw ingredients into the cauldron to make the "Grewell thicke, and *slab*". These are probably less noted as likely neologisms, thrown by the poet into the seething cauldron of the play. Who better than Macbeth to first name the "*unreal*", one of a series of new 'un-' words that appear in the play ("*undeeded*", "*unfix*", "*unprovoke*", "*unsafe*", "*unspeak*", "*unshirking*" and, of course, "*unsex*")? He confronts "*direness*", challenges Fate to "*champion me*". "Hell is *murky*", says Lady Macbeth desolately, and she would produce "*compunctious*" even as she asks the dark powers not to be any such thing. Other "witchlike words" in the text are "*shipwrecking*", "*tempest-tossed*", the verb "*sliver'd*", "*bodements*", and "*botch*". There are the privative forms "*confineless*", "*stanchless*" "*marrowless*", words to register versions of being "*unsafe*" (as above, new itself), such as "*assailable*", "*vulnerable*", "*exposure*". "*Intrenchant*", "*rooky*", "*yeasty*", "*fitful*" and "*dareful*" are more verbal apparitions. "*Pauser*" and "*poster*", "*galloping*", "*stealthy*", "*skirre*", "*vaulting*" and "*impede*" are words for the fitful movements of *Macbeth*, where everything either happens too fast or too slowly. New compounds include "*even-handed*", both "*be-all*" and "*end-all*", "*cream-faced*", "*bear-like*", "*shard-born*", "*summer-cloud*", "*over-red*", and a term diminished by a later sense, but in *Macbeth* expressive of something like denial of your own best nature, even loss of the eternal jewel, "*self-abuse*". A double-check against the Chadwyck-Healey database sometimes shows that the *OED*'s archive did suffer from the early loss of many of its sixteenth- and seventeenth-century citations. "*Fiendlike*", in the dictionary as previously unrecorded, had appeared in Marston's *Antonio's Revenge* (1602), and "*Grimalkin*" has another antedating in a very witchy context.[51]

The delirious concocting of all those severed or extracted items into a "slab" gruel, a "firm" charm, is the point where Shakespeare's imagination most indulges witchcraft. The grimoires of spells tend

---

[51] "Ile name thee no more Mother Red-cap upon paine of death, if thou wilt Grimalkin", *Satiro-mastix* III.1.190–91. *Dramatic Works of Thomas Dekker*, ed. by Fredson Bowers (Cambridge: Cambridge University Press, 1953), I.

to require bizarre ingredients, as if to guarantee the potency of the
charm by ensuring practical irreproducibility ("Take the foreskin of
a freshly-killed wolf ...").[52] A major task of witchcraft, from Ovid's
Medea onwards, was the world travel involved in putting together such
recondite materials. In the art of the period, witches assemble around
cauldrons—and a truth about shamanism is that mankind has always
gone to a lot of trouble to create hallucinogens.[53] There do not seem
to be any literary prototypes that are as grotesquely detailed, sordid, as
hallucinatory as the "deed without a name" achieved in Shakespeare's
cauldron scene.[54] The engravings of Jacques de Gheyn II alone equal
it in imagining what witchcraft might traffic in.

Responding to the scene he has glimpsed, Macbeth sets off with a
résumé of stereotypical malefice which turns into a vision of universal
destruction (IV.1.50–61). The sisters' concoction, even though it plays
with taboos of disgust, and reflects the statute of 1604, doesn't seem as
powerful as the total destructiveness Macbeth can imagine for witchcraft.
Without consuming the loathsome potion itself, Macbeth will eventually
have "supp'd full with horrors" (V.5.13), like a witch he experiences an
"old age" that is cursed by all who dare curse (V.3.22–28), but he is
still capable in his despair of a universal malevolence (V.5.49–50). He
enters last as another severed body part, a cursed head, by which the
revenger Macduff can confidently speak the future.[55] Macduff divines
that the nobility "speak my salutation in their minds" (V.9.22), and
asks for their vote to endorse his: "Hail, King of Scotland!" Unseen by
Scotland's nobility, as they second his cry, the dead lips should move, and

---

[52] The quotation is the opening of an *aiguillette*, the twelfth charm in the *Petit Albert*.
See P.G. Maxwell-Stuart, *The Occult in Early Modern Europe* (Houndmills: Basingstoke:
Macmillan, 1999), p. 127 for a talisman from Croll's *Basilica Chymica* (1609) against
both the plague *and* the pox involving two ounces of powered toads, the menstruum
of young girls, pearls, sapphire, emerald and saffron. Audrey L. Meaney, 'Women,
Witchcraft and Magic in Anglo-Saxon England' in *Superstition and Popular Medicine in
Anglo-Saxon England*, ed. by D.G. Scragg (Manchester: Manchester University Press,
1989) gives some archaeological evidence of the strange contents of elf-bags.
[53] The title page of Ulricus Molitoris, *de lamiis et phitonicis mulieribus* (c. 1500) has an
early image of witches putting items into a cauldron, which becomes a cliché in the
art of Hans Baldung Grien, Teniers the Younger, etc.
[54] Erictho in Lucan's *Pharsalia*, Book VI, has the gruesome aspects, the Bawd in *La
Celestina* has a more heterogeneous collection of organic ingredients for love-charms
(tongue of a viper, ass brains, a badger's foot, hedgehog prickles, the caul of a colt, etc.,
alongside the rope used to hang a man). In Brian P. Levack, *The Witchcraft Sourcebook*
(London and New York: Routledge, 2004), p. 327.
[55] See Keith Thomas, *Religion and the Decline of Magic*, p. 230 for an attempt to divine
using a severed head.

the unheard voice of this second bloody head should join in, with an ironic whispered "Hail!" For after all, Malcolm is confidently embarking on a regal future that, despite Macduff's vision, belongs instead (as the witches have previously told us) to the "seed of Banquo".

This investigation has ranged over the circumstances that might have prompted and shaped *Macbeth*, its sources both in print and among those less tangible notions that could have been transmitted by the English actors who had been in King James VI's Scotland. It seems likely that under their impetus, Shakespeare's company seems briefly to have collectively believed that the king would accept on the English stage re-enactments of events in his own life. *Macbeth* was written after the Gowrie play, and observed the normal prohibition on representing living monarchs on stage. Some re-imagining of what *Macbeth* might have been like if it had more fully reflected the king's beliefs has been offered here: but Shakespeare's circumspection even extends to representing James's ideas. A characteristic caution about taking overt positions in controversial matters might be deduced, but there is another possibility: some recognition, or inward repudiation, of the way King James could exploit 'witchcraft' as a confected political charge to neutralise opponents.[56] For whatever reason, or combination of reasons, Shakespeare avoided giving the company's royal patron a fully demonological play. Nobody could say, however, that *Macbeth* is a text that lacks imaginative engagement on Shakespeare's part. If it can be thought of as manifesting (in Shakespeare's decisions about what to show, and what to leave out), something that might be moral dubiety over some of the most insidious of the King's repertoire of words of power (specifically, the denunciation for witchcraft by a royal accuser), the text is fascinated by witchcraft's words of power. So it is not, in the end, to beliefs about witchcraft, but to the language of witchcraft that Shakespeare responds most creatively.

---

[56] As previously caught by Shakespeare in the worst possible exponent, Richard of Gloucester (*Richard III*, Act 3, scene 4).

WITCHCRAFT AND POSSESSION AT THE ACCESSION OF JAMES I

THE PUBLICATION OF SAMUEL HARSNETT'S
A DECLARATION OF EGREGIOUS POPISH IMPOSTURES

CLIVE HOLMES*

This paper considers a number of problems concerning the publication of Samuel Harsnett's *A Declaration of Egregious Popish Impostures*, a tract registered with the Stationers' Company on 16 March 1603, as an introduction to a more general discussion of the views on witchcraft circulating in the English government at the time of the passing of the 1604 Witchcraft statute. Not least, the publication gives some indication of the attitudes of a key player in the making of the statute—the new king, James I.

The tract has been the subject of considerable scholarly interest, but largely from students of English literature, and one of them, F.W. Brownlow, has produced a full scholarly edition of Harsnett's treatise.[1] This interest stems from the fact, first noted by an eighteenth-century editor of Shakespeare's works, that the names of the devils that Edgar (disguised as the madman "Poor Tom") lists as tormenting him in *King Lear* are derived from Harsnett's tract: the latter can be added to the list of works read and used by the playwright. Twentieth-century scholarship has both extended the range of borrowings from Harsnett,[2] and focussed on the issue of what drew Shakespeare to this text. One obvious answer to this question is that Shakespeare was intrigued by the

* This paper has been discussed at seminars in Oxford and St Andrew's: I should like to thank the participants, particularly Tom Freeman, Bridget Heal, Felicity Heal, Andrew Pettigree, and Jenny Wormald for their comments and suggestions.

[1] F.W. Brownlow, *Shakespeare, Harsnett, and the Devils of Denham* (Newark: University of Delaware Press, 1993). Pages 9–189 of this work consist of Brownlow's discussion and scholarly apparatus. Pages 191–415 are a transcription of Harsnett's text: of this, pp. 191–335 consist of Harsnett's account; pp. 337–413 are copies of the examinations of the five witnesses taken by the officers of the Court of Ecclesiastical High Commission. References to Harsnett's work will be given in the text, to the pages of this edition.

[2] Notably Kenneth Muir: see his *Shakespeare's Sources* (London: Methuen, 1957), pp. 147–61.

treatise's remarkably rich vein of references to the stage. This emerges early in the tract, and is a leitmotiv throughout. Harsnett continuously employs a series of references, tropes and metaphors drawn from the theatre: he refers to classical playwrights; to the old miracle plays; to stage technicalities. Harsnett presents himself as a theatre critic, assisting his readers to evaluate the play at Denham: "that every part may be considered, how well it hath been plaied and what actor hath best deserved the *plaudite* [...] for his good action and wit" (203). Harsnett develops a sustained metaphor in which acting and the theatre come to typify exorcism and, ultimately, the Roman Church in general. This analysis was floated in an earlier Harsnett treatise, in which exorcism is described as "a singular foundation to uphold the Pope his play-house and to make religion a pageant of Puppittes."[3] Its climactic statement informs the opening lines of the concluding chapter of the *Declaration*: "the end of a Comedie is a *plaudite* to the Author and Actors." (319)

As Richard Wilson has written, consideration of Harsnett's text "prompts most current discussion of the playwright's Catholic sympathies among literary scholars."[4] Those disposed to see Shakespeare as deeply sympathetic to traditional Catholicism, even a committed recusant, have argued that the playwright was using a fiercely anti-Catholic polemic with the intention to subvert it. Harsnett's style of exuberant, coruscating satire, often prurient and bawdy, was not universally appreciated even by fiercely anti-Catholic writers: one of them remarked with distaste his "immodest style and lascivious pen".[5] Shakespeare, it is argued, was both fascinated and repelled by Harsnett's dirty amalgam of ridicule, vitriol and prurience. In *King Lear*, with its sympathy to the possessed and to exorcism, Shakespeare distanced himself from the crude and mechanistic universe of official Protestant culture that Harsnett had sought to promote. This kind of analysis, shorn of its confessional engagement, has been developed brilliantly by the 'New Historicist' commentator, Stephen Greenblatt. For Greenblatt, Harsnett was a spokesman for the state, for the ruling elite who were seeking to obliterate "pockets of rivalrous charisma", and to impose their own

---

[3] [Samuel Harsnett], *A Discovery of the Fraudulent Practices of John Darrel* (London, 1599), sig. A3.

[4] Richard Wilson, *Secret Shakespeare* (Manchester: Manchester University Press, 2004), p. 54: and see pp. 55, 189–92, 289.

[5] John Swan, *A True and Briefe Report of Mary Glover's Vexation* (London, 1603), p. 68: Swan's tract is reprinted with the original pagination in *Witchcraft and Hysteria in Elizabethan London*, ed. by Michael MacDonald (London: Routledge, 1991).

re-defined conceptual categories—Protestantism, certainly, but far more than this—by which they constructed the world and legitimised their hegemony. Shakespeare is again seen as a formidable critic of the values of the new establishment; *King Lear* as a radical indictment of a hollow and insincere philosophy.[6]

This is clever and persuasive. And much of it is unexceptional. But, while Samuel Harsnett was certainly a spokesman "of established religious and secular authority", as Chaplain to the Bishop of London, Richard Bancroft, and licenser of the press, he was not the voice of a hegemonic elite. He was a member of a faction within the elite, a faction engaged in a fierce struggle for supremacy in the state. To understand this, we need to examine the polemical context of the *Declaration*, and we can begin this critique of a new historicist argument, by resort to an old historian's technique: chronology—and a puzzle that emerges from it.

The *Declaration* was listed in the Stationers' Register on 16 March 1603: the exorcisms it described occurred in Catholic households around London, notably at Denham and Hackney, in 1585–86; these were finally interrupted that summer when Denham was raided and the priests arrested. Government agents questioned captured priests concerning the exorcisms—these "conjurations, witchcraftys, sorceries and illusions to deceive the world".[7] But the Privy Council did not pursue the issue, despite the fact that one of the first to be exorcised, Nicholas Marwood, was a servant of Anthony Babington, the conspirator executed in 1586, who, with several of his friends, had "oftentimes" (391) attended the exorcisms.[8] Subsequently various manuscript accounts of the exorcisms circulated in Catholic circles, and became known to the authorities in 1594. But not until March 1599 did the Court of Ecclesiastical High Commission interrogate some of those involved. Another delay followed until the spring of 1602, when two of the key demoniacs and a renegade priest were interrogated. These depositions and confessions form the basis of Harsnett's tract.

---

[6] Stephen Greenblatt, 'Shakespeare and the Exorcists' in *Shakespearean Negotiations* (Berkeley and Los Angeles: University of California Press, 1988), pp. 94–128: quotation from pp. 96–97.

[7] 'The true and wonderful story of the lamentable fall of Anthony Tyrell' in *The troubles of our Catholic Forefathers*, ed. by John Morris, 3 vols. (1872–1877), II, at p. 326.

[8] Brownlow, p. 31.

Harsnett felt obliged to answer the obvious question—the reasons
for these delays—in his tract. He argued that the triumphalist Catholic
account of the exorcisms, "the Miracle Book", as he derisively named
it, "came but lately to hand" in 1598 (199) and then the authorities had
to find and interrogate the major participants. This is implausible. First,
the authorities knew of the accounts long before that year. The Council
had seized a draft account of the exorcisms from Anthony Tyrell, one of
the priests involved, in 1586. In 1594 a fuller compilation, "an English
treatise in a written hand" (201), which contained a re-worked copy of
Tyrell's account and other material fell into the hands of the repellent
recusant-hunter, Richard Topcliffe, after he arrested the Catholic agent
and courier, Robert Barnes. Barnes, in July 1598, implied that Topcliffe
had shown the work to a number of government officials some time in
the intervening period.[9] Harsnett also used a Latin treatise by Weston,
concerning the dispossession of the first of the demoniacs, Marwood,
which may have been in the government's hands even earlier. Second,
Harsnett's disingenuous chronology certainly cannot explain the three-
year delay that preceded the second tranche of interrogation in 1602.
Harsnett's prefatory remarks may not be persuasive in terms of the
detailed chronology, but his reference to "the Miracle Book" as a key
text does suggest the centrality of government-recusant relations in the
decision to commission his book in 1602–03, as does his dedication of
the work—"To the seduced Catholiques of England" (195).

The priests involved in the exorcisms saw them as a triumphant proof
of the Catholic faith. Harsnett had great fun savaging the debating
points, naïve, manipulative and self-serving by turn, scored by the priests
in their homely "dialoguizing with the devil" (332) during the process of
exorcism. The devils' testimony was used to 'prove' the power of relics
(particularly of those recently executed by the government), the sacro-
sanctity of the priestly office, the doctrines of the Real Presence and of
the Immaculate Conception. The devils would also conveniently praise
the Protestant establishment, particularly Elizabeth and her courtiers,
as their obedient disciples. Harsnett was ruthlessly cutting and pasting
material from the Miracle Book to sustain his polemic,[10] but his satire
is in some measure confirmed by a surviving section of that volume,

---

[9] HMC Cecil, VIII, p. 274, Robert Barnes to Sir Robert Cecil, 23 July 1598.
[10] The version of the 'Miracle Book' used by Harsnett is no longer extant; one
of the accounts that was part of the compilation, by the priest, Anthony Tyrell, and
describing the exorcism of Sara Williams does survive: see the next note.

an account of the exorcisms at Lord Vaux's house at Hackney. Maho, the devil, volunteered the information that Protestants sat on his right hand; schismatics—church papists—on his left, "somewhat further off": he called out "the lord save the Quene and her mynisters".[11] Not only did exorcism confirm the Catholic faith, it was, argued the exorcists, a spectacular evangelical weapon against Protestantism. William Weston, S.J., one of the major participants at Denham, believed that if people were given the opportunity "of observing the majestic power of the Church over evil spirits and monsters", they would immediately "see and acknowledge at once the difference between the two religions and award the victory to the Catholic faith".[12]

The priest, Anthony Tyrell, claimed that five hundred people were converted by the exercises in 1585–6; others were even more sanguine.[13] But this seems very doubtful. The Denham and Hackney exorcisms were very much a manifestation of seigneurial Catholicism. They took place in the enclosed Catholic households of Sir George Peckham and Lord Vaux; the lay participants were recusant gentry and their servants, who arrived in coaches. The successful exorcisms might reinforce such people in their convictions, but they had—despite the claims of the priests—negligible evangelical potential. Even when the Book of Miracles came to the government's attention, there was little reason to change this evaluation.

However, at the end of the 1590s reports reached the Council of the evangelical employment of exorcism in more troubling contexts, in popular assemblies in the north-west of England. In June 1598 Sir Richard Molyneux reported exorcisms in Lancashire attended by crowds in excess of five hundred, concluding "thus they win daily many unto them".[14] Harsnett sardonically noted the activities of one of the priests, travelling the country, "as Tynkers doe [with] their bitches", accompanied by a "wench pretended by the priest to be possessed" who

<hr/>

[11] The account is part (ff. 485–91) of a commonplace book, put together in Northamptonshire in 1605–08 designed to sustain its readers' Catholic commitment. It was in the library of the recusant Brudenell family of Dene, and is now Bodleian Library, Ms Eng. Theol. B 1. I owe this reference to the kindness of Tom Freeman.

[12] *William Weston: The Autobiography of an Elizabethan*, ed. by Philip Caraman (London: Longmans, 1955), p. 27.

[13] Ibid., p. 30, note 10.

[14] HMC Cecil, VIII, pp. 213–14, Sir Richard Molyneux to Sir John Stanhope, 13 June 1598. Molyneux's letter of 3 Aug. to Robert Cecil (p. 293) emphasises the popular nature of the Lancashire exorcisms, which "drew many ignorant people".

drew "a concourse of simple people, the founders of miracles" (250).
He sneered at this Autolycus figure—a "pedling Exorcist of the rascal
crue, who wandered like a chapman of smal wares" (251) and his rustic
performance, "this puppet-play", certainly did not give Harsnett the
range provided by the altogether more professionally produced Denham exorcisms as a butt for his invective. But we might think that the
government was troubled by the emerging *popular* potential of exorcism
and decided to target it through an exposé of the Denham incident.
This would explain the 1599 interrogations, though not the subsequent
delay in following them up and publishing the *Declaration*.

But Harsnett provides another clue to the anti-Catholic focus of
his work, which brings us closer to the date of publication, when, in
his first line of the dedication he refers to the Catholics as "Seduced
and *disunited* Brethren" (195). Disunited: at the turn of the century the
missionary priests were divided, Jesuits against seculars, first over
the government of the Wisbech community and then over the role of
the Archpriest. These conflicts were actively encouraged by Harsnett's
patron, Bishop Bancroft, and were stirred with particular vigour in
1601–02, as Bancroft flirted with the 'Gallican' seculars against the
ultramontane party of Garnett and of Weston in his effort to "divide
and discredit the Catholic clergy".[15] The Declaration is a contribution
to this programme. Harsnett constantly over-emphasises the role of
William Weston S.J. (using his alias, Edmunds) as the orchestrator of
the entire slate of exorcisms, "*rector chori*" (201), "the chiefe plotter and
the arch-imposter" (322), "the author and contriver of this devil-sport"
(332), a role that does not emerge with such clarity in the evidence that
he cites. Weston is depicted as demanding the subordination of the
attendant secular priests, his dupes, and using the triumphant success
of his exorcisms to underline his own and his Order's peculiar sanctity
and access to divine power. "Heare Fa[ther] Edmunds for all, like Julius
Caesar the commenter of his owne worthy exploites, in his monster-
miracle acted upon Marwood", sneers Harsnett, before providing an
edited account of the climactic exorcism, which involved the use of as
relic of the Jesuit martyr, Edmund Campion. After furious raving, torments, vomiting "as though he would have spued out his very entralls
and guts...ipso etiam Edmunde, Edmunde clamante, liberatus est"
(295–6). "The Jesuits," Harsnett concludes, "had an ambitious desire

---

[15] Brownlow, p. 70.

to carry away the garland from the rest of their brethren and companions in this service" (335). Pompous, self-aggrandising, self-satisfied, self-deluding; Harsnett's savage depiction of Edmunds/Weston might well be read as an invention devised out of Bancroft's manipulation of the Archpriest issues.

But we are still left with chronological difficulties created by the delay in publication. These may be better resolved if we 'read' the *Declaration* as having a different audience and a different target altogether from "seduced Catholiques". The tract was, of course, designed to display to Protestants the duplicity and perversion of the priests, and the corruption of their false religion. In the preface the "seduced" Catholics are approached as naïve innocents duped by charlatans: in the body of the text they emerge as deluded fools. But the point was not just to expose to a Protestant audience the dissimulation and hypocrisy of priests. They were also warned against the activities of radical protestant ministers and their followers. Some Puritans had also dabbled in dispossession, and they were tarred with the same brushes as their Catholic counterparts—gross fraud in the clerics; credulity in their lay supporters. This is a sub-text throughout the *Declaration*, and it emerges clearly in a sardonic passage in the conclusion. Here Harsnett suggests that if Catholic exorcists lack a sufficient number of devils in Italy to practice their skills upon,

> let them come but over into London […], and wee have ready for them Darrells wife, Moores Minion, Sharpe, Skelton, Evans, Swan, and Lewis the devil-finders and devil-puffers, or devil-prayers […] And we shall as easily finde them a route, rable, and swarme of giddy, adle, lunaticke, illuminate holy spectators of both sexes, but especially a Sisternity of mimpes, mops and idel holy women that shall grace Modu the deveil with their idle holy presence, and be as ready to cry out at the mowing of an apish wench and the lowing or bellowing of a brainlesse empty fellow, *O the glory of God: O the power of prayer*, as the Romish gulls did […] cry out at the conjuration of the Exorcist, *O the Catholique faith! O the power of the faith Catholique*. (331)

Listed here are some of the dramatis personae of the two major incidents of Puritan dispossession in the late Elizabethan period. John Darrell and George More were ministers involved in the case of William Somers that had wracked Nottingham in the winter of 1596–97. The other four were preachers who had been involved in the dispossession of Mary Glover in London in November 1602. These two cases are relevant to the vexed chronology of the publication of Harsnett's *Discovery*.

Darrell had been imprisoned and degraded by the High Commission in May 1599 after an extended trial, as being the impresario of a spectacular fraud in which he had coached Somers to imitate the symptoms of possession. The subsequent dispossession, accomplished by the fasting and prayer of the godly, was, it was alleged, designed to enhance his own reputation and, by sanctioning key Puritan practices, covertly to criticise the structure and ritual of the Church of England.[16] More, who had co-operated with Darrell in an earlier dispossession in Lancashire[17] and continued to defend his colleague's reputation, joined him in the Gatehouse. Trial and imprisonment did not silence these men or their supporters, and manuscript accounts and unlicensed tracts were circulating in 1598 and 1599 defending both the general practice of the dispossession of demoniacs by prayer and fasting as employed by Darrell and his associates, and the reality of Somers's possession. The authorities' riposte to this propaganda, to which Darrell immediately responded, took the form of an official account, *A Discovery of the Fraudulent Practices of John Darrell*, which was entered in the Stationers' Register on 15 November 1599: its author was "S.H." Some contemporaries initially suggested that this tract was by Bishop Bancroft, who had masterminded the entire campaign against Darrell.[18] But Harsnett had played a major role in securing the evidence on which Darrell was convicted in High Commission and then undertook the local police work concerning Darrell's earlier experiments with dispossession, and the bulk of the work is certainly his.

Harsnett and Bancroft sought to depict not only the Somers case, but also a series of earlier dispossessions in which Darrell had been involved, as gross and palpable frauds. Darrell and his supporters sought to refute these accusations of duplicity. In this debate between the establishment of the Church of England and its radical critics,

---

[16] The article by Thomas Freeman ('Demons, Deviance and Defiance: John Darrell and the Politics of Exorcism in Late Elizabethan England' in *Conformity and Orthodoxy in the English Church, c. 1560–1660* ed. by Peter Lake and Michael Questier (Woodbridge: Boydell, 2000), pp. 34–63) replaces all earlier accounts of the Darrell case. Freeman's account of the complex history of the publications emanating from the Somers case is particularly impressive. Marion Gibson's recent book *Possession, Puritanism and Print* (London: Pickering and Chatto, 2006) builds on Freeman's work, and provides a richly textured and nuanced account of the Darrell/Somers affair.

[17] See Tom Webster, '(Re)possession of Dispossession: John Darrell and Diabolical Discourse', pp. 91–111 of this volume.

[18] Brownlow, pp. 187–88 reviews contemporary opinion on the authorship of the *Discourse*.

Catholic exorcism, perhaps surprisingly, played a major role. First, the Darrell camp frequently made the point that the Catholics triumphed in their exorcistic powers, "this great vaunt of theirs", "the Popish assertion that only their priests can dispossess",[19] and this gave them considerable standing with the populace. Arthur Hildersham, the great Puritan minister of Ashby de la Zouch, acknowledged that "the simple evrie where noted it as a great discredit to the Ministers of the Gospel, that they do want this power."[20] Darrell reported Catholic jibes during some of the early cases: "Let us see one of your ministers cast out the devils: if we might bring a preist, wee are sure hee could doe it". He insisted that it was incumbent upon Protestants to answer these mocking "wordes of challenge", and they could answer them within a proper biblical framework: popish exorcistic ritual was indeed a sham; but fasting and prayer, warranted by Christ's words, could be efficacious.[21] Second, the establishment replied to this by arguing that Puritan dispossessions and Catholic exorcisms were essentially similar, both in substance and intention: in substance both were fraudulent; their shared intention was to challenge the established church by claiming a peculiar access to charismatic authority. This is a theme upon which Harsnett dilates in his introduction, and to which he recurs several times in the body of *Discovery*,[22] but it emerges with greater clarity in the almost simultaneous appearance of another work, "published in the very nick with S.H. his Discovery",[23] by one of Whitgift's chaplains who had also been involved in the court proceedings against Darrell, Abraham Hartwell. This work, dedicated to Bancroft, begins with an extended reflection on the debates over the Somers case; but the text itself is a translation of a French work, published in Paris in July, detailing the 'possession' of Marthe Brossier, and its manipulation by priests as part of an anti-Huguenot campaign.[24]

---

[19] John Darrell, *An Apologie, or defence of the possession of William Somers, a yong man of the towne of Nottingham* ([np], [1599(?)]), p. 19; Jesse Bee, *The most wonderfull and true storie of a witch named Alse* Goodridge, ed. by John Denison ([np], 1597), sig. A2v.

[20] Bee, *Wonderfull and true storie*, p. 26.

[21] John Darrell, *A True Narration of the strange and grievous Vexation by the Devil of 7 persons in Lancashire and William Somers of Nottingham* ([np], 1600), p. 69.

[22] *Harsnett, Discovery*: compare sig. [A2v], A3 with pp. 50, 67, 210.

[23] *The Triall of Maist. Dorrel*, p. 83

[24] *A true discourse upon the matter of Martha Brossier*, trans. by Abraham Hartwell (London, 1599): the dedication to Bancroft is dated Lambeth, 17 Oct.

The official refutation of the claims of Darrell and his supporters, by insisting on the similarities between Puritan and Catholic dispossessions, focussed attention on Catholic accounts—not least the Catholic "Book of Miracles", in the government's possession. This was certainly employed by Harsnett in his account of the Somers case.[25] The *use* of Catholic accounts as a rhetorical strategy is clear, but to understand the *publication* of an edited version of the latter the pressure exerted by Darrell and his friends must be recognised.

Darrell and his friends emphasised, as we have seen, the employment of exorcism as propaganda by the priests: this spawned a further rhetorical strategy. Why, the Puritans asked, was so much official time and energy being directed against the activities of ministers of the gospel? Why were these resources not being deployed to root out and denounce Catholic exorcism?[26] Darrell himself asked why the priests involved in the populist Lancashire exorcisms, drawn to the government's attention in mid-1598, had not been arrested, and scored a neat polemical point in his marginal annotation: "more favour to preists then to ministers of the gospell".[27] The tactic of contrasting the government's lenience to Catholic dispossession with its relentless hounding of those involved in the Somers case was employed again by Darrell after he had acquired a copy of the "Book of Miracles" that had been seized from Barnes. His efforts at Nottingham had left him a broken man—degraded, imprisoned, the subject of Harsnett's savage mockery. The "Book of Miracles" had gone unremarked, despite its obviously tendentious and ridiculous content and its continued circulation in manuscript in Catholic circles, so encouraging recusants in a belief in their priests' unique control of demons. Again Darrell appended a telling marginal note: "if this treatise of theirs [...] were in the handes of all men: I am persuaded that nothing which the will of man could devise would make their exorcising of spirits ridiculous & odious as it would".[28] Harsnett ultimately agreed with this analysis, but the spin that he put on his heavily edited version of the "Book of Miracles" and his com-

---

[25] See his reference to the exorcists' employment of a bone of "traitor Sainct Campion": Harsnett, *Discovery*, sig. [A2v].

[26] This tactic was first employed by the anonymous author of *The Triall of Maist. Dorrel*, pp. 34, 75: for the publishing history of this work, see Freeman, 'Demons, Deviance and Defiance', pp. 48–50.

[27] John Darrell, *A detection of that sinful, shameful, lying and ridiculous discourse of S. Harsnet* ([np], 1600), p. 13.

[28] Darrell, *A True Narration*, pp. 69–71.

mentary upon it was designed to ensure that it was not just Catholic dispossession that would be thought "ridiculous and odious".

Problems of chronology still remain. The Denham exorcisms became the focus of some official interest early in 1599, when two of the participants were examined. Harsnett's *Discovery*, published later that year, implied his reading of the "Book of Miracles"; in 1600 Darrell challenged the authorities to publish the latter. But it was not until the spring and early summer of 1602 that the High Commission again took up the matter, questioning one of the 1599 examinees for a second time, and interrogating one of the priests involved at Hackney and Denham and two of the three demoniacs upon whose exorcism the "Book of Miracles" focussed. And it was not until March 1603 that the *Discovery* was published. Harsnett's argument, that it took time for the government to ferret out the participants, may contain a grain of truth. But the full explanation must involve further analysis of the establishment's relationship with the Puritan exorcists in the early years of the new century. The fusillade of pamphlets in 1599 was intense, but Bancroft and Harsnett refused to be drawn by the tracts by Darrell and his associates that answered the *Discovery* in 1600. In 1601, two east Midland clergymen, John Deacon and John Walker, challenged Darrell on a number of technical points of pneumatology, and suggested that his obsessive focus upon dispossession encouraged superstition and was destructive of a properly Protestant evangelisation of the laity. To this Darrell replied, and a wordy, rebarbative controversy ensued. Darrell suggested that Bancroft was behind the Deacon/Walker attack,[29] but there is no evidence to sustain the charge. It appears rather that by 1600 Bancroft had decided, as Tom Freeman has argued, that "there was no further mileage to be obtained from a debate on the specifics of Darrell's cases", and his team of writers at Lambeth went silent.[30]

There matters might have rested, but for the development of the second great case of Puritan dispossession which Harsnett contemptuously dismisses in the concluding chapter of the *Declaration*. It was in London, around the bedside of Mary Glover, that he found his "illuminate holy spectators of both sexes, but especially a Sisternity of mimpes, mops and idle holy women" (331).

---

[29] John Darrell, *A survey of certaine dialogicall discourses* ([np], 1601), sig. [A2], p. 77.
[30] Freeman, 'Demons, Deviance and Defiance', p. 50: Freeman's discussion of the Deacon and Walker volumes (pp. 51–55) is clearer and more convincing that Brownlow's attempt to semi-associate them with Bancroft. See Brownlow, pp. 71–74.

In April 1602, Mary Glover fell ill. Her symptoms mystified the doctors called in to treat her, and one of them suggested that they might
be supernaturally caused. This was an explanation with which Glover's
godly family eventually concurred, as Mary's fits grew more violent and
frightening in the course of the summer—unconsciousness; convulsions;
ventriloquism; insensitivity to pain—and were increasingly associated
with the presence of a woman, Elizabeth Jackson, with a local reputation as a witch. After the Recorder of London had visited Glover and
been convinced that she was possessed, Jackson was indicted as a witch,
and tried at the Old Bailey on 1 December 1602. She was found guilty
of harming Glover and sentenced, under the 1563 Statute, to a year's
imprisonment and four appearances in the pillory. A couple of weeks
later a group of Puritan ministers and godly lay folk, employing the
techniques of prayer and fasting, dispossessed the girl.[31] Bancroft refused
to visit Glover in her fits, but was a shadowy, clearly malign, presence
throughout this affair. In November the Regius Professor of Divinity
at Oxford preached the public sermon at Paul's Cross and denounced
exorcism—a clear warning to those convinced that Glover was possessed. In the same month Jackson—or more likely someone writing
on her behalf—petitioned the Royal College of Physicians against the
doctors who had supported accusations of witchcraft against her. The
issue divided the College, but the majority concurred that Glover was
"not bewitched but afflicted by some natural disease". At the trial, two
eminent doctors, Edward Jorden and John Argent, testified to the same
effect.[32] After the conviction nothing was done to carry out the sentence
against Jackson.[33] The conviction of Jackson and the subsequent successful dispossession then moved an infuriated Bancroft into overdrive.
Ministers involved were berated—"called Rascall and varlot"—and
imprisoned; godly laymen arrested and interrogated.[34] In the next
months a number of Paul's Cross preachers attacked the doctrine of
possession, one referred directly to the Glover case and "spake much
to the taxing of the Iudge, Iurie and witnesses, and clearinge or acquit-

---

[31] This narrative is derived from Michael Macdonald's 'Introduction' to his *Witchcraft
and Hysteria*, pp. ix–xiv.
[32] Ibid., p. xv.
[33] John Swan, who reports this (*True and Briefe Report*, p. 5) intimates that it was a
consequence of improper official interference.
[34] Lewes Hewes, *Certaine Grievances or the errours of the Service-Booke Plainely Laid Open*
([np], 1641), pp. 14–15; Swan, *True and Briefe Report*, p. 61.

tinge the Witch".[35] It is in this context that Harsnett's *Discovery* was finally published. And its appearance was exactly contemporary with the medical treatise, *A Briefe Discourse of a Disease called the Suffocation of the Mother*, written by Edward Jorden who had spoken unavailingly on Elizabeth Jackson's behalf at the Old Bailey, and who "sought earnestly, to make the case a meere naturall disease".[36]

Bancroft's strategy in the simultaneous publication of the two tracts is clear, and represents a development on that pursued against the Darrell's dispossessions. In the latter case the successful prosecution of the principals and the account offered in Harsnett's *Discovery* had depended in part on the official interrogation of the demoniac, William Somers, pliable, isolated and self-dramatising, who had proved only too ready to confess the fraud and Darrell's role in orchestrating and manipulating his possession. But Mary Glover was not a marginal figure, like the Nottingham musician's apprentice; she was the daughter of a distinguished and well-connected London citizen and the grand-daughter of a Marian martyr. In this case the official line, suggested by Jorden at the trial and developed in his treatise, was not that Glover was a fraud or a puppet, but the victim of an illness, "the suffocation of the mother"—hysteria. But this diagnosis, of course, did not exculpate those Puritans who sought to mould her symptoms and use her illness for their own religious agenda. These "devil-finders and devil-puffers, or devil-prayers" (331) were as contemptible, as guilty of self-serving dissimulation, as the Catholic exorcists, "Edmunds and his holy crue (his twelve holy disciples)" (319). This was the message of Harsnett's *Declaration*, and explains the appearance in 1603 of an account of events at Denham and Hackney nearly twenty years before.

A plausible explanation of our initial chronological problem, turning on the complex dialogue between the establishment of the Church of England and its critics, both Catholic and Puritan, has been suggested. But there is another, equally complicated, issue concerning the date of the publication of the *Discovery of Egregious Popish Impostures*. The work was registered by the Stationers' Company on 16 March 1603: eight

---

[35] Ibid., p. 5.
[36] Stephen Bradwell, 'Mary Glover's Late Woeful Case' (this manuscript account is transcribed, and separately paginated, in *Witchcraft and Hysteria*, ed. by Michael MacDonald, p. 27).

days later Elizabeth died.[37] And the new King, as the Puritans recognised, seemed highly unlikely to sympathise with Harsnett's arguments
in the *Discovery*. John Swan, one of the Puritan divines hounded by
Bancroft and mocked by Harsnett for their role in the Glover dispossession, published an account of the Glover case. His work was dedicated to James, and in the introduction Swan sedulously emphasised
the disparities between Harsnett's positions in his "immodest booke"
on the role of the devil and the power of witches and those advanced
by the King in his own reflections on these subjects in his *Daemonologie*,
first published in Edinburgh in 1597. Swan particularly drew the King's
attention to a passage in the twenty-first chapter of the *Discovery*, which
"giveth a most dishonourable counterbuffe to your *Highnes Treatise* which
handleth that argument".[38]

The passage which Swan emphasised is certainly an interesting one
in its rhetorical construction and development. The chapter ostensibly
concerns "the strange formes, shapes, and apparitions of the devills"
(304). Harsnett begins by arguing that the Catholic image of the devil,
"with ougly hornes on his head, fire in his mouth, a cowes tayle in
his breech, eyes like a bason, fangs like a dogge, clawes like a Beare, a
skinne like a Neger, and a voice roaring like a Lyon" (306) is a laugh-
able amalgam of paganism and folk-lore. He then moves on to discuss
the similar origin of the "Idaea of a Witch", and explains how the
scapegoating of poor, old, ill-educated women becomes the popular
explanation for a series of misfortunes—"a sheepe sicke of the giddies,
or an hogge of the mumps, or an horse of the staggers" (308). This
list of *maleficia* attributed to witchcraft terminates in alleged possession,
which Harsnett sees originating in the attention-seeking games of "idle",
"knavish" adolescents. Here Harsnett introduces the exorcist, who will
make capital out of this tissue of nonsense and fraud: "ye shal have

---

[37] The actual date of the publication of the tract is contended. Brownlow has argued
(*Shakespeare, Harsnett and the Devils of Denham*, p. 321 note), from a passage in the final
chapter, that it was not completed until July 1604. The passage asserts that the papists
"are at this day plotting a new invasion to set up a new Queene, who have and doe
thus desperately blaspheme God and the King". This, he argues, refers to the Bye and
Main plots, which were investigated in June–July 1603. But the plots, in favour of Lady
Arbella Stuart, did not involve an invasion, and it is not easy to see why Harsnett did
not alter the references to Elizabeth in the present tense which surround this passage
(pp. 320, 321, 322, 328, 335). The remarks—though "God and the King" is still problematic—would be more appropriate to the scheme first mooted by the Jesuit, Robert
Persons, in 1595, to secure the throne for the Infanta Isabella.

[38] Swan, *True and Briefe Report*, p. 3: emphasis in the original.

some idle, adle, giddie, lymphaticall, illuminate dottrel [...] who will take this holy advantage to raise the ruines of his desperate decayed name, and for his better glory wil be-pray the juggling drab, and cast out Mopp the devil" (309) From Catholic devils, Harsnett has clearly shifted target to the Puritans: the "illuminate dottrell" is Darrell. "Be-pray" makes this obvious, but so too does the extended analysis of the belief that possession originated in the intervention of a witch. Witch-craft barely figures in the Denham exorcisms, though there was some discussion of the possible malefic role of Goodwife White of Bushey "commonly talked of in the country as a witch" (371); but it is central to the key cases of Puritan dispossession. Witches were named by all Darrell's early experiments with demonianism; thirteen Nottingham women were arrested after Somers had denounced them; Glover's possession was attributed to the maleficence of Elizabeth Jackson, and an elaborate narrative was constructed to explain the latter's cursing the girl, "wishing an evill death to light upon her".[39]

James was unlikely, Swan thought, to welcome the kind of rationalist explanation of witch belief that Harsnett provided, nor the condescend-ing tone he adopted, in his twenty-first chapter. And the King would certainly have recognised the source from which Harsnett had derived this offensive discussion. Much of the language was lifted verbatim from the sceptical *Discoverie of Witchcraft* of 1584 by Reginald Scot, and the tone and rhythm of Harsnett's chapter was equally derivative; there are other borrowings from Scot throughout the tract.[40] Scot's "dam-nable opinions"—"that there can be no such thing as witchcraft", his "denying of spirits"—made him one of the two major targets of the King's *Daemonologie*.[41]

John Swan believed that in publishing the *Declaration* when they did Harsnett and Bancroft had made an impolitic error, insulting the new King's convictions and his intellectual pretensions, from which the Puritans could benefit. But, unless we convict them of invincible folly, it is difficult to imagine that the bishop and his chaplain were acting thoughtlessly. Neither man was a stranger to controversy, and their

---

[39] Bradwell, 'Mary Glover's Late Woeful Case', p. 3.
[40] In his footnotes to pp. 304–11 of the *Declaration*, Professor Brownlow lists the specific borrowings from Scot.
[41] James VI of Scotland, *Daemonologie* (Edinburgh, 1597), re-printed in *Witchcraft in Early Modern Scotland*, ed. by Lawrence Normand and Gareth Roberts (Exeter: Exeter University Press, 2000), pp. 353–425, at p. 353.

experiences of it hardly suggest that they would gratuitously offend
the new Head of the Church. Harsnett had preached a Paul's Cross
sermon challenging the Calvinist doctrine of predestination, that, in
the opinion of Darrell's supporters who dragged up the incident during the possession controversy, contained "12 grosse errors of poperie",
and for which, he later acknowledged, "he was checkt" by Archbishop
Whitgift.[42] In 1599, acting as Bancroft's deputy, he licensed Hayward's
First part of the life and raigne of King Henrie IIII for publication. The work,
dedicated to the Earl of Essex and with its account of the deposition of
Richard II, seriously offended the Queen and Harsnett was obliged to
grovel in the unlikely guise of "a poor divine unacquainted with bookes
and arguments of state" to the attorney general for his carelessness.[43]
Bancroft had made similar errors of judgement; his, significantly, in
relation to the King of Scots. In 1589–90 Burghley obliged him to
apologise to James for a Paul's Cross sermon in which, in a diatribe
against the Scottish Presbyterians, he portrayed the King, to his fury,
as a helpless pawn, humiliated by the Kirk. In 1593 Bancroft published
two books, *Daungerous positions* and *A survey of the pretended holy discipline*,
against the Puritans: these included further ponderous swipes against
the Kirk and similar expressions of, in Jenny Wormald's nice phrase
"tactless sympathy with a hen-pecked King".[44] Again the bishop was
obliged to undertake some rapid fence-mending. Nor could Harsnett
have been ignorant of James's opinions about the supernatural in
1603—they had too often been served up to him by his opponents in
the controversy over the Nottingham dispossession.

   Those who defended Darrell pursued a multi-faceted strategy. Two
of their lines of attack were politically charged, adroitly drawing the
attention of powerful members of the establishment to those aspects
of the High Commission trial and of Harsnett's *Discovery* that they
would find objectionable. The first of these readings was directed at
the common law judges. The conviction of the witch nominated in
one of Darrell's early dispossessions had been challenged by Bancroft's
investigators: was this compatible with "the honour which is due to the

---

[42] Brownlow, pp. 174–79: the anonymous author of *The Triall of Maist. Dorrel*, p. 65,
refers to Harsnett's unorthodox sermon.
[43] Brownlow, *Shakespeare, Harsnett and the Devils of Denham*, pp. 174–79.
[44] Jenny Wormald's 'Ecclesiastical Vitriol: The Kirk, the Puritans and the Future
King of England', in *The Reign of Elizabeth I: Court Culture in the Last Decade*, ed. by John
Guy (Cambridge: Cambridge University Press, 1995), pp. 171–91 is the best guide to
Bancroft's interventions in Scottish politics: the quotation is at p. 181.

Temporall Courts"? Did it not bring the bishop in danger of the Statute of Praemunire?[45] Some of the specific discussion in the *Discovery*, and the implicit scepticism about witchcraft in general might seem to suggest that Harsnett thought that the judges who had convicted witches were, at best, gullible fools, at worst, murderers "guilty of innocent blood".[46] This tactic had some success. At the trial of Elizabeth Jackson in December 1602 the Lord Chief Justice, Anderson, no lover of Puritans, contemptuously rejected Jorden's attempt to argue that Glover's affliction was natural, and presented his own credo on the reality of witchcraft which was directed more against Bancroft and Harsnett than the medical doctors: "The land is full of Witches; they abound in all places: I have hanged five or sixe and twenty of them; There is no man here, can speake more of them then myself".[47]

The second 'political' strategy pursued by Darrell's supporters sought to recruit James VI as an ally to the anti-Bancroft position. The earliest defence, an unlicensed publication of 1598, provided a list of church fathers and Protestant theologians who had argued that diabolic possession was a reality, and that fasting and prayer might relieve the afflicted person; the list included "the godlie learned King of Schoth."[48] Darrell's first treatise also cited *Daemonologie*, Book 3 chapter 4, "where he setteth down 3 signes off one possessed"—unnatural strength; convulsions; speaking in strange voices and foreign languages: all symptoms displayed by Somers.[49] Upon the publication of the *Discovery* Darrell and his supporters, in addition to continuing to cite James on the symptoms of possession and the propriety of using fasting and prayer against Harsnett, were quick to detect borrowings and echoes from Scot. When Harsnett claimed that his opinion was backed by "learned men" without proper citation one of his opponents offered sarcastic assistance with his footnotes "Must I helpe at a pinch? If memory faile me not [...] M. Scot" is the source for the assertion. In particular, Harsnett's account of the psychological pressures that led some to confess themselves

---

[45] John Darrell, *A briefe Apologie proving the possession of W. Somers* (Middleburg, 1599), p. 7.
[46] Darrell, *Detection*, p. 37; *Triall of Maist.. Dorrel*, pp. 84, 87–88.
[47] Bradwell, 'Mary Glover's Late Woeful Case', p. 28.
[48] *A Briefe Narration of the possession, dispossession and repossession of W. Somers* ([np], 1598), sig. [Cv].
[49] John Darrell, *An Apologie, or defence of the possession of William Somers* ([np], [1599(?)]), fol. 12.

witches, and his denial that witches could command the devil into their victims indicated his dependence upon Scot.[50]

In 1603, at the point of James's accession, Bancroft and Harsnett published a work that contained substantial direct borrowing from Scot. They did this despite their previous uncomfortable experiences of offending authority, even James himself, and despite the certainty that their opponents would draw the borrowings—clearer than anything in the 1599 *Discovery*—to the attention of the King. More remarkably, if John Swan is to be believed, they arranged for the formal presentation of the work to James I when he entered his new kingdom: "they have not foreborne to offer that immodest booke to your Maiesties own hands".[51] What did they hope to achieve by an act that seemed almost suicidal to their opponents? Bancroft and his team must have assumed that the King was now less wedded to the opinions that he had expressed in *Daemonologie*, and more sceptical in matters of possession, and of accusations of witchcraft. Were they right?

The overall trajectory of James's intellectual interest and involvement in witchcraft is clear. The energetic, vicious witch-hunter of 1590–91 became increasingly suspicious of witchcraft accusations, particularly those emanating from the victims of possession. In 1616 James humiliated the judges at the Leicester Assizes whose credulity had permitted the conviction of witches on unsafe testimony.[52] Where did he stand in 1603? This is not an easy question to answer. The evidence is limited, and, where it survives, controversial. The significance of the 1597 publication of *Daemonologie*, the text in which the Darrell supporters and Swan placed so much of their hope, divides Scottish historians. Was it written in the white heat of the 1590–91 witch-hunts, and then published as an afterthought?[53] Was it written, as Jenny Wormald has argued, not as the confident credo of a witch-hunter, but "for self-reassurance and […] as a signing off" from the subject by a man still intellectually persuaded of the possibility of diabolic witchcraft, but increasingly

---

[50] *The Triall of Maist. Dorrel*, pp. 85–86; Darrell, *Detection*, pp. 36–37.
[51] Swan, *True and Briefe Report*, p. 3.
[52] For the Leicester incident, see G.L. Kittredge, *Witchcraft in Old and New England* (Cambridge, MA: Harvard University Press, 1929), pp. 322–23. The undated letter to Prince Henry (in Kittredge, p. 319) is also relevant here; the King stresses "how waire judges should be in trusting accusations without an exact tryall."
[53] The question is reviewed in Normand and Roberts, *Witchcraft in Early Modern Scotland*, pp. 327–28: they prefer the 1591 dating.

sceptical of specific accusations?[54] This interpretation has been fiercely criticised by Julian Goodare,[55] but it has much to recommend it. The work does not consistently breathe the intellectual confidence that some scholars have found in it. The discussion of diabolic possession (which James acknowledges may be "counterfeit", manipulated by priests "for confirming their rotten religion"), and the associated explanation of the occasional success of Catholic exorcism is particularly tortuous. And, while denouncing Scot in the introduction, James was prepared to lift a number of his insights, without acknowledgement, in the text.[56] The work suggests a measure of uncertainty, if not scepticism, which is compatible with the King's public statements in the latter half of 1597 in relation to the on-going witch-hunt in Scotland. The King was actively involved in the witch prosecutions early in that year, but by the late summer was increasingly troubled by the procedures and kinds of evidence employed against the witches by the local judges. On 12 August the Privy Council issued a very strongly worded order, denouncing the partial proceedings of local tribunals, revoking many of the commissions empowering judges to act, and insisting upon due process in future trials.[57] In September the King instructed the ministers, to their annoyance, to participate in a public conference at Falkland to discuss the key scriptural texts concerning witchcraft.[58] Next March the General Assembly expressed their disgust with the King's reluctance to permit the conviction of those accused of witchcraft on the unsupported testimony of a confessed witch.[59] As with the argument and the

---

[54] Jenny Wormald, 'The Witches, the Devil and the King', in *Freedom and Authority: Scotland c. 1050–c. 1650*, ed. by T. Brotherstone and D. Ditchburn (East Linton: Tuckwell Press, 2000), pp. 165–80: quotation at p. 179.

[55] In 'The Scottish Witchcraft Panic of 1597', in *The Scottish Witch-hunt in Context*, ed. by Julian Goodare (Manchester: Manchester University Press, 2002), pp. 51–72, particularly pp. 63–64: also relevant is his 'The Framework for Scottish Witch-hunting in the 1590s' (*Scottish Historical Review*, 81 (2002), 240–50) which deals with the ancillary issue of the commissions under which witches were prosecuted.

[56] James VI of Scotland, *Daemonologie*, in Normand and Roberts, *Witchcraft in Early Modern Scotland*, pp. 415–17: for James's use of Scot, see the editors' comments at pp. 330, 336–37.

[57] The order is reproduced Normand and Roberts, *Witchcraft in Early Modern Scotland*, pp. 429–30: Goodare's suggestion ('Scottish Witchcraft Panic', pp. 60–61) that the King was only tangentially involved in the issue of this order is not convincing.

[58] Goodare ('Scottish Witchcraft Panic', p. 63) transcribes the newsletter to England which reports both the meeting, and the anger of the kirk. His reading of the letter is, however, very different from mine.

[59] John Row, *The Historie of the Kirk of Scotland* (Edinburgh: Maitland Club, 1842), pp. 447–49. John Spottiswoode (*The History of the Church of Scotland* (1655), p. 448) asserts

tone of the *Daemonologie*, none of this suggests the kind of intellectual assurance and gung-ho conviction of the propriety of witch-hunting that the King had expressed in June 1591 when he lectured a jury who had dared to question the accusation against Barbara Napier.[60]

Whatever the significance of 1597 in the development of James's convictions in relation to witchcraft, Bancroft and Harsnett obviously believed that the new King had seriously modified his position by 1603. Conversely, the Puritans assumed that the King must deeply resent the obvious challenge in the *Discovery* to the arguments that he had presented in his own treatise; how could the King overlook the sections approvingly copied from a work he had denounced as "damnable"?

James responded to the debate about dispossession with the same political intelligence, the same careful moderation, which typified so many of his policies in the first years of his English reign—the reorganisation of his court, for instance; his performance at the Hampton Court Conference. In this, as in other areas, the King insisted on following an independent line, but one which acknowledged, while not slavishly following, the concerns of the various parties who sought to influence him. Witchcraft and possession were both publicly affirmed. The reality of witchcraft was encoded in the new statute. This was largely a gesture to the English judiciary: it entailed only a slight modification of the Elizabethan Act, and certainly did not answer the concerns of those godly divines, like Gifford and Perkins, who thought English law too lenient in this matter.[61] But it did make harming by witchcraft a capital offence—after 1604 Elizabeth Jackson would have been executed upon her conviction for her actions against Mary Glover. The new Statute did not explicitly comment on possession—harm was defined largely in the Elizabethan language "wasted, consumed, pined or

---

that James insisted on this after the shocking miscarriages of justice associated with the "great witch of Balwearie", who, upon the promise to spare her life, had denounced a series of her supposed associates.

[60] A transcript of the speech was sent by the English ambassador to Burghley, see *Calendar of Scottish papers*, X (1589–93), pp. 522–55. For the background to this see *Witchcraft in Early Modern Scotland*, ed. by Normand and Roberts, pp. 211–14.

[61] For the criticisms of Gifford and Perkins, see Kittredge, pp. 292, 296. I find Kittredge's argument (pp. 281–314) that the Jacobean statute did little to modify the law more persuasive than those of modern scholars who have claimed that it was (e.g.) "more far reaching and draconian" (Gregory Durston, *Witchcraft and Witch Trials* (Chichester: Barry Rose Law Publishers, 2000), p. 179).

lamed"[62]—but diabolic possession was overtly recognised in an equally significant enactment: canon 72 of the established Church, approved by Convocation in the same year that the Statute was passed. The canon permitted "fasting and prayer, to cast out any devil or devils", but with the provision that the ministers involved secured a license from their Bishop. This formulation is very significant. Bancroft's draft of the canon had simply banned all "fasting and prayer under the pretence of Castinge out Devilles": the revised wording—James's modification?—acknowledged, as Bancroft's did not, that possession occurred and that there was an approved therapy, which could be employed if officially sanctioned.[63]

Would Swan and his fellows have triumphed in the King's rejection of a theoretically sceptical position on witchcraft and on possession? The theological inadequacies of the witchcraft statute remained, and the obligation to seek Episcopal approval for a "meanes as God hath sanctified" by Christ's explicit words was certainly resented.[64] Worse, while James never abandoned the theoretical convictions expressed in *Daemonologie*, in practice he swiftly associated himself with the scepticism of Bancroft and his cadre. In his 1604 diatribe against smoking, James suggested that the noxious stench of tobacco might assist "both for the superstitious Priests and the insolent Puritanes, to cast out devils withal"; Harsnett's message, bracketing Catholic exorcism and Puritan dispossession had clearly made an impact.[65] Early in 1605 James interrupted his hunting trip to interview two 'possessed' girls, whom he referred to the medical faculty at Cambridge University. Though intrigued, he took the matter lightly, writing to Cecil of his being "ever kept busy with hunting of witches, prophets, puritans, dead cats, and hares", and it cannot have surprised him when doctors pronounced the girls' affliction as "natural".[66] Bancroft was kept apprised of these developments, and then played a major role in the more spectacular

---

[62] 1 Jas. I cap. 12—only "pined" in the list of possible harms suffered by the victims of witchcraft, hardly a direct reference to possession, is not found in the Elizabethan enactment.

[63] Bancroft's draft of the canon is in Stuart Barton Babbage, *Puritanism and Richard Bancroft* (London: SPCK, 1962), appendix I, p. 381; for the canon as approved on 25 June, see Appendix III of this volume.

[64] Hewes, *Certaine Grievances*, pp. 13–14.

[65] James I, King of England, *A counterblaste to tobacco* (London, 1604), sig. C3.

[66] HMC Cecil, XVII, p. 121, James to Sir Robert Cecil. There is a good account of this incident in Henry N. Paul, *The Royal Play of Macbeth* (New York: MacMillan, 1950), pp. 113–17.

case of Ann Gunter in the summer and autumn of the year. Gunter's affliction involved neither Puritan nor Catholic exorcism, but it did provide an opportunity to question the category of possession through the agency of a witch. Bancroft assembled the same team of experts employed in the Glover case—Jorden and Harsnett—reinforcing them with another anti-Puritan divine, Richard Neile. Their investigations were to lead ultimately to a show trial of Ann's father in Star Chamber for allegedly bullying his daughter to fake the symptoms of possession, so that he could indict an old family enemy for witchcraft. This unlikely story owes much to the determination of Bancroft to 'explain' behaviour that might have been seen as possession by the credulous. But his success in imposing this view owes much to the involvement of the King, who interviewed Ann on a couple of occasions, and who sent her to first Jorden and then Harsnett for further diagnosis and interrogation.[67] James had quickly identified with the practical scepticism embodied by Harsnett, and had begun to display the canny suspicion of possession and its association with witchcraft which led to his denunciation of the Judges in 1616. This was hardly the outcome that Swan and his Puritan colleagues had hoped for.

Stephen Greenblatt has argued that Harsnett wrote the *Discovery* as the representative of the "joint religious and secular apparatus". This was not the case. Writing at the crucial moment of regime change, he was a member of a faction, contending fiercely for the new King's attention and for the control of the Church. He and his patron, Bancroft, were prepared to employ a dangerous strategy, challenging James's publicly expressed views, to that end. By the time Shakespeare wrote *King Lear*, however, Greenblatt may be nearer the truth. The gamble taken by Bancroft and Harsnett had paid off, and the King co-operated with them in the exposure of fraud, and, effectively, in the development of a sceptical view of both possession and witchcraft. James had promoted Bancroft to Canterbury in October 1604: nor did the publication of the *Discovery* blight Harsnett's steady ascent of the ladder of preferment—Master of Pembroke College, Cambridge in 1605; Bishop of Chichester four years later.

---

[67] James Sharpe, *The Bewitching of Anne Gunter* (London: Profile, 1999), provides a full account of this incident; see particularly pp. 175–96 on the role of the King and the Bancroft circle: see also Paul, *Royal Play of Macbeth*, pp. 119–27.

(RE)POSSESSION OF DISPOSSESSION
JOHN DARRELL AND DIABOLICAL DISCOURSE

Tom Webster

A further assessment of the activities of John Darrell, the famed 'Puritan exorcist' is open, initially at least, to several charges. The first is to suggest that the critic is merely a dedicated follower of fashion—that possession, and the Darrell episode in particular, has 'been done'.[1] The second is that explanations for, and thereby understanding of, possession and dispossession are more than adequately dealt with in the existing historiography. The third is that our comprehension of the 'victory' of Samuel Harsnett et al. in tackling Darrell's career as a peripatetic aid to the allegedly possessed is complete. An outline of what this analysis offers will, I hope, waylay such charges. What follows opens with an effort, which will prove to be ironic, to get the story straight regarding Darrell's work in Lancashire for this case study will show that our understanding depends on an inadequate representation of what happened. This narrative will rest upon the clearly positioned texts of John Darrell and his colleague George More and also upon Harsnett's relative silence in his critique of these texts. However, this is not too much of a cause for concern as there have been few reviewers more severe than Harsnett in his assessment of their accounts![2] In this context this

---

[1] For a range of works, with different emphases and purposes, see James Sharpe, *Instruments of Darkness: Witchcraft in England 1550–1750* (Harmondsworth: Penguin, 1997), pp. 96–98, 190–210; idem, *The Bewitching of Anne Gunter* (London: Profile Books, 1999); Philip C. Almond, *Demonic Possession and Exorcism in Early Modern England: Contemporary Texts and their Cultural Contexts* (Cambridge: Cambridge University Press, 2004), pp. 150–55, 192–96, 240–43; Thomas Freeman, 'Demons, Deviance and Defiance: John Darrell and the Politics of Exorcism in Late Elizabethan England', in *Conformity and Orthodoxy in the English Church, c. 1560–1660*, ed. by Peter Lake and Michael Questier (Woodbridge: Boydell, 2000), pp. 34–63. This last is best read alongside this piece as the two complement each other despite some disagreements.
[2] In fact Darrell and one of his supporters enquired why Harsnett had not been as harsh in his treatment of the Lancashire case as the cases which preceded and succeeded it: John Darrell, *A detection of that sinnful, shamful, lying and ridiculous discours, of Samuel Harsnet* ([np], 1600) To the Reader, pp. 9–10; *A Breife Narration of the possession, dispossession and, repossession of William Sommers* ("Amsterdam", 1598), p. 3.

is an advantage as these circumstances provide us with an account of possession by those for whom possession was a reality. This will provide a reassessment of the explanations of historians as the testing ground will have changed; the explanations which seem persuasive for one set of events are less so for this modified account.

Having set out the narrative before us, I will enlarge upon the symptoms which need explaining and look briefly at the structural representation of this episode by Darrell and More. This will provide a site for an engagement with current historiography in two related ways. The first is what it is that needs to be explained and the second is how far present work is sufficient as a comprehension of these events. This will lead to a suggested modification of our analysis and a field of changed questions regarding the controversies, early modern and current, over possession and dispossession.

I

The roots of the seven possessed in Cleworth, in the parish of Leigh, Lancashire, were in the marriage of the Protestant gentleman, Nicholas Starkey. His bride was an inheritrix of a family of whom "some were Papistes, of whom some partlie for Religion". Her family resented this union and its impact upon the family's inheritance and so they "wished & vowed still to pray for the perishing of her issue". The result was that four healthy children died "in most strange maner".[3] Some of her family were "moved with compassion" and told her of "the said unnatural vowe", whereupon she made a will which passed all her estate to her husband's family, regardless of her success or failure in childbirth. With the campaign against her children made pointless in practical terms, a boy and a girl were born and were healthy until Anne's ninth year and John's tenth.[4] At this point, in February 1595, Anne "was taken with a dumpish heavie countenance, and with a certain fearful starting & pulling together of her bodie". A week later John "was taken as he was going to schole, & was compelled to showte vehemently, not being able to stay him selfe. After this they waxed worse & worse falling into

---

[3] George More, *A True Discourse concerning the certaine possession and dispossession of 7 persons* (Middelburg, 1600), p. 11.

[4] Ibid., p. 12; John Darrell, *A True Narration of the strange and grevous Vexation by the Devil, of 7 persons in Lancashire, and William Somers of Nottingham* ([np], 1600), p. 1.

often strange & extreame fittes".[5] That this was blamed upon the resentful papist family, presumably out of pure vindictiveness is not made explicit, simply implied by close proximity in More's account. Nicholas Starkey spent about £200 in attempts to remedy their ills, presumably on physicians and then turned to "a Seminarie Priest"—probably for the children to be exorcised as More noted that the priest was unsuccessful "because (forsooth) he had not then his bookes".[6] Upon this failure he turned to a third source of help, as the fits had continued for nine or ten weeks.

The third source was Edmund Hartley, a "cunning man" of whom Starkey had heard. Having been offered some recompense, after "he had used certaine popish charmes and hearbes by degrees, the children were at quiet, and so continued, seeming to be well".[7] Hartley's remedies seem to have been successful for about a year and a half but there were relapses when he looked to leave and, as he seemed to be capable of at least ending the fits, Starkey offered him a pension of 40s per annum to stay. This was accepted but he started to make greater demands, wanting his own house and grounds and, upon Starkey's refusal, was heard to make threats of worse fits. Shortly after this, Starkey went to

---

[5] More, p. 12. The same episode in Darrell's *True Narration* has Anne "taken with a dumpish and heavie countenaunce, and with a certaine fearefull starting and pulling together of her body" and John, "as he was going to schole was compelled to shout, neither was able to staie himselfe. after the [*sic*] waxed worse and worse, falling into often and extreame fits" (p. 1). The similarity here and at many other points in the two texts suggests either collusion or that one had access to the earlier text of the other. More's version was published in the spring of 1600 but was completed by December 1599 while Darrell's probably appeared in the autumn of 1600 (More, p. 85; Freeman, p. 50 note). Darrell had been released from the gatehouse at Lambeth Palace before the end of September 1599 which would have made it a little easier for him to communicate with More who was still in the Clink. In addition, there was an account of the dispossession by their collaborator Dickoms circulating by 1599 and it is a possibility that this was used by the two men, separately or together, as a template. From the way in which More, Darrell and Harsnett describe it, it seems to have been in manuscript. If it was published, no printed copies survive and the same seems to be true of any manuscript version: More, p. 80; Darrell, *A Detection*, pp. 55–56; [Samuel Harsnett], *A Discovery of the Fraudulent Practises of John Darrel* (London, 1599) p. 3. Philip C. Almond states that More died in prison but gives no reference; I have, as yet, no evidence of this being the case or otherwise: Almond, p. 240. Corinne Holt Rickert, *The Case of John Darrell: Minister and Exorcist* (Gainsville, Florida: University of Florida, 1962), p. 63 considers it as a possibility; Freeman, p. 55 is more doubtful.

[6] More, pp. 12–13.

[7] Darrell, *True Narration*, p. 1 (quote); More, p. 13. Apart from spelling, the phrase is exactly the same in More's version. Neither More nor Darrell refer to him as a "cunning man". For Darrell, he is a "Coniuror" (e.g. *True Narration*, p. 1), for More he is simply "a witch" (p. 13).

his father's house at nearby Whaley, accompanied by Hartley and the latter had his own fits all night long. The following day he took Starkey into the woods,

> where he made a Circle the compas of a yard and halfe, with many crosses and partitions, which being finished he came back to call M. Starkie, telling him what he had done, and desired him to goe and tread out his circle, for he said he might not doe it him selfe. This being also dispatched, well quoth he, now I shall trouble him that troubled me, and be meete with him that sought my death.[8]

Although the exact chronology is not clear, it seems that it was after Hartley arrived that the numbers of the possessed multiplied. Clarity is lacking for the first three. These were girls placed in the Starkey household by their parents for "education and tuition". The first was Margaret Hardman, aged fourteen; then her sister Ellinor, four years younger and thirdly Ellen Holland, a twelve-year-old. It is clear that Margaret Byrom, a thirty-three year old "poore kinswoman" of Mrs Starkey, succumbed after Hartley's arrival because she became possessed immediately after restraining him during one of his fits. The last to start having fits was Jane Ashton, a maid aged thirty who Hartley had threatened after an argument.[9]

Disconcerted by Hartley's apparent appetite for such less positive magic, disappointed by the worsening of the fits and seeing "many other bad qualities in this fellow", Starkey took a sample of his son's urine to a physician in Manchester at the start of December 1596. While he was there he also made a secret trip to consult John Dee, the warden of Christ's College, Manchester and a renowned expert in the occult. Dee was evidently unwilling to get very involved, perhaps because he was not attracted to an area which would be a risk to his already fragile reputation. He may also have remembered that, much earlier, an angel had told him that to help Isabel Lister, who thought herself to be possessed, was not his business. He simply advised Starkey "to crave the help & assistance of some godlie Preachers, with whom he should ioyne in prayer and fasting for the helpe of his children". He also called Hartley to meet him on 8 December and "sharplie reprooved" him, apparently winning three weeks reprieve for the possessed.[10]

---

[8] More, pp. 13–14.
[9] Darrell, *True Narration*, pp. 2–3; More, pp. 16–17.
[10] Darrell, *True Narration*, p. 2; More, pp. 14–15; Charlotte Fell Smith, *John Dee 1527–1608* (London: Constable, 1909) pp. 268–69; Benjamin Woolley, *The Queen's Conjurer: The Life and Magic of John Dee* (London: Harper Collins, 2002) p. 213. Dee's

However, the fits resumed in the first week of January and by the end of the month Margaret Byrom decided she should take a break by returning to her mother's home in Salford. Hartley decided to accompany her and over the following time her fits intensified despite daily visits from Hartley. Indeed, now she was prone to have fits as soon as she saw him. She had many visitors, including some ministers, among whom was Matthew Palmer, Dee's curate. Palmer and the other ministers were suspicious about Hartley, a suspicion confirmed by his inability to deliver the whole of the Lord's Prayer. He was apprehended and brought before two JPs "where he was examined, and after divers witnesses had come against him" he was returned to Byrom so that she could accuse him to his face. On five such occasions she was struck dumb. The same speechlessness occurred early in March when attempts were made to take statements from the possessed in Cleworth. He was charged before the assizes at Lancaster and here John Dee seems to have helped in that one of the JPs, Edmund Hopwood, borrowed several books on witchcraft from him. Hartley was found guilty. The difficulty was that "they could find no lawe to hange him" whereupon Starkey recalled the incident in the woods. This made it possible to hang him and this was the sentence given. At the first attempt the rope broke, "whereupon he penitentlie confessed, that he had deserved that punishment, & that all whiche Mai. Starchie had charged him with, was true, and so he was hanged out the second time".[11]

When Hartley was imprisoned, Starkey took up Dee's advice and brought ministers to see the possessed at Cleworth and to see Margaret Byrom at Salford, but to no avail. What he did get was news of Darrell's dispossession of Thomas Darling at Burton a year earlier.[12] The news

time in Manchester gets scanty treatment in most of the literature. The most thorough is Fell Smith, pp. 263–89 but the referencing is minimal.

[11] Ibid., pp. 18–22; Darrell, pp. 6–7; *The Private Diary of Dr. John Dee and the Catalogue of his Library of Manuscripts*, ed. by James Orchard Halliwell, Camden Soc., first series, 19 (1842), pp. 57, 59. Starkey's evidence of conjuration might have turned the offence into a felony, although it was unusual for such an offence without a consequent death to win an execution. Some of the evidence of "divers witnesses" might have made this a second offence and therefore a capital offence. For the legal background (and the ambiguities) see Keith Thomas, *Religion and the Decline of Magic* (Harmondsworth: Penguin, 1973) pp. 525–26, 532–33. I am grateful to Stephen Bowd for help with John Dee, particularly in giving me a copy of his forthcoming 'In the Labyrinth: John Dee and Reformation Manchester'.

[12] For Darling, see Daniel Pickering Walker, *Unclean Spirits: Possession and Exorcism in France and England in the Late Sixteenth and Early Seventeenth Centuries* (London: Scholar Press, 1981), pp. 52–56.

came from Dee's butler as Darling was his uncle's son although it is
not quite clear when Starkey was told. In any case, Starkey asked Dee
to write to Darrell requesting help presumably hoping the reputation
of Dee would prove persuasive for the two men were unacquainted, as
both More and Darrell are quick to point out. Starkey also wrote himself
but neither was successful. Darrell insisted that he lacked "anie speciall
gift" for dispossession. However, about the middle of February, Starkey
sent more letters, this time including one by a local JP, James Ashton,
and this was more fruitful. Darrell, "craving first the advice of many
of my brethren in the ministry, met togither in an exercise", because,
as More put it, "he would attempt nothing in those cases without very
good advisement, and lawful consent". Sixteen ministers accordingly
met at Ashby-de-la-Zouch. It was concluded that he should go and he
requested that he should be accompanied by George More, the pastor
of Cawlke in Derbyshire, apparently to make reports of any success
more believable, having the strength of two witnesses. In his response
to Starkey, Darrell asked for "the assistance of some faithful Ministers
about M. Starkie, especially his Pastor to ioyne with us". More and
Darrell set off, arriving at Cleworth on 16 March, about the same time
that Margaret Byrom returned from Salford.[13]

When they arrived they were greeted by Mrs Starkey with Anne
and John. Nicholas Starkey rose from dinner and requested more food
for his visitors. They enquired after his children and he reported that
John had been in good shape for about a week, Anne for four days
(although Margaret Byrom and the rest had had a succession of small
fits). While they were dining Ellinor and Margaret Hardman and Ellen
Holland were called up from the kitchen to the hall and each of them
greeted Darrell and More and went straight into a violent fit. In the
course of these fits "one or more of [them] spake iocundly concerning
Edmond Hartleyes hanging", explaining that it was impossible to hang
the devil and that the rope broke because "they were two *Ed*: and the
divel". The ministers retired to the garden to discuss a plan of action

---

[13] More, pp. 49–50, 54; Darrell, *True Narration*, p. 8; Harsnett, *A Discovery*, pp. 2, 22;
*Triall of Maist. Dorrel, or A Collection of Defences against Allegations not yet suffered to receive
convenient answere* (Middelburg, 1599), p. 13; Darrell, *A Detection*, p. 25. In this last version
the first letters arrived "About some 10. weekes" before the second, which would place
Starkey's visit to Dee about the last week in December although, as we have seen, he
was there in the first week. Either he made a later, unreported visit or Darrell's dating
is confused. The surname shared by the JP and Jane Ashton, the possessed servant, is
likely to be a mere coincidence, given the contrasting social positions.

with Nicholas and decided on an exercise of fasting and prayer the following day, considering which ministers should assist and settling upon "Mr Dickoms", the minister of Leigh. The rest of the evening was spent in preparation for the fast, with the possessed brought into one chamber where "one of us applyed his speech according to the present occasion".[14]

The following day the preachers met in the parlour with the possessed placed on couches and beds. The whole family joined with "honest neighbours" making a total of thirty 'non-possessed' laity, "some holding and tending the sicke possessed, & some sitting by". The possessed were relatively quiet from 7 a.m. to 3 p.m. Then there were particularly intense fits with Margaret Hardman being the first to improve, while either More or Dickoms was preaching, and the rest following her between 5 and 6 in the evening.[15] Jane Ashton was suffering more than the others so Dickoms and Darrell took her aside to a window at the other end of the parlour to concentrate on her ills. More was focusing the prayers of the company on the other six when they were cast down and, after recovering, started to rejoice. Dickoms had already rejoined the group. After More's success, Darrell came back and, perhaps rather petulantly, "he complayned unto [More...] & told me that he sawe never a one of them when they were delivered, which he saide grieved him exceedinglie".[16] After this More turned to warning the six dispossessed that it was not over, that Satan would attempt "to enter into them againe" but that they could resist him. Darrell returned to Ashton, who continued in her fits for another two hours. She seemed to have been dispossessed (although "we [Darrell and More] thought otherwise, because the signes of dispossession were wanting") and they all retired to their beds.[17]

During the night, "the spirits sett upon the 5 little children" and Dickoms went down to support them, gaining them a little rest and

---

[14] More, pp. 51–53; Darrell, *True Narration*, pp. 8–9. Rickert (p. 30) suggests that "Mr Dickoms" was John Deacon, the preacher at Leigh but I have not been able to back this up or refute it so he will be simply referred to as "Mr Dickoms". Darrell was doubtful whether the writer "John Deacon" was anything more than an alias for Walker: John Darrell, *The Replie of Iohn Darrell to the Answer of Iohn. Deacon and Iohn Walker concerning the doctrine of the Possession and Dispossession of Demoniaks* ([np], 1602) p. 34 but cf. Freeman, p. 51.

[15] Darrell, *True Narration*, pp. 10–11; More, pp. 59–63. Darrell has More as the preacher; More names Dickoms.

[16] More, pp. 72–65, *recte* p. 73.

[17] More, pp. 65–70, *recte* pp. 73–74, Darrell, *True Narration*, p. 12.

sleep. In the morning the ministers talked to the dispossessed about their experiences in the night. Their attention then had to be turned to Ashton who was evidently still possessed. This day there were a total of fifty family and neighbours in support and they watched as the ministers worked with the servant until the early afternoon when her fits intensified and she was finally dispossessed. After she had rested and resisted an attempted repossession they asked why she had dissembled the previous night. She told them that she was very vulnerable and the spirit had promised ease. More told her not to trust Satan again, as he was untrustworthy.[18]

Over the next two or three days, the attempts at repossession continued but all seven of them were successful in their resistance. Since that time, "god in mercy kept 6. of them: who since that time (praysed be God therfore) were never more nor lesse, they nor any of them molested by satan untill this day". The odd one out was Jane Ashton. She was fine while she was with the Starkey household but she moved to stay with "her Uncle, a papist, in the furthest parte of Lancashire". There she "became popish herselfe, as I have hard". Satan saw his opportunity and she was visited by "certayne Seminarie priestes, by whose coniurations and magical enchantments, (as it is reported) the evil spirit was brought into her againe". To the best knowledge of Darrell and More, she was still possessed when they were writing.[19]

II

The preceding narrative will have provoked questions or at least reservations. At this point, I want to address a relatively straightforward reservation which is that the preceding narrative failed to make explicit the nature of the 'fits' within this representation. This omission was deliberate, in that part of the explanation for possessions that is currently dominant requires particular sorts of people to be possessed and behave in particular sorts of ways caused by particular environments.

The first area to be addressed is the environment. Possessions have been seen as a way for young people to rebel against a strict and demanding 'religious' regime, a way that makes them the centre of

---

[18] Darrell, *True Narration*, pp. 11–13.
[19] More, p. 71, *recte* p. 75, Darrell, *True Narration*, p. 13.

attention and evades parental disapproval.[20] Does this model work here? In short, no. Darrell almost laughs at such an allegation in his response to Harsnett, making it clear that "the *parents and maister* of the persons possessed, were not *Recusants*, and *for zeale* after reformation they were so farr from that, as undoubtedly they knew not what *reformation* he speaketh of meant".[21] He turns it into an opportunity to rescue the name of 'puritan' from its pejorative use. Beyond this, the narrative encourages such a conclusion. Starkey's initial response was to turn to what were probably medical solutions and then to a priest. After about ten months he was willing to try a cunning man and Hartley did fairly well for eighteen months, so well in fact that Starkey was prepared to offer him a pension to persuade him to continue. It was only after his eventual failure and outside pressure that he was to turn to the likes of Darrell. We have neither positive nor negative evidence as to whether it was a loving environment but there is at least a theme of concern rather than blame throughout these accounts.

In terms of the symptoms to be understood on a psychological level the Lancashire Seven offer a fairly broad sweep in terms of social background, gender and age which allows us to see if the symptoms of possession carry the marks of differentiation that can be traced to such variants. There was only one boy, John, who suffered from his tenth to his thirteenth year. His sister Anne was a year younger. The social background of the first three female residents is less clear but that Margaret Hardman, aged fourteen, Ellinor, her ten-year-old sister and Ellen Holland, aged twelve at the start of her troubles, were placed in a gentry household for tuition at these ages, suggests that they were above the middling sorts. Margaret Byrom, aged thirty-three, who was explicitly described as "a poore kinswoman" of Mrs Starkey, is placed rather lower on the social scale while Jane Ashton was an unmarried servant at the age of thirty.

We can start with age and social status and see how far the symptoms of Margaret Byrom and Jane Ashton differed from the others in the ones where we know who suffered what. Byrom was violent

---

[20] As in Thomas, *Religion and the Decline of Magic*, pp. 480, 572; Darren Oldridge, *The Devil in Early Modern England* (Stroud: Sutton, 2000), pp. 114, 126–27 and *Witchcraft and Hysteria in Elizabethan England: Edward Jordan and the Mary Glover Case*, ed. by Michael MacDonald (London: Routledge, 1990), pp. xxxvii–xxxviii.

[21] Darrell, *A Detection*, p. 63. The italics are in the original, being quotations from Harsnett's *A Discovery*, p. 69.

towards Hartley; the only similar symptoms were in John although his
violence was much more indiscriminate, throwing items about and bit-
ing anyone at hand, including his mother.[22] Margaret was also unusual
in her visions. The devil once appeared as Hartley and she saw a
series of animals, a black dog, a black cat and a black mouse, stealing
her senses. On another occasion she saw several spirits being violent
towards her.[23] The other two women's visions of the departing devil
were unusual in that the children (other than Ellinor) saw an ugly man
with a hunchback leave while for Margaret he was like a crow's head,
for Jane a toad.[24] Margaret was the only one to give out rancid breath
and experience foul taste.[25] Neither Jane nor Margaret were included
in a particularly curious episode. Anne and John Starkey were joined
by Ellinor and Ellen and they spent an hour together when they rushed
into the garden and collected a leaf from every sort of plant present
in a very large garden. They returned inside and each of them placed
one leaf of the same plant in each room with remarkable speed and
precision.[26] The way in which the bodily swellings suffered by Jane and
Margaret were described may be a matter of age in that Margaret's
"belly swelled as bigge as a woman with childe" and Jane "compared
her bellye to a womans great with child".[27] That much said, internal
movements and swellings were a common factor but the others were
too young (or male!) for the comparison with pregnancy to spring to
the minds of either the victims or authors. Indeed, the vast majority of
their symptoms were in common with their companions. It was common to vomit, to cough up blood; gluttony and fasting were common
as were barking and howling.

Initially, gender looks a little more fruitful as a source of differences.
The first symptoms of John's affliction was uncontrollable shouting,
a very masculine activity. He displayed his possession through "verie
extraordinarie knowledge", denouncing sins throughout the land, calling all present to repent. Then he prayed for the Queen, praising her
for "peaceable governement" and then for the gospel and for good

---

[22] Darrell, *True Narration*, pp. 3, 2. Although More notes that they "were all of them
verie fierce, offering violence both to them selves and others" (More, p. 44) these are
the only specific instances either offer.
[23] Darrell, *True Narration*, pp. 7, 6, More, 30–31, 34.
[24] Ibid., pp. 79–6 *recte* pp. 83–84.
[25] Darrell, *True Narration*, p. 7.
[26] More, pp. 37–39.
[27] Ibid., p. 54, Darrell, *True Narration*, p. 9.

ministers. After two hours he sang part of Psalm 4 beautifully.[28] This was put right next to Margaret Hardman who went into a three-hour trance devoted to feminine sins, particularly women "who can not control themselves with anie sober or modest attire, but are ever readie to followe every newe and disguised fashion". Crucially, her approach was not to denounce, but to *enact* this sin, demanding a remarkable array of clothes from her spirit. On another occasion, she went in the opposite direction, performing a 'good' feminine activity with manic vigour when she assisted the maids with the laundry with an energy and speed that left them standing.[29]

However, John had no monopoly on extraordinary knowledge. Both Ellinor and Ellen "and some of the rest" answered questions delivered to them in Latin, well beyond their schooling. In addition, Margaret Byrom learnt three graces perfectly with the aid of her spirit and rehearsed them with aplomb. The only, but perhaps crucial, difference was that John's prayer was extempore while Margaret's graces were *pro forma*, thus within early modern gender expectations.[30]

Perhaps it is best to take George More's guidance in that although there were "many other very straunge things acted by every one of these in particular, which if they should be set downe every one, they would fill a large volume, for brevities sake therfore the most things be omitted". Furthermore, "so had they also many things in common one with another, and were in their fitts for the most parte handled alike". He goes on to list a total of *eighteen* common symptoms. These range from physical symptoms like facial disfiguration, paralysis, swelling, vomiting or the less of senses, to more spiritual symptoms like visions and seeking the protection of Jesus, and verbal symptoms like "fearfull schriking", howling or blasphemy.[31] There were slight differences of emphasis and the fact that six out of the seven were female should be noted but there was so much in common that it would be misleading to allow the focus to remain on the variations at cost to the similarities.

---

[28] More, pp. 24–25.

[29] Ibid., pp. 26–29.

[30] Cf. Diane Purkiss, 'Invasions: Prophecy and Bewitchment in the Case of Margaret Muschamp', *Tulsa Studies in Women's Literature*, 17 (1998), 235–53 (pp. 247–8). The issue of the likelihood of gender having an impact on *who* was possessed also needs to be addressed.

[31] Ibid., pp. 41–46. It may not be irrelevant that elsewhere Darrell noted that Scripture provided eighteen symptoms of possession: John Darrell, *A briefe Apologie proving the possession of William Somers* (Middelburg, 1599), p. 9.

III

A more fundamental reservation might have been nagging at the reader throughout the narrative and analysis delivered so far. That is that it is dominated by clearly positioned texts, working within a specific discourse. An initially unsatisfactory response would be that that is all we have. It is less unsatisfactory once it is made clear that I mean something more than 'all we have is More and Darrell'; it is that there is no account of any dispossession that is 'discourse-free', there are just some which are closer to *our* discourses than others.[32] Of course Darrell and More wrote within a discourse that assumed the reality of possessions but accounts which assume medical, psychological or 'political' explanations are just as positioned, it is just that the latter are seen as easier to fit in with our own worldviews and so tend to be less clearly limited in their explanatory value. If we have learnt anything from the fitful relationship between history and anthropology it is that the effort to squeeze other cultures into a supposedly ahistorical explanatory scheme is usually counterproductive.

It is my intention to take the positioned nature of the texts of Darrell and More; to take their appropriation in what I see as a more profitable direction. I will give a relatively brief sketch of how these texts operate[33] and then use that as a means with which to critically engage with the current historiography.[34] This will modify some of the 'givens' with which we approach these texts and, hopefully, open new avenues of analysis.

Both Darrell's *True Narration* and More's *A True Discourse*, of course, emerged shortly after the trial at Lambeth Palace where attention was focussed on the treatment of William Somers in Nottingham. In terms of the public sphere, it is also crucial that they were published after Harsnett's *Discovery* and Darrell's attempted rebuttal, *A Detection*. The forms in which they approached this position were different and this

---

[32] Cf. Michel de Certeau, *The Writing of History*, trans. by Tom Conley (New York: Columbia University Press, 1988), pp. 248, 254.

[33] I am currently working on a broader critique of the literature spawned by the controversy over Darrell's work which will make Harsnett's work more central and address the question of his 'success' in this dispute.

[34] Limitations of space mean that I will only be assessing the historiography relating to the possessions in England apart from where that work imports works from other geographical regions or countries.

was not a necessary consequence of More having been present only at Cleworth while Darrell was involved in both.[35]

George More's *A True Discourse* has a more complicated structure than Darrell's text, not least as it has a constantly absent presence in Harsnett's *Discovery* with cross-references and a much more explicit engagement with his version. The flip side of this is his occasional denunciation of the actions and allegations of "Atheistes and Papistes".[36] The purpose of this is made clear early on when he states that "if the Church of Englande have this power to cast out devills, then the Church of Rome is a false Church"[37] thus implying that anyone who contests this dispossession is in league with the papists, and casting himself as an advocate not of Puritans but of the Church of England. This is, effectively, to shift the goalposts. His polemic is explicitly integrated with the narrative, operating on the assumption that if one side is found convincing, the 'truth' of the other will follow. It also draws attention to the travails of the possessed as present previous to and independent of the presence of the godly preachers.

Darrell's form is both simpler and more sly. He took his experience and turned it into a sermon. His narratives of the seven in Lancashire and Somers in Nottingham are book-ended by an epistle to the Church of England and the separately paginated *The Doctrin of the Possession and Dispossession of Demoniakes out of the Word of God*. This 'objectifies' the narratives and the fact that Darrell not only draws out the doctrine of possession using these examples as his primary source but goes on to provide lengthy 'uses' almost makes them into Scripture! His narrative is set up as a representation to be referred back to in the course of his exegesis as a 'pure' representation. The first consequence was that this gave the narratives a greater authority than a simple engagement with Harsnett but the second is that the epistle encourages them to be read if not as re-enactments of, at least within a framework of, particular parts of Scripture. He opens with Acts 11, with Peter having been rebuked by the Apostles and the brethren for having been taken from Joppa to preach to the gentiles at Caesarea. After Peter explained how he had been given a vision and was called to preach, his actions acquired divine approval and he was forgiven. With Ashby-de-la-Zouch and

---

[35] See Freeman, pp. 48–50 for the finer points of the publishing history.
[36] For instance, More, pp. 4–6, 11–12, 23 (quote), 63, 71 *recte* p. 75.
[37] Ibid., p. 5.

Cleworth/Nottingham substituted for Joppa and Caesarea, Darrell's
identity and the 'proper' conclusions of the reader are plain. Not only
will Darrell's innocence be accepted; readers will "not onely cease to
be offended with me, but acknowledging the workes of god, magnifie
him for them".[38]

The playing field was made to function further in his favour with
the second Scriptural models, the Pharisees gainsaying Christ's giving
sight to the blind man (John 9) and the allegation that He cast out
devils through Beelzebub, the Prince of Devils (Matt. 12.24). In case
the analogy was thought to be too subtle Darrell concludes with the
watchmen at the tomb suggesting that the disciples stole Christ's body,
"whereunto they were hired by the Hie Preistes and Elders", a plainly
unflattering comparison for Harsnett, Bancroft et al.[39] The intention
is plain. It is to set up Darrell simply as a zealous Christian, willing to
follow a calling and to set out his experience in the sure and certain
hope that similar Christians will accept the truth and shift their attention to the doctrine of possession and dispossession and benefit from
and praise the great works of God.

One of the points where More and Darrell, and modern historians diverge is a matter of nomenclature. Part of the stated intention
of More's account of their time at Cleworth is that it "may serve to
discharge us of those grievous calumniations contayned in the discoverie [by Harsnett]: charging upon us both the names and practize of
cousiners, iuglers, exorcistes, imposters, &c".[40] Darrell puts the title of
"exorcist" in similar company when one of his first complaints in his
response to Harsnett is that he "and his master, togeather with such
others, whom they with theire crooked conveyances, have be witched"
have claimed "that *Darrell* is forsooth a *cogger, a cousener, a Iugler, an
Exorcist, a counterfeite, a devil-flinger, a devill-driver, a Seducer, a deceiver, an
Imposter....*".[41] The connotations of the term, which must have been
as plain to Harsnett as to its recipients, was made plain by More at
the end of this section. He claimed to have shown that "neyther in
dealing with these straunge afflictions, have we used eyther delusions,

[38] Darrell, *True Narration*, Epistle.
[39] Ibid., Epistle. That this is a change of tactic rather than a disinclination for direct
abuse is shown by his willingness elsewhere to describe Harsnett's *Discovery*, not unfairly,
as "written in such scoffing and raylinge characters": Darrell, *A Detection*, p. 19.
[40] More, p. 49.
[41] Darrell, *A Detection*, To the Reader.

iuglings, exorcismes, or any such vayne and ridiculous fooleries as they have detected in the popish Priestes".[42]

This is in stark contrast to the writers of the last and present centuries. Without exception, Darrell is "the Puritan exorcist", he "performed exorcisms" or in some way or another they have accepted Harsnett's nomenclature. This is not even a matter of noting the competition, weighing it up and explicitly coming down on Harsnett's side; it is simply a given.[43] In terms of nomenclature, Harsnett's is the dominant discourse. This is at its most extreme in Stephen Greenblatt's, "Shake-speare and the Exorcists", a piece employed by Sharpe and accepted and described as "brilliant" by Michael MacDonald. Greenblatt goes beyond citing and quoting Harsnett about thirty-five times compared to Darrell's six; Darrell's voice is given through Harsnett's *Discovery* on three occasions.[44] As Greenblatt was surely aware of Harsnett's intention to discredit Darrell he should at least have checked these quotations. Had he done so, he would have become aware of Harsnett's willingness to misquote, or to quote out of context for his own purposes. This is particularly clear where he quotes Harsnett's account of one particular performance. In his *Detection*, Darrell reproduces the quote and simply

---

[42] More, p. 63. The only point at which either seem to apply the term to themselves is in a quotation from Harsnett: Darrell, *A Detection*, p. 62, quoting [Harsnett], *Discovery*, p. 61.

[43] This is present in the classics, C. L'Estrange Ewen, *Witchcraft and Demonianism* (London: Heath Cranton, 1933), pp. 181–85 and Wallace Notestein, *A History of Witchcraft in England from 1558 to 1718* (Washington, 1911), pp. 73–92. More recently, see R. C. Marchant, 'John Darrell—Exorcist', *Transactions of the Thoroton Soc.*, 64 (1960) passim; Thomas, *Religion and the Decline of Magic*, p. 576; Walker, *Unclean Spirits*, pp. 3, 4; Stephen Greenblatt, 'Loudun and London', *Critical Inquiry*, 12 (1986), 326–46 (pp. 334, 335, 337–38); idem, *Shakespearean Negotiations* (Oxford: Oxford University Press, 1990), pp. 94–128; *Witchcraft and Hysteria*, ed. by MacDonald, pp. xvi, xix, xxiii, xxvi, xxxix, xl; James Sharpe, 'Disruption in the Well-Ordered Household: Age, Authority and Possessed Young People', in *The Experience of Authority in Early Modern England*, ed. by Paul Griffiths, Adam Fox and Steve Hindle (London: MacMillan, 1996), p. 194; idem, *Instruments of Darkness*, pp. 55, 97, 98, 190, 194; Oldridge, *The Devil*, pp. 12–15, 112–32. Freeman, pp. 35, 36–7, 50. F. W. Brownlow, *Shakespeare, Harsnettt, and the Devils of Denham* (Newark: University of Delaware Press, 1993), p. 54 and passim. Almond, pp. 1, 9, 10, 195 and passim. MacDonald describes Darrell as the "Puritan thaumatugist" (p. xvi), which Darrell would have objected to on the grounds that it meant that *he* was performing miracles. To be fair to Walker, he always described Darrell's "dispos-session", without ever explaining his choice of words and gives a helpful etymology of "exorcise", *op. cit.* pp. 5–6.

[44] Greenblatt, *Shakespearean Negotiations*, pp. 94–128; Sharpe, *Instruments*, pp. 203–04; *Witchcraft and Hysteria*, ed. by Macdonald, pp. xxxix–xl. This is aside from the fact that Greenblatt seriously overstates the trope of theatre in both Harsnett and Darrell.

adds "false" after it.[45] My complaint is not that Greenblatt should have published without thoroughly examining the sources involved so much as the hermeneutic and heuristic consequences of such work. To silently place Samuel Harsnett in the driver's seat is to enliven some candidates for 'truth' and to disengage with others. This reading implicitly authorises Harsnett's explanation and limits the breadth of the analysis. Above all it masks the contested nature of these readings.

It is not my intention to employ Greenblatt as a synecdoche for all writers on this dispute. In James Sharpe's textbook account of possessions, the narrative of Somers and the trial could have been taken straight out of Harsnett.[46] In discussing the controversy over Mary Glover's case he sets up a dichotomy between "*popular* godly preachers" and "the *more sceptical* élite" (my emphasis) with implicit credit being given to the latter.[47] When he sets up a 'typical' possession case, he states that "the arrival of somebody claiming to have expertise in matters of witchcraft or possession might speed the process" and then 'proves' this by quoting Harsnett without any indication that Darrell repeatedly denied having any such expertise. Similarly he notes the assessment of "sceptics" who turn out to be Harsnett alone.[48] The point is not to say that Darrell told the truth and that Harsnett lied so much as to say that the facticity of neither should not be taken as an uncontested given. To portray Darrell as "an exorcist" and Harsnett as "a sceptic" definitely weighs the scales in the latter's favour; it is much easier to dismiss an exorcist than a zealous Christian and much easier to find a sceptic convincing than a polemical satirist.[49]

If we turn away from the closed door of Darrell's explanation for a moment, what doors of understanding are open to such assessments? One of the contemporary explanations that is available to historians is physical sickness. Darren Oldridge has noted the similarities with the early modern sleep disorder, 'the hag'. He is more interested, however, in imposing a more 'modern' diagnosis.

---

[45] Greenblatt, pp. 102, 105, 106; [Harsnett], *Discovery*, pp. 118–19; Darrell, *Detection*, p. 93; cf. [Harsnett] *Detection*, pp. 231, 186 and Darrell, *Detection*, pp. 160–61, 123–24 for their disagreement.

[46] Sharpe, *Instruments*, pp. 97–98.

[47] Ibid., p. 191.

[48] Ibid., pp. 197, 203.

[49] Greenblatt allies himself with Reginald Scot in describing how "Puritan exorcists throw themselves into histrionic paroxysms of prayer" (p. 100) with the implicit question being how could anybody take them seriously.

In some instances, the drama of possession probably offered an explanation for physical symptoms which might, in different contexts, have been diagnosed in medical terms. For victims of the 'falling sickness', or epilepsy, the notion of possession offered one option for understanding a condition that was notoriously difficult to treat.[50]

Considering the adoption of Harsnett noted above, it is striking that he is the sole witness called up to observe how easy is was for young people "suffering from 'natural' diseases such as epilepsy" to feign possession.[51] When Keith Thomas noted the suggestion of natural causes put by Edward Jorden regarding Mary Glover's troubles, it was a "powerful exposé" and given as the beginning of the end for possession, at least among the elite.[52] Jorden's diagnosis of hysteria as causative was unusual and historians have been more attracted to the possibility of epilepsy. Walker's 'typical' case had fits "often of an epileptic character" and when he weighs up the evidence of Somers against Darrell he is surprised that the former was believed, given that he "was probably a mentally unbalanced epileptic".[53] James Sharpe is a little more cautious in that he merely observes that the subject needs "a full-scale examination by modern medical doctors". However, slightly earlier he simply states, in a rather patronising tone, that modern doctors (or psychologists) "would probably be able to reduce most of what appears to have happened to the categories of modern medicine".[54] The attractions of explanation through a 'natural' illness might be plain but, as they stand, so too are their limitations. Epilepsy might be suitable as an estimated cause of fits but it looks simply inadequate for most of the symptoms in the seven possessed of Lancashire. It offers no explanation for the vocal symptoms, the visions or the collection of herbs, for instance.[55] Neither does it explain how seven people in one household were suddenly taken with epileptic fits. It is to the more popular explanations using psychology or psychiatry that we must turn.

---

[50] Oldridge, pp. 141–42, 119.

[51] Ibid., pp. 13–14, citing Harsnett, *A Declaration of Egregious Popish Impostures* (London, 1603) pp. 136 ff.

[52] Thomas, *Religion*, p. 584. He notes that it was the same year as Harsnett's *Declaration*, perhaps implicitly attaching him to this Whiggish reading.

[53] Walker, pp. 16, 64–65. Sharpe mentions the possibility of either or both hysteria and epilepsy: *Instruments*, p. 205.

[54] Sharpe, 'Disruption', pp. 204, 197; cf. Walker, p. 16.

[55] Cf. Almond, p. 5.

How do historians justify such means of analysis? The first is through precedence or similarity. Oldridge proposes such analysis, with the backing of Roy Porter, because the diagnosis of possession explained "symptoms of conditions later understood as forms of 'neurosis' or 'schizophrenia'".[56] Sharpe makes a similar move to that of Thomas noted above, whcn he observes that "practically every well-documented case of the time includes references to physicians being called in, while some of the incidents became a contested field between those who adduced medical explanations and those who preferred supernatural ones".[57] This is taken further when he offers the work of John Demos as a suitable model. Demos mentions possession accounts and claims that "comparison with psychiatric case reports in our own time does not seem far-fetched".[58] Frankly, the comparison is rather attenuated. The second option is 'our' superior understanding of such phenomena. Walker resists the temptation to use "psycho-pathological terms" not because it would be wrong to use them but because it is not his field.[59] Sharpe advises caution because we need further awareness of family life in early modern England, rather than due to any impropriety in the tools of analysis.[60] He is still willing to state that the relevance of puberty is "obvious (especially given our awareness of modern psychology)".[61]

If these reasons are accepted, what do we gain from such analysis? In the historiography of English possessions the application is not too over-confident and not too determined to force the evidence into a modern model. The most common observation is that possession provided a licence for bad behaviour, sometimes repressed desires, sometimes simply being naughty.[62] On one level, this makes sense. The possessed person became the centre of attention and was not castigated for actions outwith their 'normal' behaviour. However, a pattern is present once

---

[56] Oldridge, p. 119; Roy Porter, *A Social History of Madness* (London: Weidenfeld and Nicolson, 1987), pp. 83–89.

[57] Sharpe, 'Disruption', pp. 192–93.

[58] Ibid., p. 204, quoting John Demos, *Entertaining Satan: Witchcraft and the Culture of Early New England* (New York: Oxford University Press, 1982), p. 99.

[59] Walker, p. 16.

[60] Sharpe, *Instruments*, pp. 202–03.

[61] Sharpe, 'Disruption', p. 191. It is striking that Brownlow, refers to the dispossession of "seven *children*" (emphasis added) in Lancashire: Brownlow, *Shakespeare*, p. 55.

[62] Thomas, pp. 573–74; Sharpe, 'Disruption', pp. 198–99; Oldridge, pp. 126–27; Sharpe, *Instruments*, pp. 202–03, 205, 207; Arnold, pp. 23–24, 26. This is touched upon in Purkiss, pp. 240–42.

we turn our attention to the examples chosen to illustrate or prove this thesis. Thomas mentions blasphemies and obscenities and the act of throwing a Bible across the room.[63] Sharpe's examples are a little broader. There is the child who plays with her food, sometimes missing her mouth and laughing. There is immodest humour, verbal abuse and slovenly behaviour. There are also two examples from the possessions in Lancashire. Margaret Hardman's lecture and performance about women's taste for fashion is mentioned. An occasion when three of four of them "gave themselves to Scoffing and Blasphemy, calling the holy Bible being brought up bible bable, bible bable" is mentioned, followed by John Starkey's inability to say the Lord's Prayer.[64] The symptoms as they are presented might be described as the 'pleasurable' symptoms. However, Sharpe chooses not to make it clear that Margaret's performance lasted for three hours which might change the perception a little. In addition, how far does this thesis account for Ellen and Ellinor's three day fast, John's profuse bleeding from his nose and mouth, Margaret Byrom's vomiting of "much fleamy and bloudy matter" or her being thrown at the fire, Jane Ashton's coughing up blood or vomiting?[65] It should also be noted that these less attractive symptoms appear regardless of gender, age or social status, as do the more pleasurable ones, placing question marks against the idea of possession as adolescent rebellion.[66]

IV

What has preceded may have seemed unmitigatedly negative. It is not intended to suggest that explanatory schemes of physical or psychological causation are to be seen as wholly inapplicable, so much as to recognise their limitations. If we were to propose a wholly physical explanation that would necessitate a substantial separation from the early modern frame of reference.[67] Similarly, diagnoses drawn from psychological understandings were made by contemporaries but we

---

[63] Thomas, pp. 573–74.
[64] Sharpe, 'Disruption', pp. 199–201; Darrell, *True Narration*, p. 9; More, p. 56.
[65] More, pp. 34–36, 13; Darrell, *True Narration*, pp. 10, 4–5, 13.
[66] It will be recalled that Margaret Byrom was thirty-three and Jane Ashton was thirty.
[67] Stuart Clark, *Thinking with Demons: The Idea of Witchcraft in Early Modern Europe* (Oxford: Oxford University Press, 1999), p. 410.

must appreciate that this is not a carte blanche authorisation of current psychological or psychoanalytical means.[68] To import such schemes and employ them as the primary means of explanation fits into what Michel de Certeau described as "'soft' interdisciplinarity", a practice "that allows each science the ease of assigning to others what exceeds the limits of its own explanation".[69]

My proposal is that the recentralising of demonology would be of immeasurable benefit to such studies. D.P. Walker announced that "the first possibility [of explanation], a devil, must be excluded", as historians "should not ask their readers to accept supernatural phenomena".[70] I am *not* asking for the agency of Satan per se to be taken into account so much as saying that the perception of Satan should be taken seriously; we should accept the reality of the discourse of possession. In a culture where possession is part of the worldview, possession is part of the reality; people can be possessed. Medical (both 'physical' and 'mental') explanations were offered, as were explanations through 'politics' and dissimulation. But causation simply by possession and dispossession was also proffered. Why do the first group qualify as sources for 'our' causative schema but the last tend to be denigrated or ignored?[71] The immediate response would be that Darrell et al. had an axe to grind, that their accounts are positioned. The point is both accurate and its analysis is necessary and laudable. It is right to be sensitive to the positioned nature of early modern accounts of possession. However, this agreement is qualified. Such analysis should be applied to *all* of the accounts; all the early modern texts explaining such phenomena have an implicit or explicit purpose and we can never be in a position to deliver a value-free account through them. The recognition of such conceptual location should not be employed simply to denigrate, to rule out of court, some of them and not others. This is true particularly if it is done in order to 'authorise' a privileged 'modern' explanation.[72]

---

[68] David Harley, 'Explaining Salem: Calvinist Psychology and the Diagnosis of Possession', *American Historical Review*, 101 (1996), 307–30 (pp. 308, 328–29). One particularly useful note made by Harley is that there are a myriad of current schools in these disciplines; this is a highly contested field and historians should be cautious in transferring such tools without an appreciation of such contestations: ibid., p. 308 note.

[69] De Certeau, *Writing of History*, p. 291.

[70] Walker, p. 15.

[71] Almond notes that contemporaries identified three possible causes, genuine possession, illness and fraud, but concentrates his analysis on the second and third possibilities: Arnold, pp. 38–42.

[72] Cf. de Certeau, *Writing*, pp. 254–55.

That is the point of the title of this piece: Darrell has been dispossessed of his contribution to the explanation of possession.

The current tendency to adopt (and/or adapt) Harsnett's judgement on these issues has four regrettable consequences. The first is that it encourages us to misunderstand why Harsnett 'won' this struggle, or even not to ask the question.[73] The second is that making Harsnett 'one of us' tends to mask the contest for meaning, that it was a much more thorough semiotic wrestling-match than we tend to appreciate.[74] Related to this is the third consequence, that it allows us to be unaware of the cultural specificity of our analysis, to believe that we have a transcendent rational understanding.[75] Finally, it allows historians to perform 'an exorcist's task', that is to eliminate or at least sanitise 'the strangeness of history'. To reinstate the discourse of possession in our explanatory schemes will lessen the tendency, in de Certeau's phrase, "to eliminate the danger of the *other*".[76]

---

[73] Cf. Harley, pp. 309–10. I intend to develop this argument elsewhere. Although this was not the centre of his attention, Tom Freeman's work has improved our perspective on this.

[74] De Certeau, *Writing*, pp. 246–47, 262; idem, *The Possession at Loudun*, trans. by Michael B. Smith (Chicago: Chicago University Press, 1996), pp. 2–3; Clark, p. 391; Harley, p. 330.

[75] Harley, p. 330; de Certeau, *Writing*, pp. 248, 250.

[76] De Certeau, *Possession*, pp. 227–28.

PART TWO

ENGLAND UNDER THE ACT

APPLYING THE ACT OF 1604

WITCHES IN ESSEX, NORTHAMPTONSHIRE AND LANCASHIRE BEFORE AND AFTER 1604

Marion Gibson

One of the most obvious questions that can be asked of the Witchcraft Act of 1604 is this: what actual differences were made to legal and cultural practice by the alteration of the definitions of, and penalties for, witchcraft introduced in the new Act of 1604? What, if anything, changed? But this simple question is actually very challenging to answer. Processes of cultural change are frustratingly difficult to map, as all of us know, especially when they relate to the intangibles of ideology, unspoken assumption and fantasy. But a place to start, and one way to address the more specific part of the question—that relating to changes in legal practice—is an examination of contemporary accounts of witchcraft trials before and after 1604.

News pamphlet accounts are a good source of information in that they give us far more contextual detail about trials than the brief records of indictment that survive in some areas, and for some periods, before and after 1604. There is, however, a problem in that we are reading accounts whose main purpose was not to note legal niceties, but to tell a general, instructive and entertaining story of a witch's activities and his or her downfall in court, apparently aimed at relatively uninformed readers. This problem can, however, also be a strength. It can tell us whether those reporting from the courtroom did care about the law and its workings, whether they thought their readers did, and whether they, as outsiders or insiders, remarked upon any changes. Did they know the legal context in which witches were being accused and tried? Did anything strike them as being of particular interest to the judges, magistrates, or the courtroom audience? Broadly, in their view did the Witchcraft Act of 1604 change anything about the perception and representation of witches and thus how they were treated in the courts?

Three incidents within twenty-five years on either side of 1604 were particularly well-documented by pamphleteers. In 1582, Brian Darcy, a Justice of the Peace from Essex, collected a large quantity of evidence against around twenty people accused of witchcraft in St. Osyth, Clacton, Little Oakley and Essex other villages. Thirteen were eventually tried at Chelmsford Assizes. The evidence against the accused was subsequently published in a pamphlet by one W.W., under the title *A True and Just Recorde*.[1] His identity remains mysterious, but his pamphlet was based on pre-trial informations and examinations, and when compared with surviving indictments can give us some sense of which accusations came to court and which there resulted in successful prosecution.

In 1612 several communities in Northamptonshire were troubled by accusations. In Guilsborough, Raunds, Thrapston and Stanwick about ten women and men were suspected, and at least eight sent to be tried at the Assizes at Northampton.[2] An anonymous pamphlet, entitled *The Witches of Northamptonshire*, gives accounts of some of their supposed crimes and their trial. There is also a second, and rather different, account of the cases in a related manuscript.[3] We can learn from these more than is usual about how witchcraft was tried after the 1604 Act, because we have at least two eyewitnesses commenting on the same events.

Another particularly good source is Thomas Potts' famous pamphlet about the Lancashire witches, *The Wonderfull Discoverie of Witches in the Countie of Lancaster*.[4] Potts was a court clerk, probably the Clerk of Arraigns, on the Northern Assize Circuit when he wrote his pamphlet, also in 1612. If anyone would have cared about details of indictments and legal interpretation, it would have been Potts. He described the trial of nineteen accused, and his pamphlet is the most detailed account we have of an early modern English witch trial.

What, then, were the main changes made by the 1604 Act to the provisions of the 1563 one, to which these pamphlet accounts might revealingly allude? The 1563 Act expressed concern that "fantastical and devilish persons" were devising and practising invocations and conjurations of evil spirits; were practising witchcrafts, enchantments, charms and sorceries, to the destruction of the persons and goods of their neighbours and other subjects of the realm. They were imperil-

---

[1] Published by Thomas Dawson, senior; licensed 6 April 1582.
[2] Published by Arthur Johnson and printed by Thomas Purfoot and his son, of Newgate; licensed 16 October 1612.
[3] B.L. Sloane 972, Sig. f.7.
[4] Printed by William Stansby for John Barnes; licensed 7 November 1612.

ling their own souls, and bringing infamy and disquiet to the realm. Accordingly, if anyone now practised any invocations or conjurations of evil spirits, for any intent or purpose, or practised any witchcraft, enchantment, charm or sorcery which killed anyone, they were to be tried, and if convicted put to death. Anyone aiding or counselling them would face the same punishment. There would be no benefit of sanctuary or clergy, but the wife and children of any man so convicted might inherit his property without further penalties. Anyone using witchcraft, enchantment, charm or sorcery which consumed or lamed any victim, or harmed his or her goods, would be tried, and if convicted would be imprisoned for a year. Once each quarter the prisoner would appear in the pillory at a market. Again, aiders and counsellors were liable to the same charges. There was no bail, and a second offence meant the death penalty. Seeking treasure or lost goods and provoking unlawful love by witchcraft was also forbidden: the penalty, imprisonment and pillory. A second offence meant forfeiture of all goods to the Crown and life imprisonment.[5]

The 1604 Act made substantial changes—although Kittredge regarded it as "not really a new law at all, but simply a modification and extension of the statute of Elizabeth".[6] The Act's creators certainly presented it in that light, as it set out its aims as "the better restraining" of such offences, "and more severe punishing the same". This suggested that the existing law was thought to be ineffective because too lenient. But far from simply doing "better" in deterring and punishing offenders as presently defined, it was clear from its provisions that the new Act was intended to abolish all witchcraft practices utterly. Now, therefore, if anyone practised any invocation or conjuration of an evil spirit, or "should consult, covenant with, entertain, employ, feed or reward any evil and wicked spirit to or for any intent or purpose" the penalty was death. It was also death to "take up any dead man, woman or child out of his or their grave, or any other place where the dead bodie resteth, or the skin, bone or any other part of any dead person, to be employed or used in any manner of witchcraft, sorcery, charm or enchantment". Finally, as before, killing anyone by witchcraft was a capital crime, but so was the previously less serious offence of consuming or laming them.

---

[5] For the text see Appendix I.
[6] George Lyman Kittredge, *Witchcraft in Old and New England* (Cambridge, MA: Harvard University Press, 1929), p. 308.

Any treasure hunting or love magic, damage to a victim's goods, or the intent to harm any person (even if ineffectual) meant imprisonment for a year and pillory. A second offence meant death.[7] All kinds of witchcraft were thus in theory far more dangerous to practice. Notestein read into the Act the desire to "make the fact of witchcraft as a felony depend chiefly upon a single form of evidence, the testimony to the use of evil spirits", but clearly the redefinition was a far wider one.[8]

It is these changes that should be reflected in accounts of witchcraft trials, indicating that the new Act had been noted by judges and magistrates at least, and that all the new (or newly capital) crimes specified were being pursued. But despite the substantial nature of the changes made overall, some were rather subtle in their detail. For instance, invoking or conjuring an evil spirit had always carried the death penalty. Apparently invoking good spirits was allowed, and continued to be so—although how might one prove that the spirit was a good one? But now, feeding or rewarding an evil spirit (even if one had not summoned or made a pact with it) also carried the death penalty. So did even vaguer communications with an evil spirit that one had not invoked or conjured (consulting, entertaining). Simply to be in the same room with an evil spirit—should anyone admit to such a thing—might conceivably be seen as entertaining it. Did any kind of dialogue indicate consultation? These were unusually complex questions for justices and lawyers to interpret.

Behind these subtle adjustments, wider cultural movements could be detected by those who were thoughtful about such matters—and this synergy with some existing trends might have flagged up ways of reading the law's changes to those who had to apply them in practice. The law's focus on covenanting was, of course, of particular interest to the godly in another sense. Godly groups, and radical separatists going beyond them, felt themselves to be enacting a covenant with God. A blasphemous parody of that was what the Act represented as the central transgression of witches. It was perhaps unsurprising that covenant was specifically described in the legislation now, as a capital crime in its own right, by the new Scottish king—who was well acquainted with godly and especially Scottish Presbyterian conceptions of covenant,

---

[7] For the text see Appendix II.
[8] Wallace Notestein in *A History of Witchcraft* (1911), cited in James Sharpe, *Instruments of Darkness: Witchcraft in England 1550–1750* (London: Hamish Hamilton, 1996), p. 91.

and under pressure from English godly to move closer to these in his ecclesiastical policy.[9]

The new Act also responded to some of the concerns of godly complaint literature that what was being punished was merely the injury done to God's creatures, and not to God himself, by witches.[10] It might now be inferred that any contact with an evil spirit or devil created an implicit pact, and was thus punishable in the severest fashion, whether it resulted in injury to a human being or not. Here might be straws in the wind, for magistrates and judges to observe. But Catholic demonologists had made precisely the same charges against existing legislation—and nothing was sure in the early years of James' reign.[11] He had written *Daemonologie*, it was true, from which some of his views might be inferred, but that was over a decade before and it certainly contained some assertions divergent from English belief and practice.[12] No matter how thoughtful about such implications and wider trends James's country justices and judges of Assize were when they applied the new law, what might be the King's and his ministers' intention? Did they, perhaps especially the godly among the magistracy, leap at the chance to harden their acculturative stance on such matters? Or did they take a conservative stance, and await developments?

One of the key changes between the Acts that might help us measure magisterial responses was in the attitude to spirits. Had feeding and rewarding a spirit been an offence in Elizabethan times, then many witches could have been charged and convicted. In the 1582 Essex

---

[9] It has been argued that the 1591 pamphlet *Newes from Scotland* demonstrates the tendency of Scottish divines, magistrates, and James himself, to figure witchcraft as an inversion of covenanting practice: see *Witchcraft in Early Modern Scotland: James VI's Demonology and the North Berwick Witches*, ed. by Gareth Roberts and Lawrence Normand (Exeter: Exeter University Press, 2000) and Stuart Clark, 'Inversion, Misrule and the Meaning of Witchcraft', *Past & Present*, 87 (1980), 98–127.

[10] See in particular George Gifford's *A Dialogue Concerning Witches and Witchcraftes* (London, 1593), and also restatements of such a position in providentialist writings and witchcraft trial reports such as *A true and just Recorde* (above), Richard Galis, *A Brief Treatise* (London, 1579), and *The Apprehension and confession of three notorious Witches* (London, 1589).

[11] The section on legal reform in *A true and just Recorde* is directly translated from Jean Bodin's *De la demonomanie des sorciers* (Paris, 1580), see Marion Gibson, *Reading Witchcraft: Stories of Early English Witches* (London and New York: Routledge, 1997), p. 215.

[12] James VI and I, *Daemonologie* (Edinburgh, 1591); see *Witchcraft in Early Modern Scotland*, (see Roberts and Normand above) and Stuart Clark, 'King James' *Daemonologie*: Witchcraft and Kingship' in *The Damned Art*, ed. by Sydney Anglo (London, Henley and Boston: Routledge Kegan Paul, 1977), pp. 156–81.

account, based on examinations taken by the magistrate and available to the Assize court, Ales Hunt admitted that

> Shes[13] had within vi. dayes before this examination, two spirits, like unto little Coltes, the one blacke, and the other white: And saith she called them by the names of *Jacke* and *Robbin*.[14]

Another witch, Ursley Kempe, had provided details of Hunt's familiars:

> shee went to the house of William Hunt to see howe his wife did and shee beeing from home, shee called at her chamber window and looked in, and then espied a spirite to looke out of a potcharde[15] from under a clothe, the nose thereof beeing browne like unto a Ferret. And sayeth, that the same night shee asked *Tyffin* her [Ursley Kempe's] white spirite, what Huntes wives spirite had done: And then it told this examinate, that it had killed Haywarde of Frowicke six beastes which were lately dressed of the gargette.[16] And sayeth, that her sayde spirite tolde her, that Huntes wives spirite had a droppe of her blood for a rewarde: but shee sayeth, that shee asked not her spirite upon what place of her body it was.[17]

Hunt's eight-year-old daughter, Febey, provided confirmation of her mother's familiars, saying:

> yt shee hath seen her mother to have two litle thinges like horses, the one white, the other blacke, the which shee kept in a litle lowe earthen pot with woll, colour white and blacke: and that they stoode in her chamber by her bed side, and saith, that shee hath seene her mother to feede them with milke out of a blacke trening dishe, and this examinat being caried after this confession by the Constables to her fathers house, shee shewed them the place were they stood and the borde that covered them: And this examinate chose out the dishe, out of which they were fedde, from amongst many other dishes.[18]

This, with Ales Hunt's confession, would have made perfect evidence with which to convict her after 1604. By the standards of proof of her time, she clearly had consulted, entertained, employed, fed and rewarded an evil spirit. But, in accordance with the law, in 1582 no

---

[13] *Sic.*

[14] *A True and just Recorde* ([np], 1582), sig. C3v.

[15] Rosen suggests "pot sherd", a shard or a broken piece of pot (Rosen, *Witchcraft in England*, p. 118).

[16] Recently killed, because they had inflamed throats (see Rosen, *Witchcraft in England*, p. 118 note 23).

[17] *A True and just Recorde*, sig. B3v.

[18] Ibid., sig. 2A5v–6.

mention was made of this in surviving court records. Hunt was, more-over, acquitted of bewitching cattle, and killing Rebecca, the daughter of Henry Durrant.[19]

However, the level of interest in the familiars, their housing and feeding, and the detailing of conversations with them, is striking. It is perhaps not surprising that in 1604 caring for such magical creatures was made an offence, and it may have had little to do with specifically godly concerns about covenanting with spirits. Before 1604 trouble was clearly taken in a very high proportion of cases, in many of which godly involvement cannot be detected or proven, both to record assertions that such creatures existed, and even to discover physical evidence of their presence in the accused's home. English accusers, suspects and questioners were all interested in the keeping of familiar spirits, and some wanted physical proof of it that they could take to court. This was sought in the case of Elizabeth Bennett, a woman also from St. Osyth who ended her long examination with a confession of employing spirits to kill her neighbour. Bennett had also been accused by Ursley Kempe, and although there is ambiguity over the order of events, Darcy had Bennett called before him. He was careful to have recorded his discussion with her about Kempe's accusations, especially "whether she had not a pot or pitcher of earth standing under a paire of staires in her house & wool in the same, in the which usually the said two spirites did lie". Elizabeth Bennett denied this "with many othes, saying yt she was wel assured yt she had none such". But Darcy carefully moved in for his proof of guilt:

> wherupon it was said to her, if it be proved to your face, what will you say to al the other matters you have bin charged with, are they true? To that she made answere & said yea: Then was the pot brought before her, the which she then confessed to be her pot, but denied yt the wool therin was any of hers.[20]

Interest in the physical acquisition of this kind of evidence was certainly not unique to the 1582 case. In 1579 the house of accused witch Elleine Smithe of Maldon was searched for evidence of spirits living in wicker

---

[19] *Calendar of Assize Records: Essex: Elizabeth I*, ed. by J.S. Cockburn, 10 vols (London: HMSO, 1975–85), record 1301.

[20] *A True and just Recorde*, sig. B6.

and leather bottles and a wool pack. The bottles and pack were found but, unsurprisingly, "the Spirites were vanished awaie".[21]

James Sharpe suggests that Darcy's activities in 1582 show already "a firming-up of legal proceedings against [witchcraft]".[22] It was not within the law's powers to indict a person for possessing familiars, but that did not deflect some magistrates and constables from their practical attempts to find evidence of it, or stop some attempt being made to turn this into part of the legal proceeding. The most striking example is the indictment of Margerie Barnes, almost certainly Ales Hunt's sister. Margerie played a major role in 1582, apparently advising her sister to confess and providing evidence against a neighbour, Joan Pechey. She told Darcy that she had inherited two spirits from her and Ales' mother, Mother Barnes, and passed them onto Pechey—though not before she had fed them twice on milk herself.[23] Two years later, in March 1584 she was herself indicted for murder by witchcraft, and the indictment noted that she kept and maintained three spirits, a mole, a grey cat and a dun dog. This was with the intention of bewitching men and beasts, it was specified. The main part of the indictment was for collaborating with another witch to kill a man by witchcraft, of which she was acquitted.[24] It seems from the care taken with evidence of spirit-keeping and the wording of Barnes's indictment that some justices, constables and court officials (who would have to draft such an indictment) were straining at the leash, keen to include evidence of spirit-keeping not only in pre-trial statements but in indictments themselves. It is not possible to determine precisely how such discussions about indictments might have proceeded, but the result here shows that in one instance at least they did take place.

Yet in the two trials so carefully documented in 1612, after the introduction of the new Act, there is—paradoxically—relatively little evidence of judicial concern with evidence of the keeping of familiars.

---

[21] *A Detection of damnable driftes* ([np], 1579), sig. A6v. Maldon did have a substantial godly presence, as indicated by the presence of George Gifford and the repeated conflict between townspeople and prelacy over his position; see, *The Second Parte of a Register*, ed. by A. Peel, 2 vols (Cambridge: Cambridge University Press, 1915) II, p. 260; Alan Macfarlane, 'A Tudor Anthropologist: George Gifford's *Discourse* and *Dialogue*' in *The Damned Art* (see Anglo above), pp. 140–55 and Alan Macfarlane, *Witchcraft in Tudor and Stuart England* (Prospect Heights, Illinois: Waveland Press, 1991).
[22] Sharpe, *Instruments of Darkness*, p. 98.
[23] *A True and just Recorde*, sig. C4v–C5.
[24] Cockburn, *Calendar of Assize Records*, record 1432.

In the Northamptonshire pamphlet and the accompanying manuscript it was certainly assumed that the witches had spirits. Victim William Avery had a vision of one of the witches bringing a mole to him and trying to persuade him to let it suck his toe, and a vision of a spirit of hers called Cramega.[25] He also believed that the spirits had physically restrained him from attacking the witches, although the pamphleteer seemed a little sceptical of their power to do this.[26] The writer did however include a long discussion, citing King James *Daemonologie*, of "the marke where the Spirits sucke", which he believed to be insensible.[27] The manuscript, meanwhile, described how some of the accused were "searcht by women sworn, who found marks or teates on some of them but on some none" and others were searched for teats in their mouths at which spirits might suck blood.[28]

The pamphleteer gave the most detail of actual familiars, describing the three spirits which "it is said" accused witch Arthur Bill possessed, and discussing how spirits might manifest themselves as solid bodies.[29] His interest in them seemed largely theoretical, however:

> It seemes to me that these vilde Spirits, which these Witches have at com-
> maund, and by their imployment are suffred to have power to hurt the
> bodyes of others, have a greater Power over them that set them a worke,
> For they doe not onely feed uppon them participating with the blood of
> humane flesh for the redemption wherof Christ shed his owne precious
> blood, But it appeares that they have also power even over their Soules,
> leading them into wandring by-waies, and such erroneous Laberinths, that
> in the wilfull obstinacie and perverse sufferance of their owne minds to
> stray in this daungerous desart of obduracie, they are lost for ever.[30]

Despite this lengthy concentration on spirit-keeping, there is no further record of familiars or evidence of their housing and feeding being searched for, and the two indictments recorded by the author of the manuscript are simply for attacking William Avery and his sister Elizabeth Belcher, and for killing and harming animals.[31] There is no

---

[25] Gibson, *Witchcraft and Society*, pp. 55, 57.
[26] *The Witches of Northamptonshire* ([np], 1612), sig. B3v, Gibson, *Witchcraft and Society in England and America*, p. 55.
[27] King James VI and I, *Daemonologie* (Edinburgh, 1597); *The Witches of Northampton-shire* (1612), sig. C2.
[28] Gibson, *Witchcraft and Society*, pp. 57, 58.
[29] *The Witches of Northamptonshire*, sig. C3v.
[30] Ibid., sig. C4v–D.
[31] Gibson, *Witchcraft and Society*, pp. 54, 58.

complaint, or report of the complaint of others, from either writer that the law is being misapplied, or that theologically-speaking the trial's focus is not the correct one. This is all the more striking, of course, because Northampton was one of England's most obviously godly localities.[32]

Similarly, and in a very different and contested county, none of the many indictments recorded by Thomas Potts in the massive Lancashire trial mentioned consulting, covenanting with, entertaining, employing, feeding or rewarding evil spirits.[33] Spirits were once again plentifully in evidence: a brown dog belonging to the Device family and known as Ball, a black dog belonging to James Device called Dandy.[34] The idea of covenant was, however, stressed repeatedly in the examinations. Alizon Device described how:

> her Grand-mother, called *Elizabeth Sothernes*, alias *Dembdike*, did (sundry times in going or walking together, as they went begging) perswade and advise this Examinate to let a Divell or a Familiar appeare to her, and that shee, this Examinate would let him suck at some part of her; and she might have and doe what shee would. And so not long after these perswasions, this Examinate being walking towards the Rough-Lee, in a Close of one *John Robinsons*, there appeared unto her a thing like unto a Blacke Dogge: speaking unto her, this Examinate, and desiring her to give him her Soule, and he would give her power to doe any thing she would: whereupon this Examinate being therewithall inticed, and setting her downe; the said Blacke-Dogge did with his mouth (as this Examinate then thought) sucke at her breast, a little below her Paps.[35]

The familiars in this trial account are, more often than before, in humanoid and Satanic forms: the most prominent are Tibb and Fancie, spirits belonging to the 'chief' witches Elizabeth Southerns alias Demdike and Anne Whittle alias Chattox. Tibb was a shape-shifting creature, once in the likeness of a spotted bitch, but originally introduced as "a spirit or Devil in the shape of a Boy", to whom Elizabeth Demdike gave her soul in exchange for "any thing that she would request".[36] Fancie

---

[32] See in particular W.J. Sheils, *The Puritans in the Diocese of Peterborough 1558–1610* (Northampton: Northamptonshire Record Society, 1979).

[33] *The Lancashire Witches: Histories and Stories*, ed. by Robert Poole (Manchester and New York: Manchester University Press, 2002); Jonathan Lumby, *The Lancashire Witch-Craze: Jennet Preston and the Lancashire Witches 1612* (Preston: Carnegie, 1995).

[34] E.g. Thomas Potts, *The Wonderfull Discoverie of Witches in the Countie of Lancashire* (London, 1612), sig. Gv–G2, Iv.

[35] Ibid., sig. R3v.

[36] Ibid., sig. B2v, B4.

was in "the likenes of a Man", and sometimes referred to simply as "the Devill". He visited Anne Chattox who agreed to "become his Subject, and give her Soule unto him", and to give him one part of her body to suck upon. He promised her "thou shalt want nothing; and be revenged of whom thou list" and later "Gould, Silver, and worldly Wealth at her will".[37] These were straightforward covenants with a devil, and it would be hard to find more glaring examples. Yet they do not appear in Potts's transcriptions of the indictments at all. Anne Chattox is charged simply with killing Robert Nutter, whilst Elizabeth Demdike died in prison and never came to trial. The members of the Device family were also charged with conventional offences of killing and harming victims. Indictments continued to assert that the accused had been seduced into their crimes by the instigation of the devil—but nothing more specific, and certainly nothing new. There are a few examples of indictments for the new offence of consulting with, entertaining, feeding and rewarding evil spirits (1611, 1645) but they are exceptional.

If there was no change in the drawing up of indictments themselves, was there any change in the content of informations and examinations, which might suggest an alteration in the conceptualisation of witchcraft offered to the court? The answer is, broadly, no—like the idea of spirit-keeping, the idea of covenant was not itself a new one. In 1589 Joan Cunny had reported that:

> making a Circle as she was taught, and kneeling on her knees, [she] said the praier now forgotten, and invocating upon Sathan: Two Sprites did appeere unto her within the said Circle, in the similitude and likenes of two black Frogges, and there demaunded of her what she would have, bee-ing readye to doo for her what she would desire, so yt she would promise to give them her soule for their travaile, for otherwise: they would doo nothing for her. Wher-upon she did promise them her soule, and then they concluded with her so to doo for her, what she would require.[38]

But the idea of covenant is more strongly present in Potts' pamphlet than elsewhere in trial accounts. Potts was writing on behalf of the Assize judges, who provided a preface for his work, and he had clearly read the King's *Daemonologie*, perhaps in order to prepare himself for this

---

[37] Ibid., sig. B4–B4v, D3.
[38] Cecil L'Estrange Ewen, *Witch Hunting and Witch Trials* (New York: Dial, 1929), pp. 203, 223–31; *The Apprehension and confession of three notorious Witches* ([np], 1589), sig. A3.

official task. So he was more likely than most to note that covenanting with the devil was supposedly a newly-prominent vice. If so, however, he still gave little time to it in the opinionated introductions that he wrote for each witch's case. It was unmissable in the evidence placed before the court, but Potts spent rather longer discussing the ingratitude of witches and the likelihood that they would be very ugly.[39]

If there was good and now usable evidence of covenant in Lancashire in 1612, then there was even better evidence of the newly-delineated offence of grave-robbing for the purposes of necromancy. James Device reported that:

> twelve yeares agoe, the said *Anne Chattox* at a Buriall at the new Church in Pendle, did take three scalpes[40] of people, which had been buried, and then cast out of a grave, as she the said *Chattox* told this Examinate; and tooke eight teeth out of the said Scalpes, whereof she kept foure to her selfe, and gave the other foure to the said *Demdike*, this Examinates Grand-mother.

In this case, as earlier with spirit-keeping, physical evidence had actually been sought and brought to court, as the account reveals:

> which foure teeth now shewed to this Examinate, are the foure teeth that the said *Chattox* gave to his said Grand-mother, as aforesaid.[41]

The teeth had been buried in close proximity to a clay image of a victim, James Device said. Evidence of even more sensational grave robbing and cannibalism, against three women from Samlesbury, was also brought forward, but rejected because it was believed to have been fabricated by the witness under the tutelage of a Catholic priest.[42] Yet neither of these incidents appears in the wording of an indictment. Again, the concerns were not new—in 1566, for example, John Walsh patiently explained to his church court accusers in Exeter that witches used "the earth of a new made grave" and "the ryb bone of a man or woman burned to ashes" in their spells.[43] But it was now possible to record formally official concerns about such practices. This opportunity was clearly not taken up.

---

[39] Potts, sig. D2, G, M2, O3–O3v.
[40] Skulls.
[41] Potts, sig. E3v.
[42] Ibid., sig. L2, L3v–N.
[43] *The Examination of John Walsh* ([np], 1566), sig. A7.

Later pamphlet accounts of trials did once again make mention of spirit-keeping as one of the key indicators that the accused was a witch, and also discussed searching his or her home for evidence of spirits. Covenant was also named as a vital indicator of witchcraft.[44] These were particularly prominent features of some of the pamphlets describing Matthew Hopkins' and others' witchfinding activities in the 1640s. The anonymous pamphlet *The Lawes against Witches* (1645) reprinted the Jacobean statute and began its "Observations for the discovery of Witches" with the assertion that witches usually had a familiar which appeared to them, and sucked them. But the pamphlet then argued that:

> for the better riddance of these Witches, there must good care be had, as well in their examinations taken by the Justices, as also in the drawing of their indictments, that the same be both set down directly in the materiall points, &c. As
>
> That the Witch (or party suspected) hath used invocation of some Spirit.
> That they have consulted or covenanted with their Spirit.
> That they imployed their Spirit.
> That they fed or rewarded their Spirit.
> That they have killed, or lamed, &c. some person, &c.
> And not to indict them generally for being Witches, &c.[45]

This clearly documents the writer's belief that, even 40 years after the passing of the Jacobean Act, indictments were not detailing offences with sufficient zeal, and were thus not prosecuting witches with the severity or successfulness that the 1604 law was designed to allow.

In fact it seems from this admittedly brief survey of trial reports that the 1604 Witchcraft Act had little or no effect on how witchcraft was prosecuted by the courts—or reported from them. The law may have been far more severe, and it may have caught up with some existing concerns, most evidently about the keeping of familiars. But its new emphases on spirit-keeping, covenant and necromancy made no major modification to the structure of trials. Witches went on being indicted for killing and harming people and animals, as before. Neither did the

---

[44] John Gaule, *Select Cases of Conscience* (London, 1646), pp. 55–74 discussed covenant as "the formall cause of a Witch". He was much less impressed with Hopkins' evidence about familiars.

[45] *The Lawes against Witches* (London, 1645), p. 6. Matthew Hopkins' *Discovery of Witches* (London, 1647) reiterates concerns with spirit-keeping; see Sharpe, *Instruments of Darkness*, pp. 128–47.

writers and purveyors of popular literature, sometimes thought to be
more sensitive to godly and other cultural ripples than the heavy machinery of state authority, offer as much comment as might be expected
upon the carefully thought-out provisions of the law.

From the asking of this chapter's initial simple question, however,
spring other questions. If the new Act made little difference in practice,
why have a new Witchcraft Act at all? What was its impact on other
texts and contexts? How did developments in demonology, theology
and politics relate to its theoretically quite sweeping provisions, here
so strangely ignored? And why did the Act of 1604 stay on the statute
book until 1736? The chapters in this volume begin to address these
and other questions about the 1604 Witchcraft Act.

THE TREATMENT OF POTENTIAL WITCHES IN NORTH-EAST ENGLAND, *C.* 1649–1680

Jo Bath

The Witchcraft Act of 1604 made some clear and apparently straight-forward statements about the characteristic features of a witch, and the actions for which a criminal conviction could be brought. To paraphrase, the invocation or entertaining of spirits, necromancy, and malefic magic that killed or wasted a person, constituted felonies. There was also a second rank of criminal charge, involving the finding of objects, love magic, magical damage to property or to the human body, the punishment here being a complex one as it increased on the second offence.[1] As with all laws, however, theory was not neces-sarily reflected in practice. The vast majority of 'witches' visible to the historian are so precisely because they *were* at some point facing the force of the law. In spite of this we can still see a wide range of attitudes towards those considered to possess supernatural power. This article considers the range of behaviours exhibited in the north-east of England by ordinary men and women interacting with those they considered capable of witchcraft; and the relationship between these behaviours and the new law.[2]

There is no real way to establish how common self-professed charmers were in the north-east, but it seems that those people known to have used one did not have to travel far, and they could be called upon to help in a wide range of circumstances.[3] The commonest procedure that charmers were called on to perform was the sieve and shears, which was in use

---

[1] 1604 Witchcraft Act 1 Jas I, c. 12. See Appendix II.

[2] The main evidence for this comes from informations presented to the assizes courts of Northumberland and Newcastle, which are substantially complete from 1655 to 1690—Public Record Office, PRO ASSI 45/5/6–17. Durham as a palatinate dealt with its accusations of felony separately—some informations survive from the era, but none relate to witchcraft. Supplementary evidence comes from a few contemporary publications and other documents.

[3] Peter Rushton, Women, 'Witchcraft and Slander in Early Modern England: Cases from the Church Courts at Durham, 1560–1675', *Northern History*, 18 (1982), 116–32, uses the surviving records of the church court of Durham to detail many examples of the use of cunning folk, and the punishments meted out.

to find lost or stolen goods from the fifteenth to the nineteenth century.[4]
Cunning folk also helped in cases of suspected bewitchment—some
believed that the best way of combating magic was through the help
of another magic practitioner. When an unnamed woman bewitched a
child, the mother and her friend resolved to ask for the help of Margaret
Stotherd, "a reputed charmer for such distempers". Stotherd "put her
mouth to the child's mouth and made such chirping and sucking that
the mother of the said child thought that she had sucked the heart
of it out and was sore affrighted" and then transplanted an illness to
an animal which subsequently died. Despite this unusual method, and
cost in terms of livestock, no action was taken at the time—although
the incident was remembered in years to come.[5]

Another testimony involving Stotherd also demonstrates the ambivalent position of the charmer. She was asked—via a third party (ostensibly for reasons of practicality rather than caution)—to lift a curse
on milk. Stotherd then visited the afflicted farm to offer more help,
apparently going out of her way to be useful, and refusing more than
"a little of anything" in payment. The testimony is entirely positive
towards Stotherd but for one thing—at the end, the witness allegedly
told her that she would never have anything to do with charms again.
Whether this was a true change of heart about magic (easily done, now
the cheesemaking had resumed), or merely a statement made with an
eye to the listening justice, who after all was gathering evidence for
a *maleficium* trial, we cannot say. Either way, the previously positive
testimony seems to jar, demonstrating that no transaction was entirely
straightforward or risk free.[6]

It made sense to treat a cunning man or woman with caution, and
keep an eye on his or her behaviour—and this very caution could be
self-reinforcing. Mark Humble walked past a woman "formerly suspected
of witchcraft", and this suspicion led him to look back at her over his
shoulder, and see that she "(held) her hands towards his back". This
does not seem terribly frightening, but when he fell ill soon after he

---

[4] For example, the 1567 confession of Alice Swan, *Depositions and other Ecclesiastical Proceedings*, ed. by James Raine, Surtees Society, 21 (1845), p. 117.

[5] Eneas MacKenzie, *An Historical topographical and descriptive view of the county of Northumberland and those parts of county Durham situated north of the river Tyne with Berwick upon Tweed* (Newcastle, 1825), reprints the informations of the Margaret Stotherd case (which are otherwise lost), v. ii, pp. 34–36. For a similar transference, also not prosecuted at the time, see PRO ASSI 45/6/1/167.

[6] Mackenzie, pp. 34–36.

must have voiced suspicions to his neighbours, as eventually the gossip got round to the woman and she came to visit him to ask about it.[7] The bewitchment so strangely cured by Stotherd was seen as caused by the seemingly innocuous words "Here's a fine child", surely an interpretation indicative of an earlier prejudice, even given the child's sudden illness soon after.[8]

Given the apparent ease by which, it was thought, a witch could work her *maleficia*, it was only natural to try to avoid having anything to do with those with powers. The very existence of a suspected witch nearby created a dilemma—to enter into transactions and risk coming out the worse, or to turn the witch away and risk the witch's displeasure.[9] That said, the latter situation left its traces in the court record more often than the former—there is very little evidence in the northern record of people trying to stay in a cunning woman's good graces. Conversely there are six clear instances of what might be called the MacFarlane pattern of broken neighbourly relations.[10] Four of these are cases of refusal of simple help or alms, and all four occurred because the person's reputation was already tarnished. So, Frances Mason refused to give a drink to a woman who "turned the sieve for money and hath been reputed a witch".[11] Respectable woman Katherine Cudworth curtailed her habit of buying oatcakes from Jane Watson when she was told of her evil reputation, and Mrs Nickle refused to give alms to Margaret Stotherd "being afraid of her by ill fame she bore in the country".[12] Some of these suspicions could have been for ill-behaviour in some other sphere, but the female reputation was such that a slur in one area could leave one vulnerable to suspicions in others. Additionally a reputation for cunning magic clearly had cons as well as pros for a

---

[7] PRO ASSI 45/10/3/128.

[8] Mackenzie, pp. 34–36. Stotherd herself was said to have bewitched a child by "waving a white thing."

[9] Malcolm Gaskill, *Crime and Mentalities in Early Modern England* (Cambridge: Cambridge University Press, 2000), p. 64.

[10] Alan MacFarlane, *Witchcraft in Tudor and Stuart England* (London: Routledge Kegan and Paul, 1970) pp. 195–97. In most other cases we do not know what event, if any, provoked the identification of a witch, and it is important to note that this thesis is not universally applicable (for instance others have viewed the context of witchcraft as more rooted in competition between near-equals, although this is less clearly visible in the north-eastern record)—Gaskill, *Crimes and Mentalities*, pp. 32–36.

[11] PRO ASSI 45/5/7/95.

[12] PRO ASSI 45/6/1/165; MacKenzie, p. 35. For the fourth case see Emy Gaskin below.

marginal woman trying to go about her daily life, and was just as much a catalyst for suspicion of *maleficium* as street disputes—with or without the possibility that the suspect really did intend to curse their victim.

However, cunning folk continued to profess their own abilities in spite of this, and there are several examples of people practising magic for several years before this reputation caught up with them—and in most of these cases, as with those above, *maleficium* was the charge. It is instructive to look at the very few cases which made their way to the state courts but did *not* involve a clear-cut case of *maleficium*, in order to see why people might try to accuse a witch, and how the system had to treat these accusations to make them fit the legal mould.

Peter Banks spent several years living in Newcastle, allegedly prac-tising learned magic. Amongst his services, he sold charms to make husbands behave better to their wives, and granted "leases" of life which kept sailors from by charging unnamed forces "in the high sword name to assist and bless" their ships. In the event, Jane Burrell, who initiated prosecution, said that her motivation was fear, for "she trusts in God (and is not afraid of the Devil) yet the said Peter Banks affrights her"—she thought he was hurting her family because she had burnt a charm he had made to protect her sea-faring husband. In some ways this can be seen as akin to the earlier testimonies, in that a previous arrangement—albeit for magical services, not oatcakes—was broken and revenge apparently taken for this. She was not specific as to the damage he was doing, speaking of Banks "plaguing" the family, leaving them "mightily perplexed and in great straits". Another witness said that after "contention" between them, she had been "affrighted with visions" of Peter Banks standing "in flames of fire, and [she] could never be at rest". Jane Burrell also reported that Banks admitted to "conjuring evil and malicious spirits" (although the example she gives, of a written charm given to a young woman to draw a spirit from her, bears more resemblance to a homespun exorcism than a conjuration). Interestingly rather than focussing on this *maleficium* and trafficking with spirits, which are specifically covered by the Act, the indictment was that he "exercised arts magic called charms or spells, and assumed upon himself by the same art to procure safety at sea". Certainly the prosecution of a practitioner of charms and spells was broadly covered by the Act, but this emphasis is interesting. It suggests that the Clerk of the Court, unused to dealing with such non-straightforward accu-sations, was uncertain how to frame the indictment in order to give it maximum weight according to the law.[13] Certainly the case did not persuade the jury and Banks was found innocent.

The second accusation at the assizes for charming practices was the case of Mrs Pepper, a midwife who seems to have mixed orthodox practice with Catholic trappings and other ritual. The accuser believed that her husband was made worse by Mrs Pepper's treatment for what she diagnosed as bewitchment. However this can hardly have been a unique situation, charms must often have failed. Perhaps the attempt to make the man well by placing his child to his mouth "to suck the evil spirit out of him", was a step too far for the woman, or perhaps the hints of Catholicism encouraged her hostility.[14] Nonetheless she waited a further half a year, watching her husband's condition get worse, before accusing Mrs Pepper of causing harm. Sadly in this case the indictment does not survive to show how, and how successfully, this accusation was translated into something chargeable under the Act, or what happened to Mrs Pepper.[15]

One of the region's two mass accusations was initiated by servant girl Anne Armstrong, who in 1673 took to the magistrates an involved story of forcible participation in sabbats and devil worship in rural Northumberland.[16] Although the indictments do not survive, there is no evidence of punishments taking place, perhaps because few of the alleged victims became directly involved (leaving only Anne's evidence, which was second-hand in its account of anything other than the sabbats themselves). Although Anne gave second-hand evidence of

---

[13] PRO ASSI 45/12/3/6–7.
[14] The association of witchcraft and Catholicism, while only relevant to a minority of cases, is perhaps also visible in two cases brought before the Durham church courts, also in the 1660s, in which recusants were also accused of "spinning crosses on a corpse going to be buried"—Rushton, 'Women, Witchcraft and Slander', p. 124. Rushton notes that in spite of this suspicious activity, and in reflection of the differing priorities of the church court system, "there was no attempt to extend this to form a more serious case." We can say that, at least in the previous generation, some of the trappings of Catholicism survived in the popular religion of the region—in 1629 Sir Benjamin Rudyard reported that for the "common people [...] at the utmost skirts of the north" of England, "prayers were more like spells and charms than devotions". See David Harley, 'Mental Illness, Magical Medicine and the Devil in Northern England, 1650–1700', in *The Medical Revolution of the Seventeenth Century*, ed. by Roger French and Andrew Wear (Cambridge: Cambridge University Press, 1989), p. 115, Roger Howell, *Newcastle upon Tyne and the Puritan Revolution* (Oxford: Clarendon Press, 1967), p. 79.
[15] PRO ASSI 45/7/2/62, 103.
[16] PRO ASSI 45/10/3/34–54.

maleficium, albeit in most cases against animals (having heard the witches confess their activities to the devil), the questioning of the justices to the suspects focused primarily on whether they were "in company" or "conversation" with the devil, along with a general refutation of all accusations. Despite this, Rushton suggests that judicial scepticism in this case (visible in repeated questionings of Anne herself) reflects an English interest in *maleficium* above any suspiciously exotic stories of diabolism (noting that the comparatively late date may also be a factor).[17] Perhaps similar doubts held true of the other more esoteric aspects of the law—certainly it is clear is that without the thought that actual damage had been done, people were not concerned with taking to court the more esoteric crimes of spirit summoning. As this examination of the non-standard cases shows, no-one was accused of necromancy, and accusations of damage to goods, love magic, finding goods and so on were rare and always secondary in state court trials.

The interpretation of symptoms of witchcraft is of course not inevitable. Witchcraft suspicions sprang up where there was a belief in the mundane reality of witchcraft, a suitable choice of tormentor, a suitable set of symptoms or problems, and (almost always) an exchange which could be interpreted as catalytic. Some simply did not accept this position, as can be seen for instance in the husband of the Moore family, steadfastly refusing his wife's convictions of her daughter's bewitchment (a position so different from her own that she blamed the witch for hardening his heart). Mrs Moore also had to go before several legal authorities before finding a sympathetic ear, although vagaries of legal jurisdiction also played a part in this.[18] Despite this, and the evident doubts of the magistrates to whom Anne Armstrong spun her long tale of satanic sabbats, scepticism did not follow lines of social status. Indeed, a range of people might be consulted to determine witchcraft, including priests, doctors, and local gentry like Lady Widdrington who gave the answer "that she could not understand any distemper the

---

[17] Peter Rushton, 'Crazes and Quarrels: The Character of Witchcraft in the North East of England, 1649–1680', *Bulletin of the Durham County Local History Society*, 31 (1983), 2–40 (p. 16).

[18] M. Moore, *Wonderful News from the North, or a True Relation of the Sad and Grievous Torments Inflicted upon the Bodies of three Children of Mr George Muschamp late of the County of Northumberland, by Witch-craft* (London, 1650). Frances Dolan, *Dangerous Familiars: Representations of Domestic Crime in England, 1550–1700* (Ithaca: Cornell University Press, 1994), discusses this case from the angle of the inter-personal and familial relationships which underpinned it.

child had by the circumstances they told her, unless [...] the child was bewitched".[19]

As to the choice of 'witch', several statements regarding the age, marital status and gender of those labelled witches have become well known.[20] While most were indeed women, many were married and age is rarely known; a neat profile is not viable. One interesting factor is the previous reputation of the person.[21] In nearly half of the accusations for which there are depositions there is a background of poor reputation, usually magical—and this of course is a minimum.[22] Someone with a reputation was clearly the obvious choice of suspect. As suggested above, they were closely watched and almost any action could be retrospectively judged suspicious. Furthermore such thought processes were often self-reinforcing in a situation where the delirious visions of the attacker were a crucial part of the process. Thus when Mrs Moore's daughter wrote down "Jo. Hu." as the name of her attacker, those around quickly interpreted this as John Hutton, "one it was suspected that could do more that God allowed of", as perhaps the child had known. Cleverly at this point John Hutton diverted opinion from himself by offering to help, and pointing the finger at Dorothy Swinhow—whether he somehow knew that "Do. Swi." was the second cryptic identification, or whether it was merely a lucky guess on the basis of other locally notorious charmers is unknown, but it worked.[23]

To some extent, this factor applied even in the region's two periods of mass accusation. There is some evidence that Anne Armstrong's choice of thirty sabbat-attendees was not entirely random. At least two were "formerly suspected of witchcraft"—easy targets indeed—and Anne Usher was "a mediciner", and so also potentially suspect. Many were related through blood or marriage, familial relationships through

---

[19] MacKenzie, p. 36. Margaret Wilson's testimony that her bewitchment was identified by a *Scottish* physician is particularly noteworthy—*Depositions from York Castle*, ed. by James Raine, Surtees Society, 40 (2), p. 177.

[20] See Gaskill, *Crimes and Mentalities*, pp. 37–49 for a discussion of aspects of the stereotype.

[21] Clive Holmes, 'Popular Culture? Witches Puritans and Divines in Early Modern England', in *Understanding Popular Culture*, ed. by Steven Kaplan (Berlin: Mouton, 1984), p. 88.

[22] Excluding the long lists of names given by Anne Armstrong.

[23] The latter option seems less likely given that Dorothy Swinhow was the wife of a Colonel. *Wonderful News from the North*, p. 7.

which it was believed witchcraft could often be passed.[24] Others were only named after locals had brought those they suspected to her, asking if she knew them from sabbats; and several were old. As Rushton puts it, Armstrong made her case by "mixing undeniable fact with what was currently suspected."[25]

More obviously, the suspects in the Newcastle trials of 1649 were not a random sample but were rather selected by residents after a bell-man had gone through the streets advertising the presence of a Scots witchpricker ready to do his job in the Guildhall. His method was based on an initial visual identification followed by pricking. This does at least relate to the Act inasmuch as the witchmark may be interpreted as 'proof' of entertainment of spirits, although his visual assessment is highly suspect and may have more to do with the twenty shillings he was paid per witch than any legal definition.[26] The witchfinder's use of a pin to identify witches seems to be an isolated instance in the north-east, and in any case seems to have been seen as simply confirmatory by him (he found witches' marks in twenty-seven out of thirty cases). In any case, as almost half of those women escaped the gallows, others cannot have taken the method as conclusive proof.[27]

Even for those who were sure they could identify a guilty party, there was a range of options for dealing with the problem. Legally all felonies should have been prosecuted, but Sharpe suggests that in the case of witchcraft prosecution was a last resort after other methods failed.[28] Stoicism and resignation was quite possible in circumstances of witchcraft, as with (most) other crimes, although stories of continuing

---

[24] PRO ASSI 45/10/3/39–40; for Anne Usher, 45/10/3/50. Gaskill, *Crimes and Mentalities*, pp. 59–60.

[25] PRO ASSI 45/10/3/36a gives a suggestion of age from the number of years already run on the accused's demonic "lease" of life. PRO ASSI 45/10/3/47 shows parishioners of Allendale orchestrating a meeting with a suspect. See Rushton, 'Crazes and Quarrels', p. 15.

[26] Ralph Gardiner, *England's Grievance Discovered in Relation to the Coal Trade* (North Shields: Philipson and Hare, [1655] 1849), p. 169. Gardner's account must be treated as propaganda, although the outlines of his story are supported by other evidence.

[27] Gardiner, *England's Grievance Discovered*, p. 169, says that one young woman was spared when a second pricking drew blood, after the Deputy Governor of Newcastle (a noted Baptist and ex-barber surgeon) exhorted the witchfinder to test her again in a situation where the blood would not rush to her head as a blush! For more on the witchfinder and the reception of his methods, see Rushton, 'Crazes and Quarrels', pp. 7–12, which notes that one Durham woman was acquitted in the same round of accusations despite refusing to be searched.

[28] James Sharpe, *Witchcraft in Seventeenth-Century Yorkshire: Accusations and Counter Measures*, Borthwick Papers, 1992, p. 11.

harassment tended to span months, rather than years. Accounts of long ago events tended to recall cunning magic. Others related comparatively innocuous details, later taken out of context or re-interpreted in the light of later more overtly suspicious circumstances. For instance, Jane Milburn in her accusation against Dorothy Stranger put forward as evidence the latter saying, seven years previously, "you shall never see Sandgate again". Stranger denied this, or perhaps had simply forgotten the conversation—as she said, they had seen each other there many times.[29]

Additionally, and compared to other crimes, a suspected bewitchment opened more avenues for a victim to gain relief. Alongside more forceful approaches, Sharpe mentions the possibility of apologising to the witch and giving gifts in order to re-establish a cordial relationship, but this doesn't seem to have occurred to the north-easterners, who had a more assertive turn of mind.[30] One Newcastle man, when told that the apparition of a 'witch' had disappeared under the bed, tried to stab it with his sword.[31] Still, some must have come to some accommodation with the witch for the sake of their own health. Three times in the court record, the taking of hair is mentioned—in each case, it seems that the witch was given hair from the head of her victim, which she used to effect a cure. In two cases, the victim was told that the spell was actually the doing of someone else—but the context suggests that this was not necessarily believed, but was a convenient fiction allowing further negotiation and resolution.[32]

Robert Johnson turned to Nicholas Johnson, who initially examined his urine and offered to send him an ointment for his arms and legs, suggesting a medical background. But when Robert argued that "he conceived he had some wrong done to him (meaning witchcraft)", Nicholas confirmed his diagnosis, named Bely Storey the witch responsible, and "desired him the said Robert Johnson to discharge him from any employment that might relate to him and then he should rate her and defy her and bid him not doubt but within a short time he should recover".[33] It is unclear who was to do the defying—Robert, as victim

---

[29] PRO ASSI 45/7/1/185–86.
[30] Sharpe, *Witchcraft in Seventeenth Century Yorkshire*, p. 16.
[31] PRO ASSI 45/6/1/168.
[32] PRO ASSI 45/10/3/128; PRO ASSI 45/12/3/7, Rushton 'Crazes and Quarrels', p. 15.
[33] The MS is unclear and partially scratched out here—an alternative reading to "rate her" would be "take her".

(via his initial accusation?), or Nicholas (in a magical capacity—but clearly not a medical one?).[34] More straightforwardly, others found strength in God, indeed a die-hard Protestant might argue that prayer was the only possible remedy for bewitchment. John Mills believed that crying out "O Lord deliver me for thy mercy's sake and for thy own name's sake" took a spell off him.[35] Similarly Robert Philip called on God to save him, averting a bewitchment, and made no effort to prosecute until nine months later (perhaps, judging by the questions asked the suspect, because he now feared for his family).[36]

More common—and more easily achieved without expert help—was the scratching of the witch. This might be done with the aim of getting proof, but it might also be aimed simply at reversing the spell. The several accusations made before the church courts show that this could be considered the end of the matter, as in 1630 Margaret Mallebar hauled a woman to her husband's sickbed and got him to take her blood—we only know about this because of the protests of the alleged witch, even though the man himself seems to have been dead by this stage.[37] However, the self-reinforcing interpretations of the victim made both avoiding a scratching, and accepting or even inviting one, potentially dangerous, especially given the possibility of psychosomatic improvement. Certainly the co-operation of Isabel Atcheson and Jane Watson, "partly condescending" to the treatment, did not stand in their favour when their alleged victim got out of bed an hour later.[38] Sometimes there was a third option—in 1687 Jane Blackburn responded to a neighbour's desire to "get blood of her" as a witch by getting her husband to prosecute for defamation.[39] Such a counter attack was rare, requiring a position of strength; it also shows the state courts taking on a role in defending against accusations of witchcraft which had previously been performed by the church courts.[40]

---

[34] PRO ASSI 45/6/1/134–5. Sadly the initial accusation of Robert Johnson seems to be missing; we have no informations before Isabel Story was examined. Then come Nicholas Johnson's evidence on behalf of Robert; and a more detailed examination.
[35] While hard to place any exact biblical citation, the language echoes that of the 1662 Book of Common Prayer (the exact phrase "deliver us for thy Name's sake" appears in the newly introduced prayers to be used at sea); and might allude to Psalms 6.4 and 79.9 or possibly 31.2.
[36] PRO ASSI 45/6/1/88–9.
[37] Rushton, 'Women, Witchcraft and Slander', p. 128.
[38] PRO ASSI 47/7/1/7.
[39] Northumberland Record Office QSB 5/2/27.
[40] Rushton, 'Women, Witchcraft and Slander', pp. 116–32.

With so many options, therefore, and so many lingering suspicions, we can question why those few who took their suspicions of *maleficium* to court did so, in spite of the slim chances of success. Prosecution could be time consuming and expensive, and could cause much bad feeling, so there is no wonder that it seems to have happened only rarely. People must have realised that chances of getting a conviction were not great, (indeed as far as we can tell no one was hanged for witchcraft in the north-east after the Civil War era). If this was true of *maleficium*, it must have been even more true of arguably victimless crimes like entertaining spirits. However, these points apply to some extent to other felonies, so additional forces must have been at work.

Most victims had visions of their tormentor, which must have made prosecution more attractive given the firmer identification, but victims and their symptoms varied widely. Perhaps each accuser believed their case was better, more believable, than others were. Strong incentive was provided by the belief that the witch's death would remove the *maleficium*. Even imprisonment could do the trick temporarily—one mother claimed that her children became better when the suspected witch was put in prison following a separate accusation of witchcraft, but their illness returned when she was let out again.[41] Given prison conditions, and the rarity of Assize week on the Northern Circuit, the simple desire to make the witch suffer in retaliation should not be discounted. Certainly contemporaries believed that some prosecutions for witchcraft were vexatious.[42] It was these things, not feelings of justice under the Act, that inspired prosecution—and even this was a minority perspective.

It was advantageous to build up evidence before trying for a conviction. We cannot know how many attempts at accusation fell at the first hurdle—convincing a magistrate that the case was worth carrying forward. This may explain the scratching, the gathering of other witnesses, the reporting of visions—and also trying to get insider knowledge, for example by asking Anne Armstrong if she had seen the person at sabbats.[43] It may also explain those who went around spreading rumours and saying that they would have their target hanged for witchcraft, as one was more likely to have the confidence to press a prosecution if

---

[41] PRO ASSI 45/6/1/165.
[42] Gaskill, *Crimes and Mentalities*, p. 72.
[43] See above.

they had the support of their neighbours. It seems that when someone had a case of *maleficium* to bring, they might ask around locally for other suspicious stories of magic use—whether or not felonious, harmful, or covered under the Act—as corroborative evidence. As Rushton puts it, previous magical actions "took on a new significance" in this role.[44] Without support and preferably backing evidence, a prosecution could be seen as less likely to succeed, more likely to be interpreted as the result of personal malice.

This meant that tensions could bubble under the surface for years, invisible to the historian except when forced into the light by unusual circumstances. The population of Newcastle in 1649 was around 12,000, of whom only perhaps a quarter were adult women—so the thirty women subjected to a pricking represented around one in one hundred adult women of the population.[45] Of course, some came from further away—Jane Martin, one of the women hanged, came from Chatton (some fifty miles from Newcastle), and was condemned in part by a confession of her sister, made at Berwick and then at Morpeth; she was indicted then, but apparently not found until later.[46] Yet there was not much time, and given that not everyone would have heard the message, or been in a position to force a suspected witch to come with them, we have to conclude that the number of women who were suspected of witchcraft, by someone who thought this accusation could reasonably levelled, was remarkably high.[47]

Notwithstanding the point made earlier about the vulnerability of those with a reputation for magic, it is impossible to say why these people were singled out. We know that most were accused individually, or occasionally in pairs, and that the only man included was a smith

---

[44] Rushton, 'Crazes and Quarrels', p. 25.
[45] Richard Welford, 'Newcastle Householders in 1665: Assessment of the Hearth or Chimney Tax', *Archaeologia Aeliana*, 3(7)(1911), 49–76 (p. 56) argues for a figure of 12,000 in 1660; Joyce Ellis, 'A Dynamic Society: Social Relations in Newcastle upon Tyne 1660–1760' in *The Transformation of English Provincial Towns, 1600–1800*, ed. by Peter Clark (London: Hutchinson, 1984), p. 194, opts for a figure of 15,000—but it would have been lower ten years earlier. The proportion of adult women may be even smaller given the high rate of employment in Newcastle for young men in industry, see Ellis, 'A Dynamic Society'.
[46] Confession of Margaret White of Chatton, appended to Moore, *Wonderful News from the North*, pp. 24–26.
[47] According to Sir Thomas Widdrington, MP for Berwick, the witchfinder had recently 'discovered' thirty witches there too—in a much smaller town—Bulstrode Whitlocke, *The Memorials of the English Affairs* (London, 1732), p. 424.

embroiled in other local legal battles. Rushton concludes that the presence of the witch finder "brings to the surface a mass of traditional
and personal disputes and hatreds".[48] Had the witchfinder not come to
the area and given an explicit outlet for these disputes, and an interpretation for all the remembered slights of the past, it is likely very
few of these women would have been accused. On the other hand,
Gardner believed that "if he had stayed, he would have made most
of the women in the North Witches, for money".[49] This was no doubt
an exaggeration, but one that made sense at the time.

Once some people had decided that prosecution was the way forward,
there was no stopping them. Nicholas Johnson's testimony that a witch
came to him offering to give him "seven pounds, nay, if it were her
house in Morpeth" to refrain from giving evidence on behalf of his
client is sadly credible despite her later denials.[50] The Sherburn family
of Newcastle is another striking example of determination to prosecute.
It appears that they prosecuted Emy Gaskin for the bewitchment of
their servant, and at around the same time a case was made against
two other women, Anne Mennin and Jane Watson, for bewitching
some young children in the Sherburn home.[51] The three women were
in prison together a few months later, and Emy was the main witness
when Anne was given a meal from her husband containing a lethal
dose of arsenic.[52] This is an interesting act in itself, perhaps spurred
by an affair with the housekeeper but also certainly inspired by the
damage to reputation of marriage to a notorious witch. Whether he
himself believed it we will never know; in any case we can only imagine the bitter conversations the imprisoned women might have had on
the subject of the Sherburns. Interestingly, an information survives in
which Margaret Sherburn tried to prosecute Emy Gaskin for a second
time in 1667—for bewitching of the same servant as before, Elizabeth

---

[48] Rushton, 'Crazes and Quarrels', p. 12.
[49] Gardiner, *England's Grievance Discovered*, p. 170.
[50] PRO ASSI 45/6/1/134.
[51] PRO ASSI 45/6/1/88–90; PRO ASSI 44/8 quoted in C. L'Estrange Ewen,
*Witchcraft and Demonianism, a Concise Account Derived from Sworn Depositions and Confessions
Obtained within the Courts of England and Wales* (London: Heath Cranton, 1933) transcribes
an indictment against "Emma Haskin". PRO ASSI 45/6/1/88–90 is the testimony
against Mennin and Watson. Since the latter was taken on 9 October 1661, and the
indictment against Gaskin, while undated, accuses her of a bewitchment from 4 July
to 9 October, it is quite likely that the Sherburns were involved in both accusations
on the same day.
[52] PRO ASSI 45/6/2/50–54a.

Gibson.[53] Emy must have been truly desperate to return to the house and beg, asking for "something God's sake". Elizabeth told her that "she had nothing for her for she had got too much ill by her already". If Emy did, as claimed, curse her for this, it was a foolish action given their history. One need not even bring into the picture the desire to avert guilt to foretell the unfolding of events when Elizabeth fell ill.

Of course different approaches to dealing with a witch were not mutually exclusive. For instance, if a witch scratching apparently worked this might end the matter or might be seen as proof to encourage a prosecution—or be seen as enough until a subsequent problem emerged. Jane Milburn scratched her bewitcher, and then reported the case to the justices while feeling "pretty well"—she went back seven months later when the witch apparently appeared in her house to revenge herself on the "thief" by drawing her blood in return.[54] Churchmen argued that it was right and proper to take a witch to court, but also that turning to God was the best response to such trials—one might suspect that they should have disapproved of witch scratching, but there is no evidence of this in the north-east.

Additionally, there are elements of the picture that there is not space to consider fully here. Most obviously there is the additional strategy provided by the use of the church courts, and the "very different definition of witchcraft" used by them.[55] Rushton notes one instance in which an unsuccessful assize trial was followed by an attempt to prosecute the same woman through the church courts.[56] This was unusual however; in general "the church courts seem to have dealt with the more ambiguous cases, and to have adopted more equivocal attitudes".[57] This was true even where accusations could arguably have been taken before the secular courts. Clearly any comprehensive examination of strategies to curtail magical activity, and the effect of the Act, must take the church courts into account, particularly for the earlier part of the century.

This paper has focussed on practical responses, and skirted the issue of more intellectual frameworks. Sadly the area did not contribute a great deal to the nation's print culture in general, and very few local

---

[53] PRO ASSI 45/8/2/34.
[54] PRO ASSI 45/7/1/185–187.
[55] Rushton, 'Women, Witchcraft and Slander', p. 116. It should be noted however that the church courts, while still active, were waning in influence by this date.
[56] Rushton, 'Crazes and Quarrels', p. 26.
[57] Rushton, 'Women, Witchcraft and Slander', p. 123.

writers touched upon witchcraft or demonology. Just enough evidence survives to demonstrate that here, as elsewhere, a wide-range of theoretical positions on witchcraft were held, and articulated, amongst members of the elite. Richard Gilpin, a prominent Nonconformist preacher and physician, based his *Daemonologia Sacra* on lectures he gave in Newcastle. Although the majority of the work was devoted to the nature of the Devil's works, Gilpin also attacked those who equated witchcraft with illusion and trickery (whether or not backed by the belief of the 'witch'). He cited biblical and continental evidences of the reality of witchcraft, and concluded that witchcraft was "a Power of doing great Things by the aid of the Devil".[58] He also argued that "there are many more diseases wherein Satan hath a greater hand, than is commonly imagined", debating the nature of the interaction between Devil and witch in the case of *maleficium*.[59] He may, in part, have been responding to Catholic physician Edward Wilson of Durham, who in his *Spadacrene Dunelmensis* of two years earlier had drawn heavily on the ideas of Thomas Willis in stressing a natural, rather than demonic, explanation for all illness, mental or physical.[60] These publications are a slim evidence of intellectual debate in the region, although certainly there was a fertile ground for theological dispute in the complex environment of Commonwealth and Restoration Newcastle.[61]

Be that as it may, it hard to demonstrate such material had influence beyond a narrow sphere. Few trial witnesses indulged in complex consideration of the nature of the witch's power—but then, the legal information was a place for more practical concerns. Moreover, as we have already seen, on the issue of witchcraft lines of social status or denomination were not so clearly drawn as to definitively determine belief. Harley argues that the outbreak of witchhunting in the north-east in 1649–50 was "one of the local factors encouraging a division between elite opinion and popular belief", and Henry Ogle, the Parliamentarian magistrate who hounded the Scottish witchfinder back over the border, might have agreed. However the witchfinder was called first

---

[58] Richard Gilpin, *Daemonologia Sacra: or, a Treatise of Satan's Temptations, In Three Parts* (London, 1677), pp. 30–33. Harley, 'Mental Illness', pp. 121–23, discusses the text. Interestingly Gilpin was educated in Edinburgh and so may have brought a Scottish perspective to bear on the subject—see Howell, *Newcastle upon Tyne*, p. 345.

[59] Ibid., p. 123. Gilpin, *Daemonologia Sacra*, pp. 34–36.

[60] Harley, 'Mental Illness', p. 121.

[61] Howell, *Newcastle upon Tyne*.

to Berwick and then Newcastle, officially invited by the ruling bodies of those towns.[62]

Additionally, even in the north-east elite opinions were changing as to the reality of witchcraft by the late seventeenth century. While many continued to resort to cunning folk well into the nineteenth century,[63] the instincts which were to lead to the legal changes of 1736 were visible in the region. One instructive case was brought against "wise man" Edward Blacket in 1690. William Langstaffe had lost or had stolen over three pounds, and went to Blacket to discover how to regain his property. They communicated through notes, "he [Blacket?] pretending to be dumb", and Blacket "pretended and promised by his Art and skill to get [...] the said money". Langstaffe was charged 15 shillings for this service.[64] That is all we know—presumably Blacket was not successful, and presumably the accusation was brought under the Act's inclusion of those who "tell or declare [...] where goods or things lost or stolen should be found or become"; and presumably Langstaffe believed Blacket could do this when he went for help, and was disappointed that he had sent good money after bad. Yet his statement is such that it would be equally valid under the 1736 Act—perhaps more so, as the crime complained of seems to be pretence or fraud rather than actual magical ability. It is even possible that some form of fraud was the charge, but even if this is the case the accusation still hints at the spread of a new way of perceiving those claiming magical power.[65]

The records available reveal much about the multiplicity of ways in which people interacted with and combated witches, and one thing that is clear is that they did so largely without reference to the legal

---

[62] Ibid., p. 126. John Fuller, *The History of Berwick upon Tweed* (Newcastle: Frank Graham, 1973), p. 155; Tyne and Wear Archives Common Council Book 1649–50, f. 326.

[63] For examples of the persistence of north-eastern cunning folk, see Rev. J.C. Atkinson, *Forty Years in a Moorland Parish: Reminiscences and Researches in Danby in Cleveland* (Leeds: M.T.D. Rigg, [1891] 1987), and Owen Davies, *Cunning Folk* (London: Hambledon and London, 2003), p. 98. Other approaches to witches continued also. In 1709 the quarter sessions of Northumberland did hear an accusation of slander when a man spread rumours about the bewitching of his cows and scratched the (male) 'witch'—NRO QSB 30/2/31–33. As late as 1868 a Framwellgate Moor family applied to the police for permission to scratch a witch, William Henderson, *Notes on the Folklore of the Northern Counties of England* (London: W. Satchell, Peyton, 1879), p. 181.

[64] PRO ASSI 45/16/2/12.

[65] Unfortunately we cannot tell if the Assizes court for the region was further troubled by witchcraft cases as the extant informations are almost absent between 1690 and 1730.

position. The range of crimes which people tried to take to court was clearly a subset of the crimes of the Act. Even when the terms of the Act were translated into a more everyday—and potentially provable—language of familiars and charms, it was secondary to malefic activity. Only one case mentions a familiar—a black greyhound—and this is in a confession with continental and satanic overtones, rather than an accusation.[66] Anxieties instead focussed on activity which would be far harder to prove in the court of law. This might help to explain why, even when the activity was believed to be malefic, people chose their own response from a much wider range of options than those suggested by the Act.

---

[66] Confession of Margaret White of Chatton, appended to Moore, *Wonderful News from the North*, p. 24.

WITCHCRAFT AND STAGE SPECTACLE
SPECTACULAR WITCHES AFTER 1604

Chris Brooks

In *The Witches of Lancashire*, by Thomas Heywood and Richard Brome, the sceptical character Mr. Generous is finally persuaded that witches are at work in his village, indeed that his own wife is one, and proclaims, "Does this last age / Afford what former never durst believe?" (V.3.101–02).[1] First performed in 1634, Heywood and Brome's play, especially given Generous's quote about "this last age," opens up the question about just how much influence the Witchcraft Act of 1604 had on the subsequent drama. For dramatists, did the Act represent a 'new age' of belief, or at least a new way to present dramatic spectacle?

Peter Corbin and Douglas Sedge argue that "the dramatists drew heavily from [early modern] intellectual discourse" and "exploit[ed] the dramatic potential of contemporary sensation." They also recognize "a significant surge in theatrical use of the more spectacular aspects of witchcraft belief".[2] Just exactly what are those "spectacular aspects" of certain plays written soon after the Witchcraft Act of 1604 came into law? It seems that the more detailed the Act's proscription of certain behaviours was, the more spectacle the dramatists could bring onto stage. Elizabeth's Act—the one which James's Act repealed in 1604—was written after Elizabeth herself declared that "my people are afraid of witches" and the writers "reacted" to that societal anxiety by producing a legislation that, roughly speaking, treated witch behavior as a misdemeanor in many cases.[3] But while Elizabeth's 1563 Act was reactive, James's 1604 Act against Conjuration and Witchcraft was heavily proscriptive, detailing numerous behaviors that could lead to the

---

[1] Thomas Heywood and Richard Brome, *The Witches of Lancashire*, ed. by Gabriel Egan, Globe Quartos Series, (London: Nick Hern, 2002).

[2] *Three Jacobean Witchcraft Plays*, ed. by Peter Corbin and Douglas Sedge (Manchester: Manchester University Press, 1989), p. 3.

[3] See *Witchcraft in England 1558–1618*, ed. by Barbara Rosen, 2nd edn (Amherst: University of Massachusetts Press, 1991), pp. 54–56.

execution of the transgressor but which also provided all the dramatic fodder that an eager playwright could ever want.

A primary example of a witch spectacle occurs in John Marston's *The Tragedy of Sophonisba*, a play first performed around March 1606—perhaps the first such drama to show the influence of the 1604 Act.[4] As Act IV closes, the stage directions indicate "Enter Erictho in the shape of Sophonobia [...] and hasteth in the bed of Syphax" (210–212). Various scholars read this scene as a succubus seduction, done only with the aid of the Devil, an act which would condemn Erictho for being in league with the arch-enemy of goodness and perhaps also Syphax for another violation. Erictho opens the subsequent act of Marston's play by lamenting, "Our love, farewell/Know he that would force love, thus seeks his hell" (V.1.20–21), thus making the role of her witchcraft clear, for the 1604 Act makes criminal "the intent to provoke any person to unlawful love." When she later conjures the ghost of Sophonisba's father to appear, the angry ghost describes himself as "thus ungraved" by the witch's power. The modern editors of the play, Peter Corbin and Douglas Sedge, maintain that "Erictho's necrophilic practices also place her within contemporary witch-belief, since the Act of 1604 specifically cites such activity as incurring the death penalty".[5] The audiences watching Marston's play and also Shakespeare's *Macbeth*, which was first acted within weeks, either way, of *The Tragedy of Sophonisba*, had perhaps previously read pamphlet literature and had certainly heard stories of witches, but now they had a chance to see them on stage. Marston took advantage of the witchcraft mania:

> Marston's boldness in the use of stage spectacle goes well beyond the creation of striking local effects, making full use of, and sometimes straining to the utmost, the resources of the Blackfriars' stage. Trapdoors not only act as a means of escape from Syphax's bed-chamber, but also act as a cave's mouth or vault opening into Belos' forest.[6]

Virtually all of the "stage spectacle" just mentioned pertains to witch activity, and enhances it in an imaginative way. For example, the fact that Syphax never leaves the stage when the scene shifts from Belos' forest to the bed-chamber serves as a visual metaphor for Erictho's ability to alter realities or conjure settings—both practices prohibited by the 1604 Act. The imagination of each member of the audience

---

[4] John Marston, *The Tragedy of Sophonisba* (1604), in Corbin and Sedge, eds.
[5] Ibid., p. 7.
[6] Ibid., p. 9.

is challenged to believe in a witch that can disappear into the earth as easily as a performer exits through a trapdoor.

All commentators on Marston's play acknowledge the power of Erictho's magic and the range of her evil. Interestingly, Anthony Harris observes, "the witch Erictho appears only briefly in Marston's work and makes no significant contribution to the play's development. The two scenes in which she appears could even have been grafted on to the work prior to its first performance in an effort to compete with [...] Macbeth".[7] But Harris also admits that "it is possible that *Sophonisba* predates *Macbeth* and even inspired the latter".[8] If this is so, then the 'grafted on' Erictho scenes serve, not to compete with Shakespeare's "weird sisters", but rather to reflect the King's attitude by depicting the ultimate harm of a witch at work. James, after all, had ordered that all copies of Reginald Scot's *The Discoverie of Witchcraft* be destroyed in 1603—three years prior to the first performance of Marston's drama.[9] Moreover, when James's *Daemonologie* was re-issued in early 1604, Marston almost certainly recognized the opportunity before him and responded by creating a witch who embodies the crimes delineated in the new legislation in the most serious and various of ways. Hence, Erictho has Marston's complete dramatic attention when he describes her activities as follows:

> But when she finds a corse[10]
> New graved whose entrails yet not turn
> To slimy filth, with greedy havoc then
> She makes fierce spoil and swells with wicked triumph
> to bury her lean knuckles in his eyes,
> Then doth she gnaw the pale and o'ergrown nails
> From his dry hand, But if she finds some little life
> Yet lurking close, she bites his gelid lips
> and sticking her black tongue in his dry throat
> she breathes dire murmurs which enforce him bear
> Her baneful secrets to the spirits of horror.
> To her first sound the gods yield any harm
> As trembling once to hear a second charm. (IV.1.112–125)

---

[7] Anthony Harris, *Night's Black Agents: Witchcraft and Magic in Seventeenth-Century English Drama* (Manchester: Manchester University Press, 1980), p. 65.

[8] Ibid., p. 64.

[9] Thomas Alfred Spalding, *Elizabethan Demonology* (London: Chatto and Windus, 1880), p. 40; for a reassessment of this view see James Sharpe, *Instruments of Darkness*, p. 55.

[10] I.e. corpse.

This is the "spectacle" of an all-powerful witch, one who makes "the gods" tremble and the first of her kind, scholars suggest, on the English stage.

Another way to understand Marston's play emerges from Sophonisba's observation early in the play: "For gods, not we / See as things are; things are not as we see" (I.1.131–32). Marston, as it were, faces the witchcraft situation much as a juror at a witch trial must have done: envisioning the truth located between the seen and unseen—as Sophonisba indicates—but also between physical and spectral, between Reginald Scot and King James. Jurors were asked to envision "spectral evidence," to act as if they could perceive talking cats, little black men, and dancing dogs. Many accused witches were acquitted when only spectral evidence was presented, leaving the charges suspended between what was charged and what could be proven. Similarly, then, as R.W. Ingram puts it, Marston sought to depict "the mingled reality and unreality of the stage world".[11] This "mingling" is most effective at the point where words end—the telling of witch stories—and where spectacle—the dramatizing of witches—begins. Enough pamphlet literature had set the stage—literally—for the dramatists to move into a 'new age' of spectacle.

Before I leave Sophonisba behind, a quick review of the reactions to it is warranted, especially given the nature of critical diction. Corbin and Sedge summarize *Sophonisba* by saying, "In his use of stage spectacle [...] Marston seems intent on integrating theatrical means with thematic purpose".[12] Though Erictho appears in only two scenes, she "represents the extreme of distorted appetite" and is "the play's most potent emblem of lust and appetite in action and agent of Syphax's moral, if not physical, destruction".[13] Likewise, Anthony Harris employs the terms "elaborate" and "spectacular" in describing Marston's play. Una Ellis Fermor, in *The Jacobean Drama*, describes the drama as "a well-articulated string of ghoulish detail",[14] while T.S. Eliot details the first Erictho scene as one of "gratuitous horror, introduced merely to make our flesh creep".[15] The language includes "emblem of lust," "elaborate"

---

[11] R.W. Ingram, *John Marston*, English Authors Series (Boston: Twayne, 1978), p. 143.
[12] Corbin and Sedge, eds, p. 10.
[13] Ibid., pp. 12–13
[14] Quoted in ibid., p. 6.
[15] Quoted in ibid., p. 8.

and "spectacular" events, and "ghoulish detail"—words suggesting the visual aspects of witchcraft "spectacle." Those who wrote soon after Marston followed suit, none more readily than Thomas Middleton.

"It certainly seems clear that *The Witch* was written to capitalize on the current interest in the supernatural," writes Anthony Harris, "and on the increasing vogue for the dramatic representation of the more repellent aspects of magic".[16] How repellent is *The Witch* and how many evil deeds gesture toward the 1604 Act?[17] The Act forbids any use of "the skin, bone, or any other part of any dead person, to be used in any manner of witchcraft, sorcery, charm, or, enchantment." Middleton wastes no time in depicting this proscription, for by Act I, scene 2, his central witch, Hecate, is shown "giving the dead body of a baby" to a fellow witch while admonishing her to "Boil it well; preserve the fat. You know tis precious to transfer our anointed flesh into the air" (lines 20–22). This dead baby belongs to "the resourceful use of stage spectacle" that Middleton quickly extended to the forbidden use of a "familiar spirit" on the stage.[18] Act I ends with the stage direction, "She conjures and enter Malkin, a spirit like a cat, playing on a fiddle" (228–29). This conjuration, along with the mention by Hecate's demon-son Firestone that Hecate shall later "lie with the great cat" (I.2.98), depicts two more violations of the recent Act. It appears that Middleton knows exactly what is forbidden, what is familiar to his audience, and what is current. When in Act V Hecate gives the Duchess "a picture made in wax" so she can harm the Duke (V.2.4), the 1604 legislation is being referred to since it forbids "Witchcraft whereby any person shall be killed, destroyed, wasted, consumed, pined, or lamed in his or her body, or any part thereof." Hecate's actual words state that the waxen image of the Duke "will waste him by degrees" until he is dead—words taken almost verbatim from the Act. Middleton contemporizes his play even further by alluding occasionally to London settings and, as various scholars have mentioned, referring directly to the Essex affair wherein witch-induced impotence led to the granting of a royal divorce.[19] The legacy becomes clear: James authors his *Daemonologie*,

---

[16] Harris, p. 79.
[17] Thomas Middleton, *The Witch*, (c. 1619), in Corbin and Sedge, eds.
[18] Corbin and Sedge, eds, p. 16.
[19] See Julia M. Garrett, 'Community and Intimacy in English Witchcraft Discourse', Unpublished PhD Dissertation, (University of California, Santa Barbara, 2004), particularly chapter 3.

which in turn influences the Act (or perhaps James has a more direct hand in the legislation), the court employs its language in the Essex affair, and Middleton dramatizes the event. In employing such a local and contemporary witchcraft case, Middleton also collapses the distance between drama and politics. Furthermore, the use of a familiar such as Malkin also anglicizes the witchcraft, for such creatures were rarely mentioned in continental sorcery cases but were often crucial to English witchcraft prosecutions. Although Middleton sets his play in Ravenna, then, it quickly becomes England under Jamesian scrutiny.

Other concerns arise when interpreting the witchcraft plays created after 1604. Anthony Harris is again useful in defining any dramatic change that occurred:

> The relatively limited concern with witchcraft apparent in Elizabethan poetry is paralleled in the plays of the period; there are scattered references to the subject in many plays but in very few is it a leading theme. This was due in part to the fact that there was no tradition for the dramatic portrayal of witchcraft before this time. The principal supernatural phenomena to be depicted on stage had been the devils who had figured in many of the medieval miracle and morality plays, especially those concerned with such themes as the Last Judgment and the Harrowing of Hell.[20]

Harris cites Marlowe's *Doctor Faustus* as a devil-oriented play, John Lyly's *Endimion* in which the witch character, Dispas, functions "as a comical character, certainly not one to be feared", and also Lyly's Mother Bombie, a witch "even more harmless than [...] Dispas".[21] And Shakespeare, in *Twelfth Night, The Comedy of Errors*, and *The Merry Wives of Windsor*, alludes to potential witchery but never fully explores the idea. All were created while Elizabeth's more moderate Witchcraft Act represented the legal and cultural views of sorcery. So, between having no tradition to depict witches on stage, and having no cultural or political momentum to create any sort of spectacular witch, playwrights simply ignored the idea until James stepped in to limit witch advocacy (by having Scot's book burnt)[22] and to catalogue felonious witchcraft behaviour.

One would miss another possible influence if that of Queen Anne were overlooked. Ben Jonson first produced his own witchcraft-oriented

---

[20] Harris, pp. 25–26.
[21] Ibid., pp. 27–28.
[22] See note 8.

drama *The Masque of Queens* in 1609,[23] but not without first taking the advice of Anne, who, as Jonson's preface to the play states, maintained that the "life of these Spectacles lay in their variety." Jonson declares that he "was careful to decline not" and creates for the Queen's approval "not a masque but a spectacle of strangeness" (line 18). A witch comes on stage carrying "a torch made from a dead man's arm" while the "sixth hag" declares that she has used her dagger and "killed an infant for his fat." The seventh hag has "bit[ten] off the sinew" of a hanged man just as the tenth hag contributes "a black cat's brain." Jonson's stage directions starting at line ninety-five assert that "a writer should always trust somewhat to the capacity of the spectator, especially at these spectacles, where men, beside enquiring eyes, are understood to bring quick ears, and not those sluggish ones of porters and mechanics that must be bored through at every act with narrations." In short, Jonson is showing instead of telling, letting his audience learn that seeing is believing.

John G. Demaray observes Jonson's problems thereafter with balancing an "antic spectacle of disorder against a concluding harmonious main masque." Jonson eventually retired from his position as court playwright after a dispute with Inigo Jones "over whether poetry or scenic spectacle was the controlling art".[24] Spectacle, now classified as antic or scenic, becomes a necessary, even mandated, element of any play that wished for royal approval; add this requirement to the King's own scholarly interest in witch justice, and the shift from the Elizabethan comic and ineffective witch to the powerful stage presences of Erictho and Hecate become not only understandable but readily foreseeable.

This idea of spectacle recurs in the more theoretical scholarship on the matter of witchcraft. Deborah Willis writes of Hecate, "The scenes with Hecate are spectacular but not frightening [... T]hey travesty more than demonize her".[25] Willis's subject is "maternal power" as located in the body of the witch. Spectacle, it seems, can serve as a means of evaluating gender and power as well as entertaining the audience. Moreover, witchcraft served as a trope for many playwrights:

---

[23] Ben Jonson, *The Masque of Queens* in *Ben Jonson: Selected Masques* (New Haven: Yale University Press, 1970).

[24] John G. Demaray, *Shakespeare and the Spectacles of Strangeness* (Pittsburgh: Duquesne University Press, 1998), p. 50.

[25] Deborah Willis, *Malevolent Nurture: Witch-Hunting and Maternal Power in Early Modern England* (Ithaca, NY: Cornell University Press, 1995) p. 163.

"Witchcraft metaphors make their appearance in many plays where
no literal witches are characters. Theater, rhetoric, even language itself
became coded as 'bewitching' [… and] stage plays suggested a parallel
between theatrical manipulation and literal witchcraft which worked
to blur the boundaries between them".[26] Hence, spectacle has also
become a metaphorical device as well as a means of conveying theme
and story. For example, Shakespeare's Iago will work "by wit and not
by witchcraft," using the black art as a comparative model. Even in
doing so, Iago leaves the audience aware that much recent evil might
well be ascribed to witchery, and while Shakespeare only occasionally
employed witches, other writers of the period employed witches for
various other reasons, some political as much as dramatic. In other
words, spectacle, like the attitude towards witches, evolved over the
years of James's reign.

While *The Tragedy of Sophonisba* first appeared soon after the Witchcraft
Act of 1604 along with Shakespeare's *Macbeth* and Jonson's *Masque of
Queens*, and *The Witch* is assigned a date as early as 1619, *The Witch of
Edmonton* is thought to be a product of about 1621. The early plays
were full of malevolent spectacle on behalf of witches, supportive of
the language of the new Act. Indeed, Wallace Notestein observes, "over
two-fifths of those who are known to have been convicted under the
new law would have escaped death under the Elizabethan statute".[27]
Middleton and Marston create notoriously evil witches who would
never have been spared death and who evoke little if any sympathy
from the viewing audience. But *The Witch of Edmonton*, co-authored by
William Rowley, Thomas Dekker, and John Ford, offers a much more
sympathetic witch in the case of Elizabeth Sawyer.[28] Moreover, virtually
all spectacle in the drama is provided by the devil dog/satanic familiar
in a return to Faustian notions of evil. More than any other witchcraft
play, *The Witch of Edmonton* casts an ambivalent light onto the subject. A
devilish familiar is depicted perpetrating evil, illustrating the power of
the Devil to seduce and ruin, facilitating murder; in this sense, the play
supports James's presentation of witches as found in his *Daemonologie*.

---

[26] Ibid., pp. 163–64.
[27] Wallace Notestein, *A History of Witchcraft in England: From 1558 to 1718* (New York:
Thomas Y. Crowell, 1968), p. 106.
[28] Thomas Dekker, John Ford, and William Rowley, *The Witch of Edmonton* (1621)
in Corbin and Sedge, eds.

On the other hand, Elizabeth Sawyer, the titular witch, opens Act II
with lines that Erictho or Hecate could never have spoken:

> Why should the envious world
> Throw all their scandalous malice upon me?
> 'Cause I am poor, deformed and ignorant,
> And like a bow buckled and bent together
> By some more strong in mischiefs than myself,
> Must I for that be made a common sink
> For all the filth and rubbish of men's tongues
> To fall and run into? Some call me witch
> And, being ignorant of myself, they go
> About to teach me how to be one [...] (II.1.1–9).

The three playwrights depict Sawyer being beaten, verbally abused,
and stripped of any human dignity before she finally breaks down and
laments, "Tis all one to be a witch as to be counted one" (II.1.118),
and only then does the devil-dog appear. All spectacle—the seduction
of Sawyer, the dowsing of Cuddy Banks, the ruining of the Morris
Dance—comes from the dog and not Elizabeth Sawyer. Furthermore,
while Erictho and Hecate show no signs of remorse, Sawyer admits to
all and begs forgiveness. This is hardly compatible with King James's
claim in the *Daemonologie*, "Further experience daily proves how loth
they are to confess without torture, which witnesseth their guiltiness".[29]
Rowley, Dekker, and Ford deem it unnecessary to provide the spectacle
of witch torture and in fact don't allude to any torture at all (but then
it never was part of a normal English witch trial). The play's final
spectacle depicts the depression that the townsfolk feel upon the execution of young Frank Thorney. When one recalls that the earlier plays
may have added on or thrown in witch scenes just to suit the vogue for
such characters, the fact that the plight of Elizabeth Sawyer is rooted
in fact, that she appears a very human character, and that she seems
more an unwitting victim than a malicious soul suggests a shifting of
opinion about the matter of witches.

   This sympathetic attitude toward Sawyer should perhaps not surprise
us, for in 1622, at York, a judge dismissed all charges against six accused
witches in the Fairfax case.[30] Wallace Notestein credits this judge "with

---

[29] *Daemonologie* in *Witchcraft in Early Modern Scotland: James VI's Demonology and the
North Berwick Witches*, ed. by Lawrence Normand and Gareth Roberts (Exeter: Exeter
University Press, 2000), p. 381.
   [30] See Edward Fairfax, *Demonologia*, ed. by W. Grainge (Harrowgate, 1882).

following the king's lead in looking out for imposture".[31] Notestein can
make this claim because he elsewhere writes, "records of imposture
were well on their way to rival the records of witchcraft" and "the king
who had so bitterly arraigned Reginald Scot was himself becoming the
discoverer-general of England".[32] Notestein cements his claim by citing
Thomas Fuller's almost stunning description of the King's reversal:
"The frequency of such forged possessions wrought such an alteration
upon the judgement of King James that he, receding from what he had
written in his *Daemonology*, grew first diffident of, and then to flatly deny,
the workings of witches and devils, as but falsehoods and delusions".[33]
The Witch of Edmonton coincides with this royal change of heart,
allowing Rowley, Dekker, and Ford, according to Deborah Willis, to
"construct [Elizabeth Sawyer] as a subject in her own right".[34] Sawyer
is not appended to or added onto the drama for reasons of spectacle.
She is a victim of the same circumstances and of the same cultural
biases that bring young Thorney to his death. By recalling her earlier
remarks about her abusive treatment at the hands of the villagers, the
reader can argue that English culture and not the devil created such a
sad witch. Sawyer thus does indeed become a "subject in her own right,"
a subject of imposture in its most ironic sense: imposed upon by age
and physical deformity, by a village that alienates and abuses her, by a
milieu that suspects her, and by a devil-dog that takes advantage of her
pitiful existence and desire for a reckoning. The spectacle here—besides
the antics of the devil-dog—sees the loss of human life as created by
human, not diabolical, prejudices. Indeed, one can argue that the true
spectacle involves the confessions of both Sawyer and Thorney. The
Justice, while weighing the evidence against Sawyer, admonishes those
accusing her that "Unless your proofs come better armed, instead of
turning her into a witch, you'll prove yourself stark fools" (IV.1.42–43).
The Justice also asks Old Banks if he is "a ringleader in mischief" and
chides him for "abuse[ing] an aged woman" (IV.1.34–35). This Justice
voices, many scholars argue, the King's new scepticism. In this model it
is proposed that King James has begun to understand by this time just

---

[31] Notestein, p. 145.
[32] Ibid., p. 142.
[33] Quoted in ibid., p. 143. For a contemporary interpretation of James VI & I's
views see Sharpe, *Instruments of Darkness*, pp. 48–50.
[34] Willis, p. 161.

how many witch charges were personally and not theologically or legally motivated, and Elizabeth Sawyer personifies his evolving attitude.

The Witches of Lancashire, first performed in 1634, continues to show the erosion of the rhetoric of the 1604 Act. Although a good deal of witchcraft occurs in the drama, critical response to both the antics of the witches and the attitudes of the playwrights leans toward seeing the work as comic, harmless, and even dismissive. Indeed, the words "spectacle" and "spectacular" do not appear in discussions of the play. Instead, various critical readers suggest the play reverses sympathies in a variety of ways. Gabriel Egan, editor of the Globe Quartos version of the play, cites "the dramatists' observation of the psychosexual impulses underlying the witch-hunting craze." He later states,

> This is not simply an anti-witch play, since their victims suffer little physical harm. [...] For these misdemeanours the witches suffer a variety of excesses from beating and amputation to arrest and threatened execution. In performance the final scene chilled those on stage and in the audience as the historical reality became immediate. Brome and Heywood explicitly name 'mercy' in their epilogue and throughout they present witchcraft unseriously while attending to the excessive response of state power. Perhaps this made a difference: unlike their unfortunate predecessors in 1612, there is no evidence that these Pendle witches were executed.[35]

The witches of Heywood and Brome's drama perform what previously Ben Jonson described as "antic spectacle." They mislead hunting dogs, snatch food from a feast, make a broom sweep on its own action, and, in a key allusion to the infamous Mary Spencer case, the witch Moll commands a pail to move by itself: "Pail, on afore to the field and stay till I come. [*She puts down the pail and it goes out the door*]" (II.6.65–66). Wallace Notestein observes that "The pail incident—of course without its rational explanation—was grafted into the play and put upon the stage", an interesting reversal of referential tactics.[36] The early plays, we recall, had grafted on 'witch scenes' in order to provide spectacle sympathetic toward the recently passed Witchcraft Act. Anthony Harris also addresses the allusion to the Spencer case, likewise acknowledging that Spencer's "clearly reasonable denial is ignored by the playwrights".[37] Hence, as happened in the early plays, the audience is left to decide

---

[35] Egan, in Heywood and Broome, pp. vii–viii.
[36] Notestein, p. 159.
[37] Harris, p. 177.

what is witchcraft and what is play. For those not familiar with the
Spencer case, this summary should suffice:

> when she was a young girl and went to the well for water, she used to
> trundle the collock, or peal, down the hill, and she would run after it
> to overtake it, and did overtake it sometimes, and then she might call it to
> come to her, but utterly denies that she could ever make it come to her
> by any witchcraft.[38]

So two scholars note the use of a witchcraft incident that was dubious
and troublesome to the justices that, by law, were forced to hear the
case. Notestein later writes that "Mary Spencer and the others owed
their lives in all probability to the intellectual independence of William
Harvey".[39] Harvey, intellectually inclined toward the disbelief of witches
and armed with enough proto-science to provide other explanations than
sorcery for events, personified "the continuance and growth of witch
skepticism" in the 1630s.[40] Though certain witches of the Lancashire
coven were prosecuted to the fullest extent of the law, it seems likely
that Mary Spencer was spared by the efforts of the enlightened advocates around her. Hence, the 'grafting on' of her pail incident gestures
directly toward the call for mercy at the end of the play, because while
Erictho and Hecate clearly were drawn as personifications of the worst
aspect of the 1604 Act, and while Elizabeth Sawyer did consort with a
devil-dog and seek to do malicious evil, the inclusion of the bewitched
pail in *The Witches of Lancashire* refers sceptically towards increasingly
'rational' approaches to witchcraft.

To conclude, the reader of theatrical witchcraft texts written between
1604 and 1634 can trace the evolution of attitudes toward witches from
fear and criminal contempt to incredulity and even pity. Moreover,
Queen Anne's insistence on 'spectacle' moving the plays also evolves,
for by 1650, Anthony Harris observes, "The operatic spectacles and
pantomime-like burlesques so much in vogue lent themselves more
readily to a light-hearted approach, and the audience [...] would
scorn any suspicion of their taking seriously a matter so irrational as
witchcraft".[41] Likewise, Ben Jonson, on breaking his partnership with
Inigo Jones around 1631, argued that "all representations [...] public

---

[38] Quoted in ibid., p. 177.
[39] Notestein, p. 160.
[40] Ibid., p. 162.
[41] Harris, p. 184.

spectacles [...] ought to be the mirrors of a man's life".[42] The depictions of witches as pitiable and victims indeed 'mirror' the attitudes of the 1630s. Although Matthew Hopkins' reign of terror was yet to come, his persecutions were rural and politically driven, not reflective of the urban playwrights. Witches are indeed hard to find in drama after 1640, save for revisions of Shakespeare at the hands of Davenant and Dryden in 1663 and 1667. More attention is given to apparitions and ghosts than is given to witches by the close of the seventeenth century, and in 1736, under George II the Witchcraft Act of 1604 was repealed altogether and forbade the prosecution of witches. George's Act serves as a reminder of the power of political influence on drama, for once witchcraft is declared a non-issue, dramatists turned elsewhere for any spectacle they might need. Witches, then, were like the gigantic monsters of 1950s sci-fi movies that were inspired by fears of atomic energy after Hiroshima. Both forms of evil were but phases in the development of the human understanding and imagination. That is where they still reside, occasionally revisited, but ultimately a spectacle of the past.

---

[42] Quoted in Roy Strong, *Splendor at Court: Renaissance Spectacle and the Theater of Power* (Boston: Houghton-Mifflin, 1973), p. 215.

WITCHCRAFT, EMOTION AND IMAGINATION IN THE ENGLISH CIVIL WAR

Malcolm Gaskill*

I

The rise and decline of English witch-trials can be explained largely in terms of the law: first, the political will to legislate against witchcraft, followed by judicial reluctance to convict. Witch-beliefs permeated English life long before 1542 when the first statute was passed and long after 1736 when the last was repealed; and yet the substance of witchcraft as a crime belongs to a period between the reigns of Elizabeth I and James II—roughly 120 years—when people saw witches being hanged or heard news of the same. Executions gave witchcraft a concrete reality, breeding suspicions and encouraging accusers to seek redress at law; naturally, a decrease in executions had the opposite effect. In between, an uneasy consensus prevailed, with sufficient common ground between communities and courts to despatch suspects to the gallows, but never reaching a point where the definition of witchcraft, and its supporting theories and alleged practices, were beyond contention.[1] As a concept and a crime, witchcraft was characterized by this fluidity of meaning, a tendency demonstrated by a revision of the law against it in 1604.

* I would like to thank Robin Briggs and John Walter for their advice, likewise Andy Wood and the participants at the "Voices and Identities in the Archival Record" day-school, University of East Anglia, March 2005, who heard and commented upon an earlier draft of this paper. I am also grateful to the Arts and Humanities Research Council who funded the leave during which much of my research on the Hopkins trials was completed.
[1] Clive Holmes, 'Popular Culture? Witches, Magistrates and Divines in Early Modern England', in *Understanding Popular Culture*, ed. by Steven L. Kaplan (Berlin: Walter de Gruyter, 1984), pp. 85–111; C.R. Unsworth, 'Witchcraft Beliefs and Criminal Procedure in Early Modern England', in *Legal Record and Historical Reality*, ed. by T.G. Watkin (London: Hambledon & London Ltd, 1989), pp. 71–98; Stuart Clark, 'Protestant Demonology: Sin, Superstition and Society (*c.* 1520–*c.* 1640)', in *Early Modern European Witchcraft: Centres and Peripheries*, ed. by Bengt Ankarloo and Gustav Henningsen (Oxford: Clarendon Press, 1990), pp. 45–81.

The Witchcraft Act of 1563 had long symbolized the disdain of a newly Protestantized state for disobedience to Church and state, while recognizing the practical need of ordinary subjects to fight *maleficium*: causing harm to person and property by magical means.[2] In contrast to its tone—stern condemnation of "fantasticall and devilishe p[er]sons" fomenting "Infamy and Disquietnes"— the terms were quite generous. Persons invoking evil spirits or causing death would be executed; but merely injuring someone or destroying livestock were lesser crimes for first offenders, warranting only imprisonment and quarterly appearances in the pillory. This distinction shows the extent to which, under Elizabeth I, witchcraft was still regarded as a social and spiritual lapse, perpetrators deserving of a chance to reform.[3] The 1604 statute was significantly different. Using witchcraft to cause any sort of harm would in future incur death; furthermore, the invocation of evil spirits was given particular emphasis, likewise the idea that witches robbed graves and kept familiar spirits which they would "consult, covenant with, entertaine, employ, feede or rewarde".[4] In theory, at least, witchcraft was no longer just a sin of ill-will connected to misfortune, but a blacker and more vivid crime of demonianism, apostasy and conspiracy.

This is not the place to explain this shift. Suffice it to say that an explanation involving James I's desire to extend the Scottish witch-hunt to England is inadequate; it is not borne out by subsequent events and overlooks subtleties in the religious politics of the era.[5] The purpose of this essay is to explore some practical effects of the Jacobean Witchcraft Act forty years on, a time when its technical innovations were most graphically translated into deeds. There were two key preconditions: first, the developing demonological notion that witches deliberately

---

[2] James Sharpe, *Instruments of Darkness: Witchcraft in England, 1550–1750* (London: University of Pennsylvania Press, 1996), pp. 88–94; Norman L. Jones, 'Defining Superstitions: Treasonous Catholics and the Act against Witchcraft of 1563', in *States, Sovereigns and Society in Early Modern England*, ed. by Charles Carlton et al. (Stroud: Sutton, 1997), pp. 187–203.

[3] 5 Eliz., c. 16 (1563), see C.L. Ewen, *Witch Hunting and Witch Trials* (London: Kegan Paul, Trench & Trubner, 1929), pp. 15–18. The text of this Act is also given in Appendix I of this volume. In general, see Gregory Durston, *Witchcraft and Witch Trials: A History of English Witchcraft and its Legal Perspectives, 1542 to 1736* (Chichester: Barry Rose Law Publications, 2000).

[4] 1 Jac. I, c. 12 (1604), see Ewen, *Witch Hunting*, pp. 19–20. The text is also given in Appendix II of this volume.

[5] Michael MacDonald, *Witchcraft and Hysteria in Elizabeth London* (London: Routledge, 1991). See also the essays by P.G. Maxwell-Stuart, Clive Holmes and Tom Webster in this volume.

resorted to rituals, spells and covenants; and, secondly, the way that the legal reality of witchcraft came to depend on material proof of such activities, as hearsay and circumstantial evidence crumbled as reliable foundations for justice and truth.[6] Of course, neither was a direct consequence of the statute; nor did every plaintiff and magistrate pay attention to its refinements when assembling a case. Yet the 1604 Act was none the less part of a changing climate of opinion where the identification of witches needed to be demonstrated not merely asserted.

Although, in contrast to continental Roman canon law, English courts did not require particular proofs, some kinds of evidence carried greater weight than others. To find a prisoner guilty of felony, a jury had to be persuaded by testimony, the value of which was linked to the reputation of the witness. Accused parties had their say, but were expected to lie and so were not required to swear. Prisoners who confessed, on the other hand, were not even required to face a jury, presumption of innocence having been nullified by the disclosure.[7] Yet for obvious reasons confessions were rare, especially in England where torture was only applied in exceptional criminal cases; by 1640 the Tudor and Stuart state had recorded only eighty-one such orders, the vast majority pre-dating the reign of James I.[8] By this time witchcraft prosecutions had also become rare, not because of subsidence of popular belief and anger but growing cautiousness among judges. When, in 1645, a witch-hunt in Essex and Suffolk released the pent-up frustrations of witch-fearing villagers, it was natural that the witchfinders involved—Matthew Hopkins and John Stearne—concentrated on extracting confessions that focussed on the sealing of satanic pacts. The results were extraordinary: two mass trials, each concluding with eighteen executions.[9]

But Hopkins and Stearne were not the sole authors of these confessions. The feelings of many people contributed, including suspects

---

[6] I explore this subject in more detail in a forthcoming article in *Past & Present*, 'Witchcraft and Evidence in Early Modern England: The Legal Significance of the East Anglian Witch-Hunt of 1645–47'.

[7] On criminal trial procedure, see J.H. Baker, *An Introduction to English Legal History*, 4th edn (London: LexisNexis UK, 2002), pp. 508–11; National Archives, London, SP 16/520/33.

[8] John H. Langbein, *Torture and the Law of Proof* (Chicago: University of Chicago Press, 1977), pp. 82–83, 134–35.

[9] In general, see Malcolm Gaskill, *Witchfinders: A Seventeenth-Century English Tragedy* (London: John Murray, 2005). See also *English Witchcraft, 1560–1736*, 6 vols, ed. by James Sharpe and Richard M. Golden (London: Pickering & Chatto Ltd, 2003), III: *The Matthew Hopkins Trials*, ed. by Malcolm Gaskill.

themselves, reflecting the traumas of provincial society in the 1630s and the ensuing trauma of civil war. In the 1640s an imbalance of power between centre and locality encouraged reformist fervour, from the sacking of Catholic homes and the ejection of 'scandalous' ministers, to the destruction of 'superstitious' church decorations and the persecution of witches. Often disorderly and sometimes illegal, such actions divided Protestant opinion. Yet in time of war and reformation ends justified means for those who took their lead from the Bible rather than from monarchs and bishops; furthermore the disruption of normal legal channels allowed zealous campaigns to proceed apace.[10] From Suffolk the witch-hunt spread to wherever Stearne and Hopkins travelled: into Norfolk, Huntingdonshire and beyond. The witchfinders sparked controversy that made them unwelcome in some places, thus limiting the duration of the witch-hunt. By the summer of 1647 Hopkins was dead, and the fruits of Stearne's labours at Ely were less convincing than two years earlier.

That the East Anglian witch-hunt resulted from an exceptional crisis explains why its significance remains obscure: it is seen as an aberration which, like most European witch-panics, broke some fairly consistent patterns.[11] Not only did trials increase, but so too did the proportion of male suspects, a tendency for households (including children) to be drawn in, incidence of brutal interrogations, output of confessions and rates of conviction. As many as three hundred accusations were made between spring 1645 and summer 1647, over a hundred of which resulted in executions. So, a unique event; and yet too rarely is the political, religious, intellectual and legal framework harnessed to parochial manifestations: grievances, feuds, factions and rumours, reaching down to basic human frailties, identities and emotions. A cosmic world of spiritual agency was connected to the inner life of

---

[10] John Walter, *Understanding Popular Violence in the English Revolution: The Colchester Plunderers* (Cambridge: Cambridge University Press, 1999); Ian Green, 'The Persecution of Scandalous and Malignant Parish Clergy during the English Civil War', *English Historical Review*, 94 (1979), 507–31; James Sharpe, 'Scandalous and Malignant Priests in Essex: The Impact of Grassroots Puritanism', in *Politics and People in Revolutionary England*, ed. by Colin Jones et al. (Oxford: Blackwell Publishers, 1986), pp. 223–73; *The Journal of William Dowsing: Iconoclasm in East Anglia during the English Civil War*, ed. by Trevor Cooper (Woodbridge: Boydell, 2001); Julie Spraggon, *Puritan Iconoclasm during the English Civil War* (Woodbridge: Boydell, 2003).

[11] For an overview of witchcraft prosecutions across the whole period, see: Keith Thomas, *Religion and the Decline of Magic* (London: Weidenfield and Nicholson, 1971), chs 14–18; Sharpe, *Instruments of Darkness*, chs 4–5; Ewen, *Witch Hunting*, pp. 1–115.

conscience, just as the war between Parliament and Crown exposed political and cultural fault-lines in neighbourhoods across the country. We need context, both synchronically for the upheavals of the 1640s and diachronically across the history of law, religion and witchcraft. To that end, this essay connects the macro-perspective seen in the work of Alan Macfarlane, Jim Sharpe and Peter Elmer,[12] to the more microscopic focus of Louise Jackson, Diane Purkiss and others who have delved into the psychological realm.[13]

II

Four main sets of confessions survive: evidence recorded by magistrates at Manningtree, Essex, in March 1645, as reported in a printed pamphlet;[14] a set of manuscript notes from the Bury St Edmunds trial in August 1645, possibly taken from original documents or from spoken testimony;[15] a pamphlet about proceedings at Huntingdon between March and May 1646;[16] and a file of original depositions made in the Isle of Ely, mostly in the summer of 1647.[17] Though far from uniform in detail, certain characteristics emerge from these accounts. Typically, the confessing witches were women, who pointed to life-crises that had resulted in moral weakness, emotional vulnerability and subsequent visitation by opportunistic demons. The scenario was based on the classic seduction, with what were often described as "soft, hollow

---

[12] Alan Macfarlane, *Witchcraft in Tudor and Stuart Essex*, 2nd edn (London: Routledge, 1999), ch. 9; James Sharpe, 'The Devil in East Anglia: the Matthew Hopkins Trials Reconsidered', in *Witchcraft in Early Modern Europe: Studies in Culture and Belief*, ed. by Jonathan Barry et al., (Cambridge: Cambridge University Press, 1996), pp. 237–54; Peter Elmer, 'Towards a politics of witchcraft in early modern England', in *Languages of Witchcraft: Narrative, Ideology and Meaning in Early Modern Culture*, ed. by Stuart Clark (Basingstoke: Palgrave Macmillan, 2001), pp. 101–18.

[13] Louise Jackson, 'Witches, Wives and Mothers: Witchcraft Persecution and Women's Confessions in Seventeenth-Century England', *Women's History Review*, 4 (1995), 63–83; Diane Purkiss, 'Women's Stories of Witchcraft in Early Modern England: The House, the Body, the Child', *Gender and History*, 7 (1995), 408–32.

[14] H.F., *A true and exact Relation Of the severall Informations, Examinations, and Confessions of the late Witches…in the County of Essex* (London, 1645).

[15] British Library, Add. MSS 27, 402, ff. 104–21. These are accurately transcribed in Ewen, *Witch Hunting*, pp. 291–313; all references here are to Ewen's transcription.

[16] John Davenport, *The Witches of Huntingdon, Their Examinations and Confessions; exactly taken by his Majesties Justices of Peace for that County* (London, 1646).

[17] Cambridge University Library (CUL), Ely Diocesan Records (EDR), E12 1647.

voices" coaxing women to surrender. Most suspects told of how they
had resisted, but in the end had sealed a covenant.

Often it seems that witch-confessions have been doubly decontextu-
alized, first by inquisitors looking for demonological signs, then again
by historians pursuing specialist agendas.[18] The problem is that, to
quote Marina Warner, "the supernatural is difficult terrain; of its very
nature, it resists discourse; or, to put it more accurately, it is always in
the process of being described, conjured, made, and made up, without
ascertainable outside referents".[19] This was actually a difficulty faced by
contemporary jurists, who struggled with their ignorance about a crime
cloaked in diabolical secrecy. "Confessions mattered so much in the
case of witchcraft", according to Lyndal Roper, "because the criminal
acts could by definition not be witnessed". Even then doubts made
interrogators suggestible. Under examination a witch might extend, as
well as merely reflect, learned demonology, adding credible substance
to the case and, in turn, forcing interrogators to adjust their theories.
Confessions must bear traces of the authentic voice of plebeian suspects,
otherwise they would have been worthless as legal evidence.[20]

Signs of demonology in the East Anglian confessions—from a belief
in *maleficium* to Calvinist ideas of covenanting—are obvious, and the
contribution of terror is equally simple to comprehend.[21] Hopkins and
Stearne were influenced by continental authors like Jean Bodin, via writers like Richard Bernard, Thomas Cooper and Michael Dalton, whose
own ideas had been shaped by James I and the Cambridge theologian
William Perkins;[22] like many, Bernard was a believer but cautious of

---

[18] Norbert Schindler, *Rebellion, Community and Custom in Early Modern Germany* (Cambridge: Cambridge University Press, 2002), p. 239.

[19] Marina Warner, *Fantastic Metamorphoses, Other Worlds* (Oxford: Oxford University
Press, 2002), p. 159.

[20] Lyndal Roper, *Witch Craze: Terror and Fantasy in Baroque Germany* (New Haven: Yale
University Press, 2004), pp. 46–52, quotation at p. 46.

[21] John Teall, 'Witchcraft and Calvinism in Elizabethan England: Divine Power
and Human Agency', *Journal of the History of Ideas*, 23 (1962), 21–36; Christina Ross,
'Calvinism and the Witchcraft Persecution in England', *Journal of the Presbyterian Historical Society of England*, 12 (1960), 22–27. In general, see also E. Brooks Holifield, *The
Covenant Sealed: The Development of Puritan Sacramental Theology in Old and New England,
1570–1720* (New Haven: Yale University Press, 1974).

[22] Richard Bernard, *A Guide to Grand-Jury Men* (London, 1627); Thomas Cooper, *The
Mysterie of Witch-craft* (London, 1617); Michael Dalton, *The Countrey Justice* (London,
1618; 1622 edn), pp. 250–51; James I, *Daemonologie* (London, 1603); William Perkins,
A Discourse of the Damned Art of Witchcraft (London, 1608). On Bodin, see Stuart Clark,
Thinking with Demons: The Idea of Witchcraft in Early Modern Europe (Oxford: Oxford
University Press, 1997), pp. 670–82.

proof.[23] By 1640 witch-trials had become a rarity and had it not been for the Civil War they might have faded from public life altogether. It seems likely, then, that the witchfinders' purpose lay in the provision of evidence. Here we should remember that European inquisitors applied torture in witchcraft cases not because they had low probative standards but because they had high ones. Their objective was to uncover truth: with witches specifically it was thought the devil might inhibit confession unless force were used. A pervasive dualism supported the idea that an assault on the body might liberate the soul, and thence to justice.[24] In England judicial decisions depended not on the power of an academic dossier to persuade a professional tribunal, as they did on the continent, but rather the ability of witnesses to convince juries. In many criminal trials guilt seemed obvious, but witchcraft was a work of darkness and deceit. As a consequence magistrates were advised that vague causes of suspicion might be acceptable at the committal stage, and probably in trials as well.[25]

By the 1630s, however, the days when a witch could be put to death solely on the testimony of her neighbours were clearly numbered. More was needed: physical marks where witches suckled familiars, sightings of familiars, and above all confessions, given freely or under duress. By 1645 Matthew Hopkins must have understood that witnesses needed to make a compelling case to magistrates and grand jurors if a prosecution was even to get off the ground. If there were confessions so much the better, especially if they described the lives of the accused in their own voices. That way it was more plausible that guilt amounted to more than a fantasy dreamt up in the overheated brains of a witchfinder.

This essay uses four categories of the personal and the quotidian: messy details that once added flesh to the bones of academic demonology, and which for our purposes are most valuable. The categories are: relationships in neighbourhoods and households; poverty and work; sexual desire and guilt; and salvation, damnation and despair. The witches' stories rarely fit this classification neatly, but they are

---

[23] See, for example, his discussion of the diabolic illusions used to make a suspect seem guilty in the eyes of others: Bernard, *Guide to Grand-Jury Men*, pp. 77–79.

[24] Langbein, *Torture and the Law of Proof*, pp. 3–4, 9–10, 77–78, 90.

[25] Bernard, *Guide to Grand-Jury Men*, ch. 17; Dalton, *Countrey Justice*, p. 251; Christina Larner, 'Crimen Exceptum? The Crime of Witchcraft in Europe', in *Crime and the Law: The Social History of Crime in Western Europe since 1500* ed. by V.A.C. Gatrell et al. (London, Europa, 1980), pp. 49–75; Barbara J. Shapiro, *Probability and Certainty in Seventeenth-Century England* (Princeton: Princeton University Press, 1983), ch. 6.

comprehensible in terms of its universal themes: political power, economic survival, the urge to reproduce, and hopes of redemption. The
examples constitute a selective sample, but are broadly representative
of confessions heard across East Anglia between 1645 and 1647.

III

The first category concerns social relationships. A society obsessed
with order was also obsessed with disorder, in particular breaches of
authority and other transgressions. Before the religious and economic
upheavals of the sixteenth century, a sense of *caritas*—"charity" by its
broadest meaning—had been more effortlessly observed in English
parishes than was so by 1600. Respect for traditional land rights was
also in decline, breeding anxiety and anger among the lower orders.
Witches personified malice, spite and greed; but these sins were just as
prominent among those who neglected their weaker neighbours. Anne
Leech of Mistley in Essex eyed Widow Rawlins's house with envy, but
only because she had been evicted from it in Rawlins's favour. Leech
admitted sending an imp to kill Rawlins's daughter—in her mind an act
of justifiable revenge.[26] This was not an isolated case. Witnesses from
Thorpe-le-Soken testified that Margaret Moone had admitted murder-
ing a couple who caused her to be evicted by offering an increased rent.
Nor was this the first time Moone had been made homeless without
redress to custom or law.[27]

   However extraordinary the stories of diabolic pacts, contemporaries
would have recognized the social backdrop. Polarization between the
well-to-do and their neighbours led to a downward spiral of estrange-
ment. In Manningtree the acquisitive entrepreneur Richard Edwards
was an obvious target, representing a growing imbalance in wealth and
power. Resentment from below and suspicion from above fed each other.
Rebecca West explained that Elizabeth Gooding bewitched a horse
belonging to another prominent townsman, Robert Taylor, because he
had once unjustly accused her—of killing one of his horses![28] Some
relationships were beyond repair, the differences inherent rather than

[26] *True and exact Relation…Essex*, pp. 8–9.
[27] Ibid., pp. 21–25; Ewen, *Witch Hunting*, p. 225.
[28] *True and exact Relation…Essex*, p. 12.

superficial. One sees this in Huntingdonshire too. Forced to explain why she attacked Mary Darnwell of Keyston, Elizabeth Chandler explained she had "received some hard usage from the said Goodwife Darnwell, by causing her to be duckt". Animosity rubbed off onto Darnwell's daughter, who claimed that Chandler wished her dead. A party Goodwife Darnwell threw for her neighbours, excluding Chandler, ended in misery when a pot of porridge boiled over so prodigiously as to preclude natural explanation.[29]

Witchcraft accusations could result from the malicious persecuting the innocent, but for 1645–47 they are mostly understandable as clashes between unusually enraged people. Folk with few material possessions took special pride in their piety, credit and authority as householders; there were boundaries, physical and symbolic, and they were ferociously defended. In 1645 Rebecca Jones of St Osyth confessed "that the cause of offence she tooke so to destroy and kill the said [Thomas] Bumstead and his wife, was because the said Thomas Bumstead did beate the sonne of this Examinant for eating up of some honey". It mattered less whether the boy was guilty than the fact that Bumstead had encroached upon a domestic jurisdiction: the fantasy of his punishment redrew the perimeter in Jones's mind.[30] Memories of uncharitable behaviour were long. Frances Moore, one of the Huntingdon witches, confessed to bewitching a neighbour to death six years earlier for threatening to "have hanged two of her children for offering to take a piece of bread". Moore may well have accepted her poverty; bad neighbourliness she could not.[31] It was the same with the witches of St Osyth. A carpenter's apprentice who had denied them woodchips was made to bark like a dog and crow like a cock, relegating him so far down the great chain of being that he joined the base creatures of the farmyard.[32]

Confessions also allow us to examine the emotions of household life. John Winnick's confession at Huntingdon displays the frustration of a servant whose savings had been stolen by someone in his household. Unable to make an accusation without offending his master, he put his trust in a bear-like spirit. Upon the return of his purse, Winnick "fell downe upon his knees and said, my Lord and God I thanke you". It is noteworthy that the only criminal act for which he used his

---

[29] Davenport, *Witches of Huntingdon*, pp. 7–9.
[30] *True and exact Relation…Essex*, p. 33.
[31] Davenport, *Witches of Huntingdon*, p. 5.
[32] *True and exact Relation…Essex*, pp. 29–31.

familiars was provoking another servant to rebel against her master by stealing.[33] Confessed witches spoke of raising their children in the cult of witches—as was claimed at Halesworth and Rattlesden in Suffolk—either by initiation or biological inheritance.[34] It could be a gift to raise the powerless, or a curse to bring them down further: one woman at Stretham in the Isle of Ely lamented: "woe was the tyme that ever I was borne of such [an] accursed mother".[35] There were homicidal urges too. Susanna Smith of Rushmere in Suffolk said that "the divill appeared to her like a red shaged dog and tempted her to kill her chilideren".[36] Mother Lakeland of Ipswich confessed that she murdered her own husband, and so was burned for petty treason.[37] In this instance, there seems to have been no clear motive, but in most other cases acts of aggression originate in vengeance for shunning the poor.

And so to the second theme: poverty. In Framlingham in Suffolk, twelve women exposed as witches all lived beyond the Saxon ditch, outside the heart of wealth and authority, and were too poor to pay taxes. Shortages of land, work and housing, unfairness in trade, parsimony in almsgiving, and inability to pay rents, tithes and levies lay behind discontent.[38] At Bacton the source of accusations was the principal inhabitants' exploitation of land for dairy farming and their campaign against unauthorized begging.[39] But poverty has been isolated here because the fantasy of enrichment did not necessarily involve social conflict. Most poor people dreamed of extricating themselves, and confessions offer insights into these dreams. Elizabeth Bradwell from the Norfolk port of Yarmouth was an old stocking-knitter who, unable to find employment, imagined that a dark stranger visited her

---

[33] Davenport, *Witches of Huntingdon*, pp. 3–4.

[34] *A True Relation of the Araignment of eighteene Witches That were tried, convicted, and condemned... in Suffolke* (London, 1645); Ewen, *Witch Hunting*, pp. 309–10; John Stearne, *A Confirmation And Discovery of Witch Craft* (London, 1648), p. 12.

[35] CUL, EDR E12 1647/7.

[36] Ewen, *Witch Hunting*, p. 296. See also the case of Priscilla Collit: ibid., p. 299.

[37] *The Lawes against Witches, and Coniuration. And Some brief Notes and Observations for the Discovery of Witches* (London, 1645), pp. 7–8.

[38] East Suffolk Record Office (ESRO), FC 101/E2/26; FC 101/G7/1–2; JC 1/29/1, pt. 1, pp. 15–17, 25, 30; Ewen, *Witch Hunting*, pp. 304–05; Sharpe, *Instruments of Darkness*, p. 240 note; R. Green, *The History, Topography, and Antiquities of Framlingham and Saxsted* (London, 1834), pp. 172–94.

[39] Ivan Bunn, 'The Suffolk Victims of Matthew Hopkins and John Stearne, 1645–46', unpublished study, 1999, pp. 10–12, 14–18. I am grateful for Mr Bunn's guidance here.

and promised she would never have to work again.[40] Alleviation of
suffering lay behind all the confessions at Bramford in Suffolk. After a
long interrogation, a man named Payne told John Stearne that many
times in his hard life the devil had encouraged him to hang himself.
In the end, though, his route to spiritual oblivion had been witchcraft.
Despairing as he sweated and cursed to push a plough, Payne had
been approached by the devil who asked for his soul. Craving relief,
Payne had relented.[41]

Many women became witches because they lacked the economic
and emotional security of a household.[42] In her confession, Elizabeth
Clarke of Manningtree blamed her witchery upon Anne West, who
had sent her a familiar in the shape of a kitten. Widow Clarke had
been collecting sticks when West told her "That there was wayes and
meanes for her to live much better then now shee did", and that the imp
would bring food. Another imp promised to "helpe her to an Husband,
who should maintaine her ever after". This dream came true when
Clarke slept with the devil, "a tall, proper, black haired gentleman, a
properer man than your selfe" she told Matthew Hopkins.[43] Compare
this to the confession of Jane Wallis of Keyston in Huntingdonshire.
She confessed that she had given herself to a spirit called Blackman,
"like a man something ancient in blackish cloathes, but he had ugly
feet uncovered". No sensitive lover he, Wallis described him as a "filthy
rough" whose sexual demands were as pressing as they were depress-
ing. Brought before the magistrates two days later she denied that she
had ever given into his demands, but had tried to care for two spirits
that begged her for food. "She said she was poor", Wallis confessed,
"and had none to give them"; from that point they brought her two
or three shillings at a time.[44]

The third theme concerns troubled feelings about love and sex. This
image of a domestic provider was closely related to intimacy and its

---

[40] Matthew Hale, *A Collection of Modern Relations of Matters of Fact Concerning Witches
and Witchcraft* (London, 1661; 1693 edns), pp. 46–48; Stearne, *Confirmation And Discovery*,
pp. 53–54; C.L. Ewen, *Witchcraft and Demonianism* (London: Heath Cranton, 1933),
p. 280.
    [41] Ewen, *Witch Hunting*, p. 294; Stearne, *Confirmation And Discovery*, pp. 26–27, 30.
    [42] This is a principal theme in Malcolm Gaskill, 'Witchcraft and Power in Early
Modern England: The Case of Margaret Moore', in *Women, Crime and the Courts in
Early Modern England*, ed. by Jenny Kermode and Garthine Walker (London: Chapel
Hill, 1994), pp. 125–45.
    [43] *True and exact Relation... Essex*, p. 6; Stearne, *Confirmation And Discovery*, p. 15.
    [44] Davenport, *Witches of Huntingdon*, pp. 12–13.

associated guilt: a chasm between ideals of chastity and modesty on one
side, and the insistence of desire on the other. Sometimes the witchfinders added a sexual edge to their questions; but the stories they got back
amounted to more than the fulfilment of their own repressed fantasies.
In confessions could be heard laments of age for youth, yearning for
sensitivity and kindness, and self-indulgence in seduction and abandon.
One sees this in the Suffolk confessions. Margaret Bayts confessed to
having two secret nipples suckled by imps which scuttled beneath her
skirts pleasuring her while she worked. One of her neighbours described
nothing less than an orgasm: "she felt 2 things like butterflies in her
secret p[ar]ts w[i]th w[a]tchings dansings and suckinge & she felt them
w[i]th her hands and rubbed the[m] and killed them". Mary Scrutton
sheepishly told her husband that suckling noises beneath the bedclothes
must be mice; and another woman, persuaded by Satan that she was
too sinful to be saved, allowed herself to be ravished by two great flying
beetles that came to her in the night.[45]

Through witchcraft the elderly restored themselves as objects of
desire. According to John Stearne, Anne Boreham of Sudbury "confessed that as she awoke out of a dreame she saw uglie men (as she
thought) a fighting, and asked them why they fought, who answered
that they would fight for all her, and then one vanished away, and then
came to her into bed and had the use of her body". As was usual, he
was heavier and colder than she would have expected—a clue, if clue
were needed, to his unnatural identity. She told him she was only a
poor widow, and he reassured her that "she should never want, but
have her desire".[46] Margaret Wyard of Framlingham said that "the
devill appeard to her in the likenes of a calfe and told her he was her
husband and asked her to have the use of her body w[hi]ch then she
did denie, after this he came to her in the shape of a handsome yonge
gentleman w[i]th yellow hayre and black cloaths & often times lay
w[i]th her". Her experience revived sensuous romance for a woman
with her courting days behind her. But the devil's promises came to
nothing and soon she was struggling to feed seven hungry imps. These
creatures—flies, beetles, spiders and mice—clamoured for space at her
body, but with only five teats "when they came to suck they fight like

---

[45] Ewen, *Witch Hunting*, pp. 304–06.
[46] Stearne, *Confirmation And Discovery*, p. 32.

pigs with a sow". She had become a drudge again; her prince charming nothing but the prince of darkness.[47]

The final theme concerns salvation and damnation. Many witches reserved their most negative feelings for themselves, regretting sin and fearing its consequences. Eleanor Shepherd confessed at Huntingdon that she gave herself to a rat-like spirit which appeared when she was "swearing and cursing about the discords of her children"; now, she declared, she did "intend to leave her former course of cursing and swearing".[48] For those whose fears were shaped by strict Calvinist soteriology, a dissolute life was not a cause of damnation but a sign; even poverty could be taken to indicate non-election. And so the devil came to the poor when their God seemed to have abandoned them. Elizabeth Weed of Great Catworth told magistrates that in about 1625 "she being saying her Prayers in the evening about bedtime, there did appear unto her three Spirits"; one asked "if shee would renounce God and Christ; she answered, shee would" and a covenant was sealed with blood, possibly a more potent covenant than that between the elect and their Saviour. She spoke in a new way about "the light of the Spirit", interpreted by the devil as an invitation to join her in bed. Now in 1646, as the time when the devil would claim her soul drew near, she repented and was drawn to sermons and catechisms, as her minister attested.[49]

The prospect of perdition and its mental turmoil is plain. A Suffolk widow named Susan Marchant confessed that the devil came to her as she sat milking, singing a psalm. He asked what good a psalm might do when she was "a damned creature"—that is, not one of the elect. Accepting his argument, she received three imps that she nursed for twenty-eight years.[50] Mary Becket of Framlingham said the devil "told her her sins weare so great that there no heven for her"; Mary Skipper of Copdock, by contrast, related how after her husband died she was visited by Satan who promised that her debts would be paid and that "he wold carrie her to heaven".[51] Either way, the devil offered escape from damnation. Anne Boreham of Sudbury said she was told "she

---

[47] Ewen, *Witch Hunting*, pp. 304, 306–07; ESRO, FC 101/E2/26.
[48] Davenport, *Witches of Huntingdon*, pp. 9–10.
[49] Ibid., pp. 1–2.
[50] Ewen, *Witch Hunting*, p. 297.
[51] Ibid., pp. 306, 313.

must goe to hell, but should not be tormented".[52] With "a great hollow voyce", three mouse-like familiars asked Joan Ruce of Polstead to deny Christ, she protested that if she did she would lose her soul; they persuaded her, however, that "they were more able to save her soule then God".[53] This was a counsel of despair; but afflicted by price inflation and the doctrine of predestination these women's lives were full of despair, not only that there would be no respite from poverty and loneliness on earth but no reward in heaven either.

IV

Two hundred years after the civil war, Thomas Carlyle wrote optimistically about recovering what he called "the soul of whole Past Time". He recognized that the greatest problem faced by historians is that their subjects are dead. In the written word, however, Carlyle believed could be found not just the dusty bones of narrative but "the articulate audible voice of the Past, when the body and material substance of it has altogether vanished like a dream".[54] This essay has built on Carlyle's optimism about the recovery of an articulate and audible voice—or *voices*—but not in the sense of an intangible national soul or Zeitgeist. Rather, it has concerned expressions of feeling made by humble people, recorded not because they were held in high esteem by society but because of suspicions that they were witches—rebels against God and man. When these people confessed, they spoke not just as subordinates paying lip-service to the ideas of their masters, but as sentient beings with powerful emotions and imaginations to match. In other words, we can detect not just sound and movement, but internal representations of an external social and political world. This might be called consciousness, defined by the mathematician Roger Penrose as "the phenomenon whereby the universe's very existence is made known".[55]

This is a plea for historians to turn up the volume on the voices of the past, not just to enhance our sense of their vital activity, but to

---

[52] Stearne, *Confirmation And Discovery*, p. 32.
[53] Ibid., p. 27.
[54] Thomas Carlyle, *On Heroes, Hero-Worship, and the Heroic in History*, ed. by Michael K. Goldberg (Berkeley: University of Nebraska Press, 1993), p. 138.
[55] Roger Penrose, *The Emperor's New Mind: Concerning Computers, Minds, and the Laws of Physics* (Oxford: Oxford Paperbacks, 1989), 447–48.

appreciate how their minds worked.[56] We need to keep breaking what Robert Darnton once called "the vast silence that has swallowed up most of mankind's thinking".[57] The quest for mentalities can be as futile as its goals are desirable, especially if one chases collective mentalities that may never have existed anyway.[58] Even at parish level what E.P. Thompson called "the ulterior cognitive system of the community" can seem intangible and elusive;[59] and when the spotlight falls on individuals it is hard to avoid the feeling not only that their mentality remains beyond reach but that what we do establish with confidence is unrepresentative.[60] For the inarticulate and illiterate majority, we can only study the records of their words and behaviour in particular situations. Geoffrey Lloyd has termed these "social contexts of communication", arguing that mentalities consist in self-representations and that the meaning of ideas depends upon the historical arenas in which they originated.[61]

Records of crime are well suited to this task, and for historians interested in mentalities witch-trials hold special promise.[62] In recent years experts in this field have played down the direct significance of witchcraft for early modern life—even for early modern criminality—defending their research instead as a means to an end. Witches may have been thin on the ground, but a single event can penetrate inscrutable mysteries of past existence, from attitudes to fertility and

---

[56] Malcolm Gaskill, *Crime and Mentalities in Early Modern England* (Cambridge: Cambridge University Press, 2000).

[57] Robert Darnton, 'Intellectual and Cultural History', in *The Past Before Us*, ed. by Michael Kammen (London: Cornell University Press, 1980), p. 343.

[58] Peter Burke, 'The History of Mentalities in Great Britain', *Tijdschrift voor Geschiedenis*, 93 (1980), 529–40 (pp. 532, 536); Gaskill, *Crime and Mentalities*, pp. 16–17. In general, see: Peter Burke, 'Strengths and Weaknesses of the History of Mentalities', *History of European Ideas*, 7 (1986), pp. 439–51; Michael A. Gismondi, '"The Gift of Theory": A Critique of the *Histoire des Mentalités*', *Social History*, 10 (1985), pp. 211–30.

[59] E.P. Thompson, 'History and Anthropology', in *Persons and Polemics: Historical Essays* (London: The Merlin Press Ltd, 1994), p. 217.

[60] The classic study remains Carlo Ginzburg, *The Cheese and the Worms: The Cosmos of a Sixteenth-Century Miller* (London: Johns Hopkins University Press, 1982).

[61] G.E.R. Lloyd, *Demystifying Mentalities* (Cambridge, Cambridge University Press, 1990). Cf. David Zaret, 'Religion, Science and Printing in the Public Spheres in Seventeenth-Century England', in *Habermas and the Public Sphere*, ed. by Craig Calhoun (Cambridge, MA: MIT Press, 1992), pp. 212–35.

[62] Malcolm Gaskill, 'Mentalities from Crime: Listening to Witnesses in Early Modern England', in *Droit et Societé en France et en Grande-Bretagne XII*-*XX*ᵉ *Siècles*, ed. by Philippe Chassaigne and Jean-Paul Genet (Paris: Publications de la Sorbonne, 2003), pp. 91–101.

ageing, and interpretations of illness and psychosis, to the practices of magistrates and witnesses working within the law yet bending it to their needs.[63] Confessions like those sampled above are particularly interesting because here we see self-representation, however distorted by the influences of interrogators and the medium of the written record. As we have seen, to be convincing as legal proof a witch-confession had to combine theory familiar to inquisitors with homespun detail of malevolence and diabolic intercourse known only to the suspected witch.[64]

To this babel of voices we can add one more. In 1647 Matthew Hopkins published a self-defensive book in which he mimicked the devil addressing his handmaidens: "What will you have me doe for you, my deare and nearest children, covenanted and compacted with me in my hellish league, and sealed with your blood, my delicate firebrand-darlings?"[65] That may not have been the true voice of the devil; but it was the definitely the voice of Hopkins, to the extent that it has been suggested he used ventriloquism to persuade the accused of the devil's proximity.[66] There is no evidence for this; but there is something in the idea that the "hollow voices" mentioned by confessing witches were projected from within, an illusion of hope superimposed onto a reality of depression and desperation. This was the witches' perception, their subjectivity of an intangible world. Hopkins the witchfinder did not create these feelings, but he did expose them and record them. His purpose was to gather evidence that would add authenticity to demonological charges made under the 1604 Witchcraft Act by the inclusion of emotion; in an age of growing intellectual and judicial scepticism, real passions might be taken to mean real witchcraft. After all, witches were like other legal witnesses, telling stories about themselves which,

---

[63] See, for example: Alison Rowlands, 'Witchcraft and Old Women in Early Modern Germany', *Past & Present*, 173 (2001), 50–89; Lyndal Roper, *Oedipus and the Devil: Witchcraft, Sexuality and Religion in Early Modern Europe* (London: Routledge, 1994); David Harley, 'Mental Illness, Magical Medicine and the Devil in Northern England, 1650–1700', in *The Medical Revolution in the Seventeenth Century* ed. by Roger French and Andrew Wear (Cambridge: Cambridge University Press, 1989), pp. 114–44; Malcolm Gaskill, 'Witches and Witnesses in Old and New England', in *Languages of Witchcraft*, (see Clark above), pp. 55–80.

[64] Roper, *Witch Craze*, p. 52.

[65] Matthew Hopkins, *The Discovery of Witches: In Answer to severall Queries Lately Delivered to the Judges of Assize for the County of Norfolk* (London, 1647), pp. 6–8.

[66] Anne Llewellyn Barstow, *Witchcraze: A New History of the European Witch Hunts* (London: HarperCollins, 1994), p. 174.

to quote Laura Gowing, "made sense of certain experiences whose meaning was being questioned by the court".[67]

The women and men who during the civil war revealed that they were witches were extremely unusual members of their society: in the previous sixty years relatively few had even been tried for witchcraft, and the proportion that confessed was tiny. Yet the fantastic fulfilments of their ambitions and daydreams, their hatreds and vendettas, have left a unique record of the emotion and imagination common to a majority of the labouring poor. These were people caught between the medieval morally reflexive universe and the demands of a changing economic world: it was possible to be poorer than ever and yet convinced this was either God's reward for sin or a providential sign of damnation. Either way, the world denied them fortune and heaven denied them grace, and this was not a sustainable mentality for getting through life; something had to give, and in time this shift would lead to a more secularized understanding of the individual's place in a world of hostile market forces.[68] Blame was still levelled and despair was still felt, but feelings of moral weakness and guilt were gradually subtracted from the equation. The day would come when the soul—whether fundamentally corrupt or a blank slate—would surrender to the mind and its malfunctions as the only reasonable focus for scientific study.[69]

Fortunately, the witchfinders of the 1640s were also caught between these two worlds—mysterious, mystical and metaphysical on the one hand, mechanical, logical and empirical on the other—meaning that the type of graphic evidence they extracted in East Anglia, though persuasive in the summer of 1645, would fail in the end as judges made jurors realize that torture did not place a suspect's guilt beyond reasonable doubt. After 1660 cases of witchcraft were still tried at law, and occasionally prisoners in the dock confessed. But increasingly what the court heard in the voices of demons was only the lament of the dispossessed and the distracted, those a sceptical writer in 1651 described as "poor, aged, deformed, ignorant people" who should be treated with food and medicine not persecuted as witches. In this he implied

---

[67] Laura Gowing, *Domestic Dangers: Women, Words and Sex in Early Modern London* (Oxford: Oxford University Press, 1996), p. 235.
[68] Gaskill, *Crime and Mentalities*, ch. 8; C. John Sommerville, *The Secularization of Early Modern England* (Oxford: Oxford University Press, 1992). On moral reflexivity, see Thomas, *Religion and the Decline of Magic*, pp. 106–08, 125–30, 675–76.
[69] Roy Porter, *Flesh in the Age of Reason* (London: Allen Lane, 2003), pp. 26–27.

not just the need to banish injustice, but the idea that society would be better served by humanitarian regard than by furious campaigns against demonianism based solely on the evidence of confessions; these he dismissed as nothing more than "imagining Erronious conceptions and novelties".[70] If only the law would make a stand, this scathing, sensible voice appeared to be saying, then not only would witchcraft prosecutions wither away but so too a whole way of thinking.

---

[70] Reginald Scot, *Discovery of Witchcraft* (London: 1584; 1651 edn), title-page.

PART THREE

THE PASSING OF THE ACT

THE POLITICS OF *PANDAEMONIUM*

Jonathan Barry

Historians of witchcraft have often cited the letter sent by Sir Francis North to Secretary of State Sir Leoline Jenkins (dated 19 August 1682) from the Exeter assizes concerning the trial of the three 'Bideford witches', a trial which also generated several accounts in pamphlets and ballads and widespread contemporary comment. North, one of the two circuit judges (though not the one trying this particular case), wrote that

> I find the country so fully possessed against them, that though some of the virtuosi may think these things the effects of confederacy, melancholy or delusion, and that young folkes are altogether as quicksighted as they who are old and infirme; Yet we cannot reprieve them without appearing to denye the very being of witches, which, as it is contrary to law, so I think it would be ill for his Majestie's service, for it may give the faction occasion to set afoot the old trade of witchfinding that may cost many innocent persons their lives, which this justice will prevent.[1]

By the faction, North meant the Whig party, which was very strong in the South West. In the life of Francis North written by his brother, Roger, these witchcraft cases are discussed immediately after a discussion of how the judge had to act very carefully when watched and tested by the factious. Specifically, he reports North's reprieve, in a Taunton assize case of 1680, of an old woman who claimed to have been tried before during the civil war period. Roger North makes much of his brother's scepticism on such matters, contrasted with the credulity of the juries.[2] Yet, as Sir Francis noted, the law was clear about the reality of witchcraft, and the royal judges could not afford to appear to flout the law lest "the faction" take advantage. The reference to "the old trade of witchfinding" suggests that North at least was conscious of the precedent of Hopkins in the 1640s, and perhaps of the wider upsurge

---

[1] SP Dom C2/420/24, cited in P.Q. Karkeek, 'Devonshire Witches', *Transactions Devonshire Association*, 6 (1874), 736–63 (p. 742).
[2] Roger North, *Life of the Right Honourable Francis North, Baron of Guildford* (London, 1742), pp. 129–32.

of witchcraft prosecutions during the interregnum in areas such as the
south west. The three Bideford witches were thus sacrificed to prevent
broader danger to the monarchy and the state, caught between rival
political factions for whom witchcraft was contested ground.

In considering attitudes to the Act of 1604, and witchcraft more
generally, between the Restoration and 1736, historians have become
increasingly aware of the malleable and conjunctural character of
responses, in the highly complex and rapidly altering ideological contexts
of the period. Both religion and politics in general were dominated by
disputes over the meaning of allegiance to crown, parliament and the
Church of England (or Protestantism more generally), and by how to
respond to the threats to national culture posed by social and cultural
change, seen by many as requiring a 'reformation of manners'. Although
one dimension of this change was often seen as the decay of religion
as a force in public life (as opposed to a spiritual or moral guide), most
people appear to have still held strongly providentialist views, linking
national well-being with God's judgement on the nation. Moreover,
all of these debates took place in an atmosphere of polarization and
conspiracy, in which disputes regarding allegiance and cultural change
were conducted, not through the acceptance of genuine differences
between parties and opinions that could be resolved, but through the
demonization of opposing viewpoints as expressions of faction at best,
and of treason against the state and God at worst. As Bostridge, Elmer
and the present author have shown, in this setting the language and
accusation of witchcraft could be deployed by all sides and in many
different settings.[3]

As North's letter demonstrates, the statute against witchcraft was
itself a potent, yet highly contested, factor in this process. As a law, it
represented the fusion of the authority of both crown (stressed by the
Tory North) and parliament. Its close association with the first of the
Stuarts, and his well-known attack on witchcraft as the ultimate crime
against royal authority in his *Daemonologie*, gave it strong royalist credentials. Yet in practice the Stuart monarchs in England, and most of

---

[3] Ian Bostridge, *Witchcraft and its Transformations c. 1650–1750* (Oxford: Oxford University Press, 1997); Peter Elmer, 'Towards a Politics of Witchcraft in Early Modern
England', in *Languages of Witchcraft*, ed. by Stuart Clark (Basingstoke: Macmillan, 2001),
pp. 101–18; Jonathan Barry, 'Hell upon Earth or the Language of the Playhouse'
in ibid., pp. 139–58. See also the introductions by Peter Elmer and James Sharpe
to volumes 4–6 of *English Witchcraft 1560–1736*, gen. ed. by James Sharpe (London:
Pickering and Chatto, 2003).

their judges and leading clergy, had proved highly suspicious both of the reality of witchcraft in specific cases and, in general, of the potential that witchcraft (especially possession) offered to critics of the established church to claim authority in matters of the spirit. Before 1640, this was a dual struggle against both Roman Catholics and Puritans, but after that it became ever more complex, with the emergence not only of more radical forms of sectarianism (themselves often seen as demonically possessed), but also of the fear of Hobbesian materialism and atheism. For the next seventy-five years, at least, it was far from clear to the establishment where the greatest threat to national security lay. The emergence of Tory and Whig political parties, and the association of each of these (by their opponents) with absolutist popery and republican fanaticism (respectively), with each party struggling to rid itself of these labels and to convince the nation that it could rid the country of atheism and enthusiasm and reform the nation's manners, meant that both the general debate about witchcraft, and specific cases (both trials and reported happenings) became overlaid with ideological readings and meanings.

The aim of this article is to uncover as many of these layers of meaning as possible for a specific text, namely *Pandaemonium, or the Devil's Cloyster* published in 1684, and for the Bovet family of the Somerset/Devon border region who produced the text.[4] Ian Bostridge has already sketched the potential of reading *Pandaemonium* from North's perspective as an example of a writer "with Whig credentials embracing witch theory and with political ends in mind [...] as the cover for an attack on Roman Catholicism", showing that "the iniquities of the Restoration court, and the advance of Popery in the bosom of the English establishment, were, quite literally, diabolical".[5] In so doing, he focuses his account on the first part of the text, rather than the second part, which has normally been seen as the most interesting part of the volume. This part "giving plain Evidence concerning Apparitions, Spirits and Witches, proving by a Choice Collection of Modern Relations (never yet Published) their real Existence" consists of fifteen cases either from Bovet's locality and own experience or sent to him by friends (in Scotland, mostly) and several of these (regarding fairies and ghosts) have

---

[4] For ease of reference I will use the modern edition, with introduction and notes by Montague Summers, published by Hand and Flower Press, Aldington, Kent in 1951. The original editions are discussed below.

[5] Bostridge, *Witchcraft*, p. 90.

become standard parts of the repertoire of supernatural stories. Russell Hope Robbins dismisses the first part as "unoriginal comment on witchcraft, violently anti-papist, some borrowed from Glanvill and the rest from the mystical theology of the unreliable Daniel Brevint", but considers that "the second part, however, contains fifteen quite amusing ghost stories (including Poltergeists) [...] In collecting such stories from his friends, Bovet shows the contemporary interest in experimental philosophy, in common with Dr Henry More (to whom the book is dedicated) and Glanvill".[6] Most other historians have echoed this last point, seeing Bovet as a follower or colleague of Joseph Glanvill, Henry More and the Scotsman George Sinclair, all publishing in the period 1681–5. Jo Bath and John Newton, for example, regard Bovet's subtitle (in the Walthoe edition, see below) "being a further Blow to Modern Sadduceism, proving the Existence of Witches and Spirits" as showing "that he was self-consciously following in [Glanvill's] footsteps".[7] Only the eccentric Montague Summers, who republished the text in 1951, has used both parts of his work, citing him uncritically in his *Witchcraft and Black Magic* both as a serious demonologist and as a source of specific cases.[8] However, Summers treats Bovet as schizophrenic—contrasting his "religious eccentricities" with the "plain and practical" work of the "absolutely unmystical" Bovet as "an investigator of psychic phenomena". He even argues that "in one sense and in a very real way, the religious bias and prejudice of the author lend a certain weight to his pages. His eccentricities, although harsh enough and foolish, today we can set aside. His 'Relations' bear the hall-mark of truth".[9] I shall argue that this completely inverts Bovet's own order of priority.

To understand Bovet's text in its entirety, we need to understand the relationship between its two parts, and what relationship it actually bears to the work of Glanvill and More. We also need to consider its title, borrowed from the court of the fallen angels in Milton's *Paradise Lost*.

---

[6] Russell Hope Robbins, *The Encyclopedia of Witchcraft and Demonology* (New York: Crown, 1959), p. 59.
[7] Jo Bath and John Newton, '"Sensible Proof of Spirits": Ghost Belief during the Later Seventeenth Century', *Folklore*, 117 (2006), 1–14 (pp. 4–5). Cf. James Sharpe, *Instruments of Darkness* (London: Hamish Hamilton, 1996), p. 266; Gillian Bennett, 'Ghost and Witch in the Sixteenth and Seventeenth Centuries', *Folklore*, 97 (1986), 3–14 (pp. 10–11).
[8] Montague Summers, *Witchcraft and Black Magic* (London: Studio Editions, 1995), pp. 18, 35, 98, 103, 200–01, 203.
[9] Introduction to Bovet, *Pandaemonium*, pp. xvii and xx.

We need to understand the two slightly different editions of the text, and their relationship to a pamphlet on one of the cases in part two, the "Daemon of Spraiton" (Spreyton near Okehampton in Devon), which Bovet had published the previous year, and how his handling of this case in each publication compares with the account of it which John Aubrey received from his Somerset correspondent, Andrew Paschall. We also need to understand how this text fits in with the experiences of the Bovet family in the second half of the seventeenth century, including the radical lives and deaths of Richard and Philip Bovet in civil war, under republican and Restoration regimes and finally in Monmouth's rebellion of 1685, and the participation of other Bovets in one of the last cases of witchcraft tried at Exeter, in 1696. This case brings home the question of whether we can or should separate the use of witchcraft as an ideological weapon against political and religious enemies, from its place in shaping the fears of families faced with everyday misfortune and tragedy, and their legal actions against their neighbours within the framework of the law. Ironically, these Bovets found themselves up against another royal judge, Sir John Holt, who was even more determined than North to use suspicion of fraud and sarcasm about the evidence to undermine the possibility of prosecution under the act of 1604. Holt passed on his notes about this and other late trials to Francis Hutchinson for his *Historical Essay concerning Witchcraft* of 1718, after which Whigs generally adopted the attitude which lay behind the new Witchcraft Act of 1736, in which the threat to the state from witchcraft was authoritatively declared no longer to be the actions of demons, but the frauds of conspiring humans and the credulity of the vulgar.

* * *

Bovet's text has normally been identified as part of the campaign to defend the existence of the world of spirits, and hence the truths of the Christian religion, against 'sadducism', revived in the form of Hobbesian materialism and fashionable scepticism. The two central figures in this campaign were Joseph Glanvill (Rector of Bath) and Henry More (of Christ's College, Cambridge), with the key work being Glanvill's 1681 *Saducismus Triumphatus*, which was More's edition of the revised and expanded version of Glanvill's earlier writings on this subject, left unfinished at his death in 1680. At the core of Glanvill's text were the details of a series of Somerset witchcraft cases from the period 1657–1664, given to him by the Somerset JP Robert Hunt, plus his own experience of the Wiltshire poltergeist case at the time attributed to witchcraft, which is generally known as the 'Drummer of Tedworth'.[10] Glanvill corresponded regularly with More, and took from More's 1653 text, *An Antidote against Atheisme*, the characteristic mixture in all these books of theological debate with detailed accounts of specific cases of the preternatural observed first-hand by the author or his trusted correspondents. Given that Bovet was also from Somerset, and drew his cases largely from that county and its close neighbours, and organised his book in a similar fashion, it is hardly surprising that his work has been seen as a minor contribution to the same tradition.

Indeed, Bovet goes to some lengths to encourage the reader to consider his book in this light. *Pandaemonium* is dedicated to More, praising "with what irrefragable reason you have opposed and vanquish't the legions of atheistical and disbelieving pretenders who seem to be incredulous of discourses of the existence of spirits and their attempts upon lapsed and degenerate men".[11] Bovet claims to be taking up the invitation in *Saducismus Triumphatus* "to contribute all I could to the asserting the reality of spiritual existencies [*sic*] and, by consequence, the advantages such subtle agents have to surprise the unwary and entrap the negligent disbeliever in inextricable snares; whil'st they who shut their eyes against the belief of daemons are imperceptibly hurried by them upon the unavoidable principles of sensuality and impenitence".[12] Later he attacks "the bold confidence of some of these Witch advocates that they durst affront that Relation of the Daemon of Tedworth, published by the Ingenious Mr Glanvil, and Attested by Mr Mompesson, a Gentleman, and a Divine, who (to all that knew them) were never over fond of crediting stories of this kind".[13] At the end of chapter five, before turning to the relations of witches, Bovet states "that atheism, idolatry, sensuality, and debauchery, have a natural tendence [*sic*] to promote this impious and diabolical confederacy, hath been hinted in the forgoing pages. Which being so regularly, learnedly and largely treated of by the excellent pens of Dr H.M. and Mr J.G. before mentioned, in the second part of *Saducismus Triumphatus*; I shall presume

---

[10] Michael Hunter, 'New Light on the "Drummer of Tedworth"', *Historical Research*, 78 (2005), 311–53, is the most recent contribution on Glanvill, More and their work.

[11] Bovet, *Pandaemonium*, p. xxiii.

[12] Ibid., p. xxiv.

[13] Ibid., p. 37.

to wade no further in the argumentative and philosophical part". Bovet also compares his cases with those in *Saducismus Triumphatus*.[14]

A Narrative of the Demon of Spraiton, edited by Bovet in 1683, is even more emphatic in its attack on "your Hobbs's, your Scots, your Websters, with their blasphemous denyals of the existence of spirits, or an eternal state in the life to come. Or how can they that deny the being of spirits suppose that there is such a thing in the world as a God? Here is one Account more of matter of fact, to those which the learned Doctor Moore, the ingenious Dr Glanvill (with divers others, the assertors of divine providence, and an eternal state) have printed in confutation of your brutish stupidity; which one would think were enough for ever to silence and confound the advocates of debauchery and sadducism and reduce their arguments into that nullity they contend for".[15] It continues "we have not room in this place to enter into a disquisition of the nature of the apparitions hereafter mentioned; but shall for that refer the reader to the learned discourses of the reverend Dr Henry Moore and the ingenious Dr Glanvill, before mentioned, who have largely treated of the nature of spirits and daemons and with undenyable arguments proved the existence of such".[16]

However, there is no evidence in any other sources that Bovet was known to Glanvill, despite their proximity, and he admits that he is dedicating his book to More despite being a "stranger" to him. Apologising for his "unpolisht" discourse, Bovet describes it as "common prudence to list myself under the banner of so victorious a chieftain" and, anticipating attacks for his work, he claims to "have this farther incouragement, that I have not only ingaged in a good design, but have put myself under the umbrage of so great a patron, that there can be no apprehensions of dangers from the attacks of the modern sadduces upon, sir, your assured humble servant R.B.".[17] This suggests that the appeal to the More/Glanvill tradition is more a defensive mechanism than an acknowledgement of authority. It is also worth noting that Bovet, while not neglecting the theological dimension of 'sadducism', emphasises the degeneracy, sensualism and debauchery which are indelibly associated with it. This reflects the very distinctive character of the first part of his text, which offers, in the words of the title-page of the

---

[14] Ibid., pp. 57–58, 103, 113, 124.
[15] *A Narrative of the Demon of Spraiton* (London, 1683), pp. 1–2.
[16] Ibid., pp. 3–4.
[17] Bovet, *Pandaemonium*, pp. xxiii and xxvii.

Walthoe edition "a discourse deduced from the fall of the angels, the propagation of Satans kingdom before the Flood: the idolatry of the ages after, greatly advancing diabolical confederacies. With an Account of the lives and transactions of several notorious witches", which the other title-page identifies as "confederacies of several Popes and Roman priests with the Devil".[18] Bovet's dedication anticipates that "some, perhaps, may be offended at the method I have used in attributing to priestcraft, so much of the original and contagion of diabolical confederacy".[19] It is doubtful if the Anglican clergymen and apologists Glanvill and More would have approved of this strategy which, if it claimed to be attacking Hobbesian scepticism, seemed to reproduce much of the anticlericalism which underlay both Hobbes's own writings and the use made of them by both radical Whigs and court wits.

Furthermore, Bovet was very clear that the first part of his text took precedence over the second. Both title-pages privilege the first part, and Bovet notes that "the collection of relations may by some be blamed for being too short, many delighting themselves more with novelty of story then to enquire, and pursue the drift of the design; to these I can only say, that being confined to such a volume, there was not room for more, tho [sic] many might have been added, which perhaps may be the subject of another volume; besides I could not without detriment to the whole have omitted anything contained in the first part, wherein I fear I have rather been too concise".[20] If one compares the "collection of relations" in the second part with More or Glanvill's publications, Bovet's can be seen to be highly sketchy, with fifteen cases related in forty-two pages of the modern edition (compared to ninety-seven pages for the first part), with the longest being the case of the "demon of Spraiton", in a slightly amended version to that published in pamphlet form the year before. Although Bovet presents this collection in the empirical tradition of the Royal Society, hoping "some sober and ingenious persons would undertake but to commend to the publick the occurrences of this nature in every county",[21] his language quoted above emphasizes the subordination of the factual details to the "drift of the design", and indeed denigrates the desire

---

[18] Ibid., p. xxi reproduces the Walthoe edition title page. The Malthus title page is on p. vi.
[19] Ibid. pp. xxiv–v.
[20] Ibid., p. xxvi.
[21] Ibid., p. 99.

for more detail, not as the product of scientific interest but of delight in the "novelty of story".

If we are looking for a true inspiration for Bovet's work, a more likely answer is given by his title, borrowed from the name given to the court of the fallen angels in Milton's *Paradise Lost*. We are now so used to the word Pandaemonium that we tend to forget both its original meaning (literally an all-demon-assembly) and that it was a word coined by Milton: indeed the *Oxford English Dictionary* records no further usages of the term until the 1690s.[22] In 1691 John Wilson's *Belphegor, or, The Marriage of the Devil* begins with the reading of a paper dated "At the Pandaemonium, or Common-Council of the Infernal". Bovet acknowledges his use of Milton when discussing the spread of idolatry among the Israelites; "nay, there was not any detestable idol among the heathens, though never so bloody and diabolical, which did not at some time or other obtain for a Deity among the hardned [*sic*] and back-sliding Jews. A list of which is excellently drawn up by the pen of the learned and profound Mr John Milton in his Paradice lost [*sic*]".[23] Reading Milton's poem as a historical account of the interdependence of diabolism and idolatry, Bovet can clearly be seen as part of the radical tradition of reading Milton which was obscured by its absorption into the mainstream of literary culture in the eighteenth century.[24]

There is no direct evidence that Bovet knew Milton except through his work, but one of Bovet's accounts in his second part suggests that he may have done. The eighth and twelfth accounts both refer to a "nobleman's house in the West of England, which had formerly been a

---

[22] For the name see R. Smith, 'The Sources of Milton's Pandaemonium', *Modern Philology*, 29 (1931), pp. 187–98 (which argues that Milton may have based his image on his memory of St Peter's in Rome) and *Poems of John Milton*, ed. by John Carey and Alastair Fowler (Harlow: Longmans, 1968), p. 505, which notes a possible precursor in Henry More's use of 'Pandaemoniothon' in his writings.

[23] Bovet, *Pandaemonium*, p. 9.

[24] For studies of Milton's early reception see R.C. King, 'Andrew Marvell', *Milton Studies*, 27 (1991), 165–82; Joseph Wittreich, 'Under the Seal of Silence', in *Soundings of Things Done*, ed. by Peter Medine and Joseph Wittreich (London: Associated University Presses, 1997), pp. 295–323; Barbara Liewalski, '*Paradise Lost* and Milton's Politics', *Milton Studies*, 38 (2000), 141–68 and especially Nicholas von Maltzahn, 'First Reception of *Paradise Lost* (1667)', *Review of English Studies*, 47 (1996), 479–99 and id., 'Laureate, Republican, Calvinist', *Milton Studies*, 29 (1992), pp. 181–98, which considers the responses of another Somerset man, the royalist natural philosopher John Beale. A recent study emphasising Milton's attack on idolatry is Achsah Guibbory, *Ceremony and Community from Herbert to Milton* (New York: Cambridge University Press, 1998), pp. 187–227, especially pp. 193–98.

Nunnery".[25] The only house which clearly fits this description is Wilton House, the home of the Earls of Pembroke. In 1667, when Bovet tells us he was staying there "with some persons of honour" and ended up sharing a room with "the Noblemans steward, Mr C", the Earl in question was the fifth Earl, Philip Herbert. Philip had been a Parliamentarian and President of the Council of State in the early 1650s, although he survived the Restoration. He had a reputation as a chemist and Behmenist and, at the very least, a sympathizer with Quakerism, and in 1665 braved the Restoration Court to warn Charles II that the end of the world would come that year (to which Charles responded by offering to buy Wilton House for seven years' purchase, since the Earl did not anticipate enjoying it for long!).[26] During the 1660s the Earl employed the radical Behmenist Samuel Pordage as his steward (presumably not 'Mr C'?) and the tutor to his children between 1665 and 1670 was Milton's nephew, pupil and literary heir, Edward Phillips.[27] If Bovet was indeed a regular guest at Wilton in 1667, which was the year when *Paradise Lost* was published, he must have known both Phillips and Pordage, and perhaps met Milton: certainly he would have been encouraged to see Milton through the lens of radical dissenting republicanism.

Bovet's other acknowledged source is Daniel Brevint, Dean of Lincoln. He admits that he has chosen "to make use of the allegations of the learned Dr Brevint" who "had the advantages of being both an eye and ear-witness of the detestable idolatries of the Roman Church, by being so long in Italy amongst them".[28] Summers and Robbins have identified the close use of Brevint's work in the first part of Bovet's text, but he may also have borrowed from Brevint the idea of using a text apparently about witchcraft to attack the idolatry of the Roman

---

[25] Bovet, *Pandaemonium*, pp. 121, 132.
[26] David Masson, *Life of John Milton*, 7 vols (New York: P. Smith, 1946), VI: *1660–1674*, pp. 763–64; Stephen Pincus, *Protestantism and Patriotism* (Cambridge: Cambridge University Press, 1996), p. 52; Samuel Pepys, *Diary*, ed. by Robert Latham and William Matthews, 11 vols (London: Bell & Hyman, 1970–83), V, p. 294 and IX, pp. 150–51 (and notes); *HMC 78 Hastings II*, pp. 150–51.
[27] Nigel Smith, 'Pordage, Samuel (*bap.* 1633, *d.* in or after 1691)', *Oxford Dictionary of National Biography*, Oxford University Press, 2004 <http://www.oxforddnb.com/view/article/22547> [accessed 31/05/2006]; Gordon Campbell, 'Phillips, Edward (*b.* 1630, *d.* in or after 1696)', *Oxford Dictionary of National Biography*, Oxford University Press, 2004 <http://www.oxforddnb.com/view/article/22148> [accessed 31/05/2006].
[28] Bovet, *Pandaemonium*, p. xxv.

Catholic Church.[29] Despite its title, Brevint's 1674 work, which Bovet used, *Saul and Samuel at Endor, or, The new waies of salvation and service, which usually temt [sic] men to Rome and detain them there truly represented and refuted*, actually contains nothing about the witch of Endor. Brevint's work also formed the source for much of the material in another work which may have influenced Bovet more directly, since it was published in London in 1683 by Thomas Malthus, with a preface by Titus Oates, namely Christopher Ness's, *The Devils Patriarck, or, A full and impartial account of the notorious life of this present Pope of Rome Innocent the 11th wherein is newly discovered his rise and reign, the time and manner of his being chosen Pope, his prime procession, consecration and coronation, the splendour and grandeur of his Court, his most eminent and gainful cheats, by which he gulls the silly people, his secret and open transactions with the papists in England, Scotland, France and Ireland, and other Protestant countreys to this very day: together with the rest of the hellish policies and infamous actions of his wicked life/written by an eminent pen to revive the remembrance of the almost forgotten plot against the life of his Sacred Majesty and the Protestant religion*. Here again we have the association of diabolism with popery, set in the context of priestcraft, plots and hellish policies. Like most publications of this period, this can only be understood in the context of the Popish Plot and its aftermath, with 1682–83 seeing the highpoint of the press struggle to define whether the greatest threat to the country came from Popery or from Whiggery. The prosecution of the Rye House plotters and the full force of the Tory reaction over the next two years, up to James's succession to the throne and Monmouth's rebellion, drove much of this press controversy underground.

It is in this context that we may be able to understand the curious publishing history of Bovet's text. It survives in two editions, whose texts are apparently identical, but with different title pages and publishers. One was printed for "Tho. Malthus at the Sun in the Poultry", while the second was printed for "J. Walthoe, at the Black Lion, Chancery Lane, over against Lincoln's Inn". The Malthus title page gives the title simply as "Pandaemonium or the Devil's Cloyster, in Two parts" and then gives in full the chapter headings of part I, before describing part II as "giving plain evidence concerning apparitions, spirits and witches; proving by a choice collection of modern relations (never yet published) their real existence". The Walthoe edition has the subtitle, "being a further blow to modern sadduceism, proving the existence

---

[29] Ibid., pp. xvi–xviii; Robbins, *Encyclopedia*, p. 59.

of witches and spirits", before giving the details of the "discourse" quoted above, and then "also, a collection of several authentick relations of strange apparitions of daemons and spectres, and fascinations of witches, never before printed". The Michaelmas 1684 edition of the *Term Catalogue* (under 'Miscellanies') gives a further variant of the title, identical to Walthoe's except that it replaces "an account of the lives and transactions of several notorious witches" with "an account of the lives of several notorious witches, some whereof have been popes". No publisher is given for the work here, but the next item was an edition of Lucan's works sold by Malthus.[30] It appears that, as I have suggested was the case within the text, there was an ongoing tension about whether this book was primarily to be identified as an anti-papal or an anti-sadducist work.

The publishing careers of Malthus and Walthoe may suggest that this reflected two potentially different markets for the work. *Pandaemonium* was not their only collaboration, and they both also co-published with D. Brown, who combined with Malthus to publish *A Narrative of the Demon of Spraiton* in 1683. Walthoe was a newly established bookseller, whose location in Chancery Lane reflected the start of a long career marked by a focus on law publishing, with no obvious ideological bent.[31] Malthus, on the other hand, although his career had also begun only in 1682, had a highly active record in 1683 and 1684, then just two publications in 1685, when he disappears from the record. John Dunton (who printed works for Malthus, including *The Devils Patriarck*) last remembered seeing him leaving for Holland in a hurry in 1685, "his circumstances being something perplexed".[32] This must surely be a euphemistic way of describing the flight into Dutch exile which many Whig radicals (such as John Locke) made in 1684–85, some returning with Monmouth, others not until 1688. Dunton noted that Malthus "midwifed several books into the world, ay! And that of his own conceiving (without help of woman). He made a shew of great trade by continually sending out large parcels, But all I can say of his industry is, He took a great deal of pains to ruine himself".[33] Many, though not all,

---

[30] Edward Arber, *The Term Catalogues, 1668–1709*, 3 vols (London: The Editor, 1903–06), II, p. 102.

[31] Henry Plomer, *Dictionary of Booksellers and Printers 1668–1725* (London: Bibliographical Society, 1922), pp. 300–01; John Dunton, *Life and Errors of John Dunton* (New York and London: Garland Publishing, 1974), pp. 284–85.

[32] Plomer, *Dictionary*, p. 196.

[33] Dunton, *Life*, p. 297.

of his publications in 1683–84 were Whig in sympathy, including works praising the Duke of Monmouth and the Earl of Shaftesbury, Dutch and Scottish publications and other anti-papal texts, and none were Tory or Anglican. In June 1683 the *Term Catalogue* advertised another Malthus publication entitled *A Whip for the Devil, or the Roman Conjurer*, which was a swingeing attack on "the folly, prophaneness and superstition of the papists in endeavouring to cast the Devil out of the bodies of men and women".[34] One might plausibly conclude that Malthus published Bovet as part of a body of work which used the sensational theme of witchcraft to sell to fellow Whigs a diet of anti-papal diatribes, but ones which, from 1683 onwards, were best disguised as fitting a moral and religious agenda which had the protective respectability of Anglican clergy such as More, and could be published, in that setting, by men such as Walthoe.

It is interesting, in this respect, to consider more closely the story of the "demon of Spraiton", which Bovet had published the previous year, and how his handling of the case in each publication compares with an account of the same events which circulated among the real colleagues of Glanvill and More. This was later published by John Aubrey, from a letter received in May or early June 1683 from his Somerset correspondent, Andrew Paschall.[35] The story involved the appearance of various spectres to members of the Furze household, notably a young male servant, with increasingly violent attacks on his body, which was also carried into the air and around the countryside, ending with a bird attacking him with a metal weight while he was in Crediton. Both accounts refer to a "person of quality" and a clergyman as witnesses to the events. Bovet names the former, who wrote the letter of 11 May to a "gentleman his friend in London" (presumably Bovet) which formed the basis of the pamphlet, as "T.C. esq a near neighbour to the place", and this is probably one of the numerous members of the Cary family of Devon and Somerset. He continues "and though it needed little confirmation further than the credit that the learning and quality of that gentleman had stampt upon it, yet was much of it likewise known to and related by the Reverend Minister

[34] Arber, *Term Catalogues*, II, p. 33.
[35] John Aubrey, *Three Prose Works*, ed. by John Buchanan-Brown (Fontwell: Centaur Press, 1972), pp. 90–94.

of Barnstable, of the vicinity to Spraiton".[36] The clergyman to whom
Bovet referred, and who was the author of the letter to Paschall which
he then forwarded to Aubrey, was John Boyse, who also held a living
at Cheriton Bishop, near Spreyton. Paschall expected Aubrey to pass
on the account to Henry More via Benjamin Whichcote in Cambridge
and also, intriguingly, expected Sir Francis North to find it of interest.
More did not use this material in the later editions of *Saducismus Triumphatus* but did use Paschall's account of the haunting of his father's
house in Soper Lane.[37] With the thoroughness of a fellow of the Royal
Society, Paschall sought corroboration of the details of the story from
another local clergyman, who had also spoken "with a gentleman of
good fashion that was at Crediton when Fry was blooded and saw the
stone that bruised his forehead, but he did not call it copper or brass
but said it was a strange mineral. That gentleman promises to make a
strict enquiry on the place into all particulars and to give me the result;
which my friend also promises me, with hopes that he shall procure for
me a piece of that mineral substance which hurt his fore-head".[38]

John Boyse, was, like Paschall, a former fellow of Queens' College,
Cambridge, now holding a living in the west country but still in intellectual contact with Anglican antiquarian and scientific circles. Paschall
also refers to an earlier episode concerning an apparition in Barnstaple
where "An account was given to me long since [by Boyse], it fills a sheet
or two, which I have by me; And to gratifie Mr Glanvill, who is collecting histories for his Sadducism Triumphatus, I desir'd to have it well
attested, it being full of very memorable things, but it seems he could
meet only a general consent as to the truth of the things; the reports
varying in the circumstances". In May 1686, shortly before his death,
Boyse was to write to Paschall again regarding "new feats played by
invisible powers in his own parsonage house in the countrey".[39]

There is not space here to make a detailed comparison of the three
accounts of the same event. Although Bovet in 1684 justifies reprinting
his earlier work, "having likewise since had fresh testimonials of the
veracity of that relation; and it being at first designed to fill this place;

[36] Bovet, *Pandaemonium*, p. 107.
[37] Aubrey, *Three Prose Works*, pp. 389–90.
[38] Ibid., p. 93.
[39] Ibid., pp. 93–4, 389–91; A.J. Turner, 'Paschall, Andrew (1631?–1696)', *Oxford
Dictionary of National Biography*, (Oxford: Oxford University Press, 2004) <http://www.
oxforddnb.com/view/article/58459> [Accessed 31/05/06].

I have thought it not amiss (for the strangeness of it) to print it here a second time, exactly as I had transcribed it then", in fact there are minor textual variations.[40] There are also minor differences in the information provided between the Bovet and Boyse versions, mostly reflecting the different viewpoint of the relators. The Boyse letter provides names and further details on the relationships between the parties, reflecting its status as a private letter rather than a public document. The crucial difference, however, comes at the end. Whereas the pamphlet ends by stressing that it is a faithful account of the original letter, "the truth of which will be attested not only by divers persons of quality in this city, but upon inquiry in the adjacent county will be confirmed beyond all exception", Boyse concludes his letter by adding details of several other afflicted people caught up in the same episode, and adds. "Indeed Sir you may wonder that I have not visited that house and the poor afflicted people, especially since I was so near and passed by the very door, But besides that, they have called to their assistance none but Nonconforming ministers, I was not qualified to be welcome there, having given Mr Furze a great deal of trouble the last year about a conventicle in his house, where one of this parish was the preacher. But I am very well assured of the truth of what I have written, and (as more appears) you shall hear from me again".[41] Even though Bovet's 1684 version promises "fresh testimonials", it offers no updating of the May letter, and indeed ends "whether the young man be yet alive, I can have no certain account. I leave the reader to consider of the extraordinary strangeness of the relation".[42]

In short, Bovet's account is, even in his longest case study, lacking in any real depth of interest in the story related, except as a source of wonder. Furthermore, both Bovet accounts omit the crucial information that the incident takes place in a Nonconformist house with Noncon-formist ministers involved, as well as Anglican ones. Glanvill and More, and their fellow Anglican clergy like Paschall and Boyse, were seeking to walk a line between popery and Nonconformist enthusiasm and using witchcraft and the spirit world to vindicate Anglicanism against both threats. Can we see Bovet as treading the same tightrope? No. His texts are unequivocally aimed against Catholicism, with no parallel attack

---

[40] Bovet, *Pandaemonium*, p. 107.
[41] *Narrative of Demon*, p. 8; Aubrey, *Three Prose Works*, p. 93.
[42] Bovet, *Pandaemonium*, pp. 112–13.

on any form of Protestant dissent. *Pandaemonium* offers, as Bostridge
rightly saw, a devastating contrast between the evils of the Restoration
regime and the virtues of the period before the Fall, which it is hard
not to read as the period of the "good old cause" of republicanism. At
issue here were both morality and religiosity—a simultaneous critique
of decadence and licentiousness which both created and reflected a
lack of proper religion, and of a form of religion which was idolatry
and priestcraft not true faith. Both these facets reflected the role of
the Devil in inciting such corruption—forms of both behaviour and
worship which he created and which led to his worship in place of
that of God.

Both the pamphlet and the book are obsessed with the "bestial
sensualities" which would inevitably follow lack of belief in spirits or
a future life, leading to an 'eat, drink and be merry' culture "whilst
with torrents of intemperate and libidinous debauches they overwhelm
their pampered and deluded selves in an eternal gulph of inextricable
misery".[43] This world of licentiousness is seen as the product of con-
stant falls from grace, in which the devil strives to "seduce and draw
off the subjects of the Almighty from their allegiance to their sovereign
creator" and "bring them into an estate of vassalage and subject to
his infernal power".[44] One form that this takes is the explicit compact
with the devil made by witches, or what he calls "those homages, offices
and oblations made him by his miscreant haggs [*sic*] and confederates
in their nocturnal cabals and night-revels".[45] But the language of this
extract makes clear that such witchcraft presents itself to Bovet as a form
of a much wider tendency to false worship, confederacy and revelling
which all amount to the "worshipping that abomination", whether in
pagan form or "in temples and pompous ceremonies". Throughout the
ages Bovet portrays a cosmic battle between a "righteous seed" and
those "still held captive in the chains of his diabolical enchantments
and fascinations, notwithstanding the dreadful and terrible judgments
of the Almighty".[46] The Israelites "had no temple erected to his infernal worship, but still he reign'd among atheistical priests, debauched
courts and wanton cities" nor "are the streets of Christian cities free,
but rather too shamefully infected with the filthy riots of these lewd

---

[43] *Narrative of Demon*, p. 2.
[44] Bovet, *Pandaemonium*, p. 1.
[45] Ibid., p. xxv.
[46] Ibid., pp. 5, 7.

night ramblers: whose shameless abominations (if not soon suppressed) will doubtless bring us under an amazing and tremendous desolation". "If the back-slidings of the Jews cost them so dear, what may we think will become of apostate Christians?" In pre-Christian times, this saw "the first National Church of the Jews perverted to the abominations of the Gentiles".[47] But worse was to come, as "the idolatrous papists of later date have been and are the great promoters of this infernal and accursed defection…the great encouragers of Demonolatry as well as Idolatry" for "idol priest-craft [i.e. the Roman Catholic clergy] and devil-worship are inseparable dependants one upon the other".[48] Papal apostasy from "primitive simplicity" involved one long series of confederacies with the Devil leading to "an adoration of images, altars and relicks". "Still the old confederacy is kept up, tho [*sic*] under new forms and notions. And perhaps it is none of the smallest policies of the agents of that communion to impose upon their credulous ones the belief that there is no such thing as a witch, so that their performances of that kind may the better pass under the notion of a miracle".[49]

Bovet's account of witchcraft itself is highly unoriginal and could have been written by any seventeenth-century English Protestant. It condemns the full Biblical range of soothsayers, charmers, sorcerers and magicians, as well as witches both black and white.[50] Given the power of the gospel, "in those countries where there is least idolatry and where the sincere preaching of the word of power is countenanced, there it is very rare comparatively to meet with instances of the Satanical craft and power".[51] Witchcraft appeals to the ignorant, the malicious and especially the superstitious "for they often become witches, by endeavouring to defend themselves against witchcraft", but others "take up the use of magical forms and simples by tradition".[52] He condemns the use of conjuring books and most judicial astrology, but notes that the latter, if kept "within the modest directions of natural speculation" can be lawful and useful. Similarly, there can be lawful divination, as God can give true knowledge of the future "to such as truly fear him and call upon his name", such as "the changes that may happen either to

---

[47] Ibid., pp. 12–13.
[48] Ibid., pp. 20–21, 68.
[49] Ibid., pp. 72, 97.
[50] Ibid., pp. 16–19.
[51] Ibid., p. 42.
[52] Ibid., pp. 53–54.

his Church in general or to particular countries, families or persons".
"Approaching calamities" "often shew themselves to us either in aerial
or other prodigies", for example "the dreadful desolations that happened in Germany and in England in the late unnatural warrs [*sic*]
(which whether or no they were presaged by them, yet certainly had
many tremendous apparitions in the air and on the earth etc before
those calamities broke forth among them)".[53]

The witch is "commonly understood" as "a female agent or patient,
who is become in covenant with the Devil, having in a literal sense
sold her selfe to work wickedness, such whose chief negotiation tends
to the spoiling their neighbours persons or goods".[54] Bovet describes the
witch's relationship to the Devil in terms of prostitution ("those hellish
compacts therefore are managed like the filthy intrigues betwixt a forni-
cator and his strumpet").[55] But because "it is very difficult to prove such
and such a one to be a witch" "it ought to be done with the greatest
caution and tenderness imaginable". Some "may have been unjustly
accused for witches; either by ignorance of causes meerly [*sic*] natural
or misapplying causes that in themselves are supernatural" especially
given the possible effects of the imagination. But "even if it be supposed
that some have been suspected for witches, barely for having deformed
bodies, ill aspects of melancholy constitutions", this does not disprove
the existence of witches.[56] That witches are "commonly of the female
sex" is explained by their Eve-like qualities, and "it has been a long
time observed" that women excel in both virtue and wickedness.[57]

There is no sense in Bovet's book that he is seeking to stir up the
prosecution of witches, but in his commentaries on the cases in the
second part, he is relatively quick to identify a witch at work. In
the first case (a 1683 report from Bristol of a case *c*. 1638) although
"there be no mention made of any suspected witch, by whose power the
aforesaid children were reduced to that deplorable state, and some of
the physicians that administered to them were of the common opinion
that there was nothing of fascination on the case, but that was purely
the effect of a natural distemper, I must crave their pardon if I dissent from them". Many of the features of the case were preternatural

---

[53] Ibid., pp. 55–57.
[54] Ibid., p. 19.
[55] Ibid., p. 48.
[56] Ibid., pp. 47–49.
[57] Ibid., p. 51.

(unnaturally powerful convulsions, levitation, vomiting of pins and sudden recovery) and revealed "the cloven-foot of fascination" and the omission of any reference to a witch appearing to the children might just be because no account survived of that particular, or "the confederate agency might purposefully avoid shewing any personal figure to them, lest the relations upon such notice should detect and prosecute the peccant party".[58] In the fifth case, a Somerset one, the "suspected agent" was a "woman that had been of ill fame among the neighbours and suspected of divers ill practices", and problems began when she was refused the loan of some small change. A "great toad" and seven "vast large" cats appeared, and the fits of the afflicted mother and son involved vomiting pins and needles. The mother saw the witch and got her husband to cut at it with his sword, and "that party had a lame hand for a considerable time after", though the "supposed malevolent" lived about five years after the afflicted. Bovet notes "I do not understand for all this any Justice was applyed to, but many Physicians who all agreed it to be notorious witchcraft".[59] Two of the Scottish cases also involved witches, although only the first, the 1678 case of Sir George Maxwell of Pollock, had led to an actual prosecution.[60]

However, there is no sign in Bovet's volume of the elaborate confessions of Sabbaths and other dealings with the Devil found in the Somerset cases published by Glanvill or in the writings of Hopkins and Stearne. Bovet's witch stories could have appeared in any of the maleficial and possession pamphlets published during the previous century. The "nocturnal cabals and night-revels" of the dedication, or the elaborate idolatrous worship of the Devil of the first part, are conspicuously absent, as is any direct role for the Devil. One other case involves a falconer "raising the Devil" by reading a book at night, but the Devil is called a "frightful goblin" and it is far from clear what took place or how seriously it is meant to be taken.[61] Another case, in which some maids hope to see their future husbands on Midsummer's Eve night, leads Bovet to discuss "magical days and seasons", noting the Devil's "aversion to the light" and concluding that "most probable

---

[58] Ibid., pp. 102–03.

[59] Ibid., pp. 114–17.

[60] Ibid., pp. 134–8. See Michael Hunter, *The Occult Laboratory* (Woodbridge: Boydell and Brewer, 2001) p. 3 for the widespread interest in the Maxwell case, which appears in both *Saducismus Triumphatus* and George Sinclair's *Invisible World Discovered*, making it the only case in Bovet that also appears in both these other volumes.

[61] Bovet, *Pandaemonium*, pp. 118–19.

this appointing of times, and hours, is of the Devils own institution, as well as the fast, that having once ensnared people to an obedience to his rules, he may with more facility oblige them to a stricter vassalage", but he leaves the "learned to judge" whether the "appearances were the spirits of two young men" or (as he is "apt to believe") "spirits of another nature, that assumed their likeness".[62] The "demons of Spraiton" are also described by Bovet as "ghosts", "spectres" and "spirits" and Bovet concludes that one came "not upon an errand of uncharitableness, but to see the will of the defunct performed".[63] The other stories all involve the preternatural, but cover a wide range of phenomena from apparitions and poltergeists of various kinds to what are labelled as "fairies". In discussing these, Bovet is cautious about drawing any firm conclusions about what is happening, and quite often reports the cases with no comment or explanation at all. Their common message would appear to be the moral drawn from the final case, which forms the last sentence of the book, namely "let no man doubt of intelligencies [*sic*] in the world, besides what are hudled up in garments of clay: we see agencies above the reach of our comprehension; and things performed by bodies seemingly aerial, which surpass the strength, power and capacity of the most robust mortal".[64]

Once again, this returns us to the question of how we can link the two halves of the text, since the mild anti-materialism of the second part seems to have little connection with the anti-idolatrous radicalism of the first. Should the second part then be seen merely as a publishing ploy, drawing in the reader with the promise of strange wonders and orthodox anti-sadducism, to encourage him to read the polemical first part? To answer this question, we need to turn to the history of the Bovet family themselves, and consider the relationship between *Pandaemonium* and the family's experience. This will offer strong support for the supposition that radical anti-popery lies at the heart of the book, and suggest that a further motive for its publication, and for the inclusion of the second part, was a desire to vindicate the gentility and worth of the Bovets; but it will also suggest that it would be wrong to rule out the fear of witchcraft as a force driving the production of such a work.

---

[62] Ibid., pp. 129–30.
[63] Ibid., pp. 107–13.
[64] Ibid., p. 140.

Who was the "Richard Bovet[t] Gent.", named on both title pages as the author of *Pandaemonium*? Most scholars have followed Montague Summers in identifying him as Richard Bovet junior, born about 1641 in Somerset, who matriculated at Wadham College Oxford in 1657 as "Arm. fil" (the son of a gentleman) and the likely author of two later anti-Jacobite congratulatory poems, praising the defeat of the French fleet in 1693 and William III's escape from an attempted assassination in 1695. Both share *Pandaemonium*'s deep-seated anti-Catholicism and its tendency to uncover Jacobite conspiracies animated by devilish powers.[65] But *Pandaemonium*'s author could be his father (or possibly uncle) Richard Bovet senior of Bishops' Hull, near Wellington (Somerset) who, together with his brother Philip, was executed in 1685 for commanding a regiment in Monmouth's rebellious army.[66] Both had been prominent parliamentarians in Somerset, where Richard briefly became MP for Taunton in 1659: his purchases of sequestered property included a Duchy of Cornwall manor at Milton Falconbridge (purchased for £7150) and, from the Stawell family estates, both the rectory of Wiveliscombe and the mansion at Cothelstone, outside whose gates he was hanged in 1685.[67] After the Restoration, "Colonel Bovet" (or Buffet) was associated with numerous plots, frequently hiding before reappearing; Philip remained a significant local figure, but was refused the title of gentleman by the heralds visiting Somerset in 1672.[68] These Bovets

---

[65] *The Registers of Wadham College Oxford*, ed. by Rev R.B. Gardiner, 2 vols (London, 1889), I, p. 225; R. Bovett, *A Congratulary Poem To the Hon. Admiral Russel on his Glorious Victory over the French Fleet* (London, 1693) (the EEBO copy contains a handwritten dedication to the King by Bovett); R.B., *A Poem Humbly Presented to his Most Excellent Majesty King William the Third. Upon his most miraculous and happy preservation from that barbarous Jacobitish conspiracy to assassinate his Royal person February anno 1695* (London, 1696). Although the latter fits Bovet's ideology, there are several other 'R.B.'s publishing at this period. Both poems are reproduced in Bovet, *Pandaemonium*, pp. 141–68. *HMC House of Lords* n.s. 1, pp. 250–51 contains a letter of Richard Bovett (apparently from London) with information on a French privateer dated 12 October 1693. A Richard Bovett also signed the Taunton Association Roll in 1696 (PRO C213/226).

[66] Arthur.Humphreys, *Materials for the History of the Town of Wellington* (London: Henry Gray, 1889), pp. 75–76 summarises the history of the Bovets of Wellington. I am grateful to many people for references that have helped me trace the Bovets, notably Nancy Cooper, Peter Elmer, Ruth Fisher, Priscilla Flower-Smith, Richard Greaves and Stuart Walsh.

[67] *Victoria History of the County of Somerset*, ed. by Robert Dunning (London: Oxford University Press for the Institute of Historical Research, 1978), IV, p. 91; *Proceedings of Somerset Archaeological and Natural History Society*, 29 (1883), Part 1, pp. 32–33.

[68] Sir Edward Bysshe, *Visitation of Somerset and City of Bristol, 1672*, ed. by G.D. Squibb (London: Harleian Society, 1992), p. 203.

were part of a larger clan of Bovets, most of them from the middling
ranks of the countryside and small towns, who straddled the borders of
west Somerset, east Devon and west Dorset, exactly the territory from
which Monmouth was to draw his rebel forces in 1685. Monmouth's
rebels included ten Bovets, from Yarcombe, Honiton, Axminster,
Membury in Devon and Stockland in Dorset as well as Taunton and
Wellington, whose occupations included yeomen, combmakers and an
exciseman. Only Richard and Philip were definitely executed, but three
others were transported to Barbados and one was reported "slain in
service".[69] The family then lapsed into relative obscurity.

The clan leader was "that beggar old Buffet", as Richard senior was
described in 1685.[70] From his rise to prominence as a parliamentary
officer in the 1640s in Somerset (especially his defence of Wellington
House against royalist siege in early 1645), as a supporter of the
radical John Pyne "Colonel Bovet", as he was regularly known, was a
rogue figure in Somerset politics. By 1651 he was mayor of Taunton,
and purchasing the properties noted above.[71] By 1653 he had joined
the county bench, his first meeting in April 1653 also featuring the
first witchcraft case in Somerset in the Interregnum period, although
there is no sign he was involved in it.[72] In August 1656 Bovet was an
unsuccessful candidate at the county elections (with 374 votes).[73] He
operated as a JP alongside such prominent families as the Carys until
1660, although he was less active from 1657. This may have brought
him into contact with the source of Glanvill's material on Somerset
witchcraft cases, Robert Hunt, since Cary and Hunt worked closely
as JPs (including in a number of witchcraft cases) from 1657 (when
former Royalists such as Hunt came back onto the Bench), but there

---

[69] Walter MacDonald Wigfield, *The Monmouth Rebels* (Gloucester: Sutton, 1985), pp. 17–18.

[70] Somerset Record Office, DD/SF 3109, letter of William Clarke to Edward Clarke 29 July 1685. The alternative spelling suggests that the 'o' of Bovet was pronounced as a 'u', as is still the case in Bovey Tracey in Devon.

[71] *Somerset Assize Orders 1640–59*, ed. by J.S. Cockburn, Somerset Record Society Publications, 71 (Taunton: Somerset Record Society, 1971), p. 39. David Underdown, *Somerset in the Civil War and Interregnum* (Newton Abbot: David and Charles, 1973), pp. 151, 159, 164–68, 171, 173, 176, 182, 187, 189–93. On p. 187 it is noted that Pyne and Bovet had been friendly towards the Quakers, unlike Cary and Hunt.

[72] *Quarter-Session Records for the County of Somerset*, ed. by E.H. Bates Harbin, Somerset Record Society Publications, 28 (Taunton: Somerset Record Society, 1912), III: *Commonwealth 1646–60*, p. 203 and *passim*.

[73] *Somerset Assize Orders*, p. 77.

is no direct evidence of Bovet and Hunt collaborating. At the Restoration, whereas both the Presbyterian Cary and the conforming Hunt remained on the bench (until purges in 1672 and 1680 respectively), Bovet lost everything.[74] The sequestered royalist and crown properties were taken back, and Bovet entered a twilight zone. He was identified, rightly or wrongly, in every radical plot of the 1660s and 1670s, as the potential military leader capable of raising thousands of soldiers around Taunton, which made him crucial since Taunton was the most anti-royalist town in the west country. Time and again he was Somerset's most wanted man and disappeared, only to resurface when things had calmed down.[75] Finally, in 1685, his status was recognized when he was made a Colonel again to command the Blue Regiment in Monmouth's army, while his daughter Catherine was the leader (or "captain") of the famous Taunton schoolgirls who greeted Monmouth, and became the particular objects of both popular memory and the revenge of Judge Jefferys.[76]

So, everything we know about the Bovet family fits easily with the radical anti-popery and hatred of the Restoration regime displayed in part one of *Pandaemonium*. But what of the collection of relations in the second part? One way of reading these is to see them as an assertion of the gentility of the Bovets, establishing their linkages with a range of leading families in the west country. Presenting himself as the correspondent, confidante and frequent guest of these families, the author presents the marginal Bovets (often on the run from arrest) as regular members of gentry society. In addition to the "noble family", these include the Ayshs of South Petherton, the Woods of Kitford (Devon), "Sir J.F. near Sherburne", and several lesser but established families, as well as merchants in both London and Scotland. His Bristol informant, "Mr J.R. a gentleman of good ingenuity and reputation" might well have been Colonel John Rumsey, the Customs Collector, a

---

[74] *HMC 51 Leybourne-Popham MS*, pp. 157–58 contains a February 1660 letter from Bovet to Monck recording his efforts to prevent the Restoration.

[75] See, from numerous examples in the State Papers, *CSPD 1671–72*, p. 161 and *CSPD January–June 1683* pp. 104, 185. He is discussed in Robin Clifton, *Last Popular Rebellion* (London: Maurice Temple Smith, 1984), pp. 46, 60–61, 219; Richard Greaves, *Enemies under His Feet* (Stanford: Stanford University Press, 1990), pp. 33, 41, 223; id., *Secrets of the Kingdom* (Stanford: Stanford University Press, 1992), p. 158.

[76] Walter MacDonald Wigfield, *The Monmouth Rebellion* (Bradford-on-Avon: Moonraker Press, 1980), pp. 44–46, 92–93; *Glory of the West, or The Virgins of Taunton Deane* (London, 1685), which picked out "Kate" "the Collonel's daughter" for comment and claimed that she "was the lass that had his [Monmouth's] heart".

leading radical, who was involved in the Rye House Plot, though he
saved his life by turning informant.[77] The use of initials in this case
(and that of "T.C." in the Spraiton case) and the coyness in naming
the "noble family" or discussing their cases in detail ("I could say much
more, only for the regard and honour I ought to bear to the family, I
dare not name them")[78] seem to be playing simultaneously with two
conventions. The one, widely discussed in the history of science at this
period, is the notion of using unimpeachable witnesses from the aristocracy and the professions to give credibility to testimonies, but avoiding
compromising their "honour" through the use of social descriptions
and initials rather than full names. The second is the convention of
the conspirator, who has to establish the strength of his potential con-
nections, but without compromising their security. The bitter irony is
that, a year later, the Whig gentry families of the south west failed to
support Monmouth, and left the beggarly Bovets to lead the middling
and lower orders of the region.

It would be perfectly plausible therefore to argue that for the Bovets,
as for the bookseller Malthus, the publishing of *Pandaemonium* was
shaped by the politics of anti-popery and the standing of the Bovets,
not by a desire to contribute to an intellectual debate on the world of
spirits, much less to "the old trade of witchfinding". Yet it need not
follow from this, of course, that the Bovets were simply exploiting the
fears of "the country" without believing in the powers of the Devil or
witchcraft. There is no evidence to link the Bovet family with any of
the Somerset cases tried in the period up to 1684. But the story of the
Bovets and witchcraft does not end with the events of 1684–85.

On 7 September 1696, an Elizabeth Harner or Horner, alias Turner,
was tried at Exeter Castle, for killing Alice Bovett by witchcraft and
bewitching her sisters Sarah and Mary Bovett. It has been argued by
Humphreys, the historian of Wellington, that the family must have
been based there, as both Horners and Bovetts were local names.[79]
But in that case a trial at Devon's assizes in Exeter is most unlikely,
and we have seen that Bovets were scattered across the region. From

---

[77] Bovet, *Pandaemonium*, p. 99; John Latimer, *Annals of Bristol in the Seventeenth Century*
(Bristol: William George's for the author, 1900), p. 418. Rumsey was named in 1686
as one of those, like Catherine Bovet, excluded from the general pardon of those
suspected of participating in Monmouth's rebellion.
[78] Bovet, *Pandaemonium*, pp. 133–34.
[79] Humphreys, *Materials*, p. 237.

some of the names in the case it is more likely that this Bovet was from Yarcombe or Honiton, and that the father in the case, Thomas Bovet, may have been another of the Monmouth rebels, perhaps the one transported to the West Indies and then pardoned by William III, or his descendant.[80]

Details of the trial are preserved in a letter written a week later by Archdeacon Blackburne to the Bishop of Exeter, who had commanded him to attend the trial.[81] The parents, Thomas and Elizabeth Bovett, were the chief witnesses, reporting the strange ailments and physical contortions of their children, the bafflement of physicians, the vomiting of pins and stones, marking of the children's skin, levitation, and the voices and apparitions of the witch, who also prevented them from saying prayers and forced them to swear and curse: all classic symptoms of possession cases and all found in *Pandaemonium*. The children "gave the same account sensibly enough", one adding details about Bett Horner playing with a toad in a basin. Four other witnesses, three women and a man, then testified in various ways. One repeated the classic story of refusing Horner drink, after which their brewing vessel began to behave oddly. A second recorded seeing the witch in the countryside when she was locked up in prison. The third reported a piece of counter-magic, driving a red-hot nail into the witch's footprint, after which the witch went lame and "being searched her leg and foot appeared to be red and fiery" until the nail was pulled out and "then the witch was well". Finally the other male witness, John Fursey, deposed "to his seeing her three nights together upon a large down in the same place as if rising out of the ground". In court "the witch denied all, shewed her shoulder bare in court, when there appeared nothing but a mole or wart", i.e. not a devil's mark, and also managed, despite some hesitation, to repeat the Lord's Prayer and the Creed.

It is tempting, given the vagaries of seventeenth-century spelling, to associate the John Fursey who witnessed in this case with the Furze family who were involved in the Spraiton case (a Nonconformist family, it will be recalled) and/or the Alice Furze against whom Alice Molland supposedly practised witchcraft in Exeter in 1685. At the Exeter Lent

---

[80] Wigfield, *Monmouth's Rebels*, p. 18.

[81] Reproduced in Humphreys, *Materials*, pp. 237–39 and summarized by C. L'Estrange Ewen, *Witchcraft and Demonianism* (London: Heath Cranton, 1933), pp. 377–78 (pp. 445–46 records the not-guilty verdict on all three charges of bewitching Alice, Sarah and Mary Bovett).

Assizes on 20 March Alice Molland was found guilty of witchcraft on the bodies of Joane Snow, Wilmott Snow and Alice Furze and hanged, probably the last witch executed in England. Four Somerset Furzes were Monmouth rebels.[82]

Despite his neutral presentation of the evidence, Blackburne was clearly a little disturbed at the behaviour of Lord Chief Justice Holt, a notorious sceptic who presided over many non-guilty verdicts at this period, of which this was one. He notes "my Lord Chief Justice, by his questions and manner of hemming up [summing up?] the evidence, seemed to believe nothing of witchery at all, and to disbelieve the fact of walking up the wall, which was sworn by the mother". Holt passed his case notes onto the sceptic Francis Hutchinson, who used them in his brief account of the case in his *Historical Essay* of 1718.[83] Both Holt and Hutchinson, like North, clearly regarded the witchcraft statute, and the uses to which it could be put by factious politicians feeding on the passions of the people, as the real danger to the establishment in state and church. For all its complexities, perhaps the example of *Pandaemonium* suggests that they were right.

---

[82] C. L'Estrange Ewen, *Witch Hunting and Witch Trials* (London: Kegan Paul, 1929), p. 43 and plate opposite (Ewen wrongly states here that the judges were North and Raymond again, as in 1682); Wigfield, *Monmouth's Rebels*, pp. 63–64.

[83] Humphreys, *Materials*, p. 239; Francis Hutchinson, *Historical Essay concerning Witchcraft* (London, 1718), p. 45. He wrongly calls the father William Bovet.

DECRIMINALISING THE WITCH

THE ORIGIN OF AND RESPONSE TO THE 1736 WITCHCRAFT ACT

OWEN DAVIES

The witch trials had long been in decline in England by the time the crime of witchcraft was removed from the statute books in 1736. There was only a trickle of cases in the first decade of the eighteenth century, with the last trial and conviction under the 1604 statute occurring in 1712. The last execution had taken place in 1685. Why, therefore, was witchcraft not decriminalised earlier? The same question could be asked, and should be asked, of the legal rejection of witchcraft in most other European states, where decriminalisation came long after judicial scepticism had become the orthodoxy amongst the central authorities.[1] Any answer regarding the case in England, however, requires a consideration of events in Scotland as well. The Union of the two countries had taken place in 1707, and while this did not have a direct impact on the history of the witch trials, the political and religious tensions it created have been shown to have permeated the discourse on witchcraft in the period.[2] The 1736 Act was not a mere afterthought or an act of legislative spring-cleaning; its passing was conducted in an atmosphere of contentious political and religious dispute. Neither should it be studied as just an act of repeal, as it instituted a new crime of 'pretended' witchcraft and sorcery. The activities of cunning-folk and diviners, which had been central to previous witchcraft legislation, remained crimes, though now interpreted as fraudulent rather than diabolic. The Act, then, was the product of social as well as religious, political and philosophical concerns.

---

[1] See Brian Levack, 'The Decline and End of Witchcraft Prosecutions', in *Witchcraft and Magic in Europe: The Eighteenth and Nineteenth Centuries*, ed. by Marijke Gijswijt-Hofstra, Brian P. Levack and Roy Porter (London: Athlone Press, 1999), pp. 74–82.
[2] Ian Bostridge, *Witchcraft and its Transformations, c. 1650–c. 1750* (Oxford: Clarendon Press, 1997).

The Last Trials

To understand why the Witchcraft Act was passed when it was, it is first necessary to consider the pattern of the last of the witch trials. Witchcraft prosecutions may have ended in 1675 in that heartland of prosecutions, and most intensely studied of counties, Essex, but they continued elsewhere in the country for another forty-two years. In 1707 Maria Stevens was indicted for witchcraft and held in Wells gaol awaiting the next assizes, but the case was apparently thrown out by the Grand Jury.[3] In January 1711/12 the Wakefield Quarter Sessions ordered the arrest of Margaret Whiteley of Sowerby, Yorkshire, as a suspected witch, though there is no evidence she was put on trial.[4] The prosecution of Jane Clarke and her son and daughter at the Leicester assizes in 1717 also never got to trial, as the indictment was rejected by the Grand Jury.[5] This was the last indictment for witchcraft in an English court, though there is a tantalising reference in the records of the Wakefield Quarter Sessions, sitting at Pontefract in 1721, that an allowance be paid to a woman acquitted of witchcraft.[6] Across the border in Scotland the last execution of a witch mentioned in the central court records was in 1706 (though there is a doubtful secondary reference to the execution of two witches in Perth in 1715).[7] The last confirmed successful prosecution before the criminal courts was in 1709, when a Dumfries woman, Janet Hairstanes, was sentenced to be branded on the cheek. What is often cited as the last trial for witchcraft in Scotland was that of a woman found guilty by a sheriff's court in Dornoch in 1727. She was supposedly burned for her crime.[8] There is no surviving contemporary documentation for the case, however, and

---

[3] Charles L'Estrange Ewen, *Witchcraft and Demonianism* (London: Muller [1933] 1970), p. 446.

[4] West Riding QS1/51/2.

[5] Ewen, *Witchcraft*, p. 390.

[6] West Riding QS1/60/4.

[7] On these last Scottish cases see Christine Larner, *Enemies of God: The Witch-Hunt in Scotland* (Oxford: Blackwell 1981), p. 78; Peter Maxwell-Stuart, 'Witchcraft and Magic in Eighteenth-Century Scotland', in *Beyond the Witch Trials: Witchcraft and Magic in Enlightenment Europe*, ed. by Owen Davies and Willem de Blécourt (Manchester: Manchester University Press, 2004), pp. 84–85; Edward J. Cowan and Lizanne Henderson, 'The Last of the Witches? The Survival of Scottish Witch Belief', in *The Scottish Witch-Hunt in Context*, ed. by Julian Goodare (Manchester: Manchester University Press, 2002), pp. 205–06; Stuart Macdonald, *The Witches of Fife: Witch-Hunting in a Scottish Shire, 1560–1710* (East Linton: Tuckwell Press, 2002).

[8] See Cowan and Henderson, 'The Last of the Witches?', pp. 205–09.

it is possible that the execution never took place. Even if the event, or at least the trial, did occur it was a tragic anomaly, pursued by a local sheriff-depute backed by the local community, but lacking the sanction of the senior judiciary. Despite the geographical and administrative challenges, central government in Scotland maintained considerable control over witch prosecutions for much of the early modern period, but with the abolition of the Privy Council in 1708 there was greater potential for local authorities, as in Dornoch, to be swayed by popular opinion.[9]

Yet, although the last formal execution for witchcraft in Scotland occurred twenty years after that in England and a large-scale witch trial had taken place in 1697,[10] an examination of the eighteenth-century records of the secular courts shows that Scotland's reputation for persisting in persecuting witches with more vigour than the English judiciary seems largely unfounded. By 1710 the Scottish central judiciary was just as reluctant to enforce the 1563 Scottish Witchcraft Act as their English equivalent was the 1604 Act. In fact, at the parish level, the English magistracy seems, from the surviving records, more proactive for longer in pursuing witchcraft prosecutions than their Scottish counterparts. The reason Scotland has a reputation for being a belated witch-persecuting country in the age of Enlightenment is because the Kirk, and its ministers, continued its campaign to suppress witchcraft and magic through the church courts until the mid-eighteenth century.

The Anglican ecclesiastical authorities had pretty much given up trying to police popular 'superstition' by the time the courts were restored in 1660. Even when they were most active in this area, during the Elizabethan period, they conscientiously left the crime of witchcraft, as distinct from other magical practices, to the secular authorities. In Scotland, however, the presbytery had worked closely with the secular authorities in pursuing witches, and many cases heard by the criminal courts began as cases in the kirk sessions.[11] That relationship was broken by the early eighteenth century when the criminal courts closed the possibility of pursuing suspected witches, but the Kirk continued to deal with the same potent mix of accusations and suspicions of

---

[9] See Julian Goodare, 'Witch-Hunting and the Scottish State', in *Scottish Witch-Hunt* (see Goodare above), p. 142.
[10] Michael Wasser, 'The Western Witch-Hunt of 1697–1700: The Last Major Witch-Hunt in Scotland', in *Scottish Witch-Hunt* (see Goodare above), ch. 9.
[11] See Goodare, 'Witch-Hunting and the Scottish State'.

witchcraft, as it had done for the previous century and a half. The kirk
sessions did not prosecute witchcraft as such, but rather related cases
of cursing, defamation and counter witchcraft. Yet, to a certain degree,
those accused of witchcraft were also still on trial before the community. When, in 1747, Margaret Robertson successfully complained to
the Kenmore Kirk Sessions that her name was being besmirched by
accusations of witchcraft, the session expressed its unanimous view
that she was no witch but nevertheless publicly rebuked her for her
"sin and scandal".[12]

Peter Maxwell-Stuart is right to caution against overemphasising the
Kirk's continued interest in witchcraft. The number of cases they dealt
with was relatively small and the sessions were far more concerned with
fornicators and adulterers.[13] Yet the fact they continued to adjudicate
formally in witchcraft disputes gave witchcraft a relevance and a sense
of reality years after the secular courts in both countries had rejected
the concept. It is no surprise, then, that it was a section of the Scottish clergy that proved amongst the most vocal critics of the repeal of
witchcraft legislation.

The two eighteenth-century witch prosecutions that lodged most
strongly in the intellectual consciousness, and which would, after 1736,
form part of the bedrock of criticism and mockery levelled at the witch
trials, were that of Sarah Moredike before the Surrey Assizes in 1701,
and that of Jane Wenham, the last convicted witch in England, at the
Hertfordshire Assizes in 1712.[14] The enthusiasm shown by the London
magistrate Sir Thomas Lane in having Moredike strip-searched for
witch's marks, and his sanctioning that she be scratched by her supposed victim Richard Hathaway, was later singled out for particular
criticism in some quarters. An explanation for Lane's zealousness may
be found in his religious persuasion. He was, it would seem, a prominent member of the Presbyterian congregation at Salter's Hall, Canon

---

[12] Cited in Cowan and Henderson, 'The Last of the Witches?', p. 209.
[13] Peter Maxwell-Stuart, 'Witchcraft and Magic in Eighteenth-Century Scotland',
p. 85.
[14] On Moredike see *The Tryal of Richard Hathaway, Upon an Information for being a Cheat
and Impostor* (London, 1702). The Wenham trial provoked a flurry of pamphlets, which
have been studied in Phyllis J. Guskin, 'The Context of English Witchcraft: The Case
of Jane Wenham (1712)', *Eighteenth-century Studies* 15 (1981–82), 48–71. See also Anne
How, 'Jane Wenham of Walkern, England's Last Witch?', *Herts Past & Present*, 3rd s.,
1 (2003), 3–11.

Street.[15] The subsequent prosecution of Hathaway for fraudulently feigning possession and making false accusations was later used as an exemplar of the folly of belief in witchcraft. Writing sixty years after the Moredike affair, Oliver Goldsmith recounted the case and remarked that "there are many alive now, who must, I suppose, remember the famous impostor Richard Hathaway".[16] Likewise the magistrate and clergymen who pursued and publicly defended the prosecution of Jane Wenham would later be held up as examples of the bigotry and credulity of witch believers.

Prosecution under the Witchcraft Acts was not the only context in which suspected witches found themselves in court. With assize witch trials petering out during the later seventeenth century, prosecutions for defamation at the quarter sessions become more obvious to the historian's gaze. In 1680, for example, a spinster named Elizabeth Hole of Wingerworth, Derbyshire, was charged with scandalous behaviour by bringing unfounded charges of witchcraft against Henry Hunloke and other people. The Northumberland Quarter Sessions heard a similar defamation case in 1687/88 concerning John Richardson of Ellington, who did "unlawfully scandalize and defame Jane Blackburne of the same widow and maliciously called her a Witch and sayd he wished that he could get Blood of her". The Northumberland Sessions heard another such case in 1709 and again in 1725. In the latter a Hexham woman lodged a complaint that her name had been scandalized, it being said that she was "a witch & had witched a cow, that this cow dropped down dead" after she "had cast her eye upon it."[17]

Such defamation suits had occurred in England before of course, in both the secular courts and the pre-Civil War ecclesiastical courts. But there is a sense that from the late seventeenth century onwards, poor victims of witchcraft accusations were more willing to counter-sue in the secular courts. While witchcraft remained a capital offence, suspected witches would surely have been generally reluctant to pursue their persecutors through the secular courts. Even in nineteenth-century reverse trials one finds nervous prosecutors emphasising to magistrates

---

[15] The Presbyterian clergyman, William Tong, who was elected minister at Salter's Hall in 1702, wrote an admiring dedication to Lane in *A sermon preached at Salter's-Hall* (London, 1704). On Tong see the *New DNB*.

[16] Oliver Goldsmith, *The mystery revealed; containing a series of transactions and authentic testimonials, respecting the supposed Cock-Lane ghost* (London, 1762), p. 28.

[17] Derbyshire Record Office, Q/SB/2/1214; Northumberland Record Office, QSB/5, QSB/30, QSB/65.

that they were not witches.[18] So, if there was an increase in quarter sessions defamation suits, it would suggest a growing popular consciousness of the increased caution and scepticism of the magistracy in general towards witchcraft. The lack of research renders this mere speculation, and only more systematic cataloguing of quarter sessions will reveal whether there is substance to it. However, Brian Levack has detected signs of a similar increase in counter-prosecutions against witchcraft accusers in other countries from around the time that witch trials went into terminal decline.[19]

It can be confidently assumed that fear of witchcraft and witchcraft accusations remained widespread in the early eighteenth century. As well as defamation cases, we find proof of it in manifestations of individual violent retribution against suspected witches. In 1710, for example, James Sawford, of Woolershall, Worcestershire, was examined by magistrates for assaulting one Jane Pace, he having tried to drag her to a pool saying she was an old witch and that he intended to swim her. In 1728 Joan Best, a butcher's wife of Barnstaple, was brought before the magistrates for assaulting a suspected witch.[20] In the year of the Witchcraft Act, Margaret Goldsbrough of Baildon, West Yorkshire, applied to the justices to have a neighbouring family bound over after they had accused her and her mother of witchcraft, and had shouted in the street, "kill them all and let them live no longer".[21] Explosions of communal anger against witches also periodically erupted in the form of actual witch swimming. In 1709 the villagers of Horninghold, Leicestershire, swam several people in their search for a witch, and in the same county Jane Clarke and her children were swum by the villagers of Great Wigston in 1717. In 1730 three men of Frome, Somerset, were charged with manslaughter following the death of a woman after being swum.[22] It is intriguing that hardly any instances of such popular justice against witches have been record in Scotland in

---

[18] See Owen Davies, *A People Bewitched: Witchcraft and Magic in Nineteenth-Century Somerset* (Bruton: privately published by the author, 1999), pp. 119–20.

[19] Levack, 'Decline and End of Witchcraft Prosecutions', pp. 83–84.

[20] Worcestershire Record Office QS 1/1/215/51; North Devon Record Office, B1/2260. For some other examples see Malcolm Gaskill, *Crime and Mentalities in Early Modern England* (Cambridge: Cambridge University Press, 2000), pp. 83–84.

[21] James Sharpe, *Instruments of Darkness: Witchcraft in England 1550–1750* (London: Hamish Hamilton, 1996), p. 280; James Sharpe, *Witchcraft in Seventeenth-Century Yorkshire: Accusations and Counter-Measures* (York: Borthwick Institute, 1992), p. 20.

[22] See Davies, *Witchcraft*, pp. 90–95.

the same period.[23] The only comparable case concerned a suspected witch, Janet Cornfoot, who after being released from custody in 1705 was stoned and then pressed to death by villagers from Pittenweem, Fife. A pamphlet decrying the event stated that several of those involved were arrested on the charge of murder but that on the word of the local minister they were released.[24] If it is not a mere consequence of gaps in the source material, the apparent lack of communal justice in Scotland could be due to the continued involvement of the Kirk and its ministers in investigating witchcraft allegations, which helped diffuse communal tensions.

It is safe to say, then, that the repeal of the laws against witchcraft would certainly not have attracted widespread public support, though James Sharpe is right to note that, despite the paucity of evidence, there were undoubtedly voices of scepticism in popular as well as learned cultures by the early eighteenth century.[25] Yet the extent of scepticism amongst the burgeoning middling-sort and elite is also very difficult to gauge accurately. The last weary punch of the intellectual bout over the reality of witchcraft was thrown by the medical writer Richard Boulton in his *Vindication of the Compleat History of Magick* (1722). From then on, there is little opinionated public discourse on witchcraft until the passing of the 1736 Act, and what there is, is largely from a sceptical point of view. The most vocal commentators were anti-clerical, Whig polemicists such as Thomas Gordon, who followed in the footsteps of 'Free Thinkers' and Deists such as John Trenchard (*d.* 1723) and Anthony Collins (1676–1729).[26] In 1725 Gordon published an essay on witchcraft in which he stated that many had been condemned as witches "for no other Reason but their knowing more than those godly Blockheads who accus'd, try'd, and pass'd Sentence upon them". "Credulity", he continued, "is a much more mischievous Error than Infidelity, and it is safer to believe nothing, than too much. A Man that believes little or nothing of Witchcraft, will destroy nobody for being

---

[23] The point was made by Larner, *Enemies of God*, p. 78.

[24] *An answer of a letter from a gentleman in Fife, to a nobleman* (Edinburgh, 1705), p. 4.

[25] James Sharpe, *Witchcraft in Early Modern England* (London: Longman, 2001), p. 83.

[26] For their opinions on witchcraft see, for example, Anthony Collins, *A discourse of free-thinking* (London, 1713), pp. 27–32; John Trenchard, *The Natural History of Superstition* (London, 1709), pp. 21, 27–28. Michael Hunter rightly criticised Ian Bostridge for neglecting to consider fully the views of such polemicists; Michael Hunter, 'Review Essay: Witchcraft and the Decline of Belief', *Eighteenth-Century Life*, 22 (1998), p. 146.

under the Imputation of Witchcraft". Gordon recognised the popular
enthralment to the belief though, and wearily remarked that it was "one
of the most unthankful Offices in the World, to go about to expose the
mistaken Notions of Witchcraft and Spirits".[27]

But, as Jonathan Barry's detailed analysis of the educated response
to the Bristol Lamb Inn possession case of 1761–62 demonstrates, the
tenor of public debate was not necessarily a reflection of private belief.[28]
The published opinion on witchcraft in the decade prior to 1736 thus
provides us with little insight into how belief was changing and declining
amongst the gentry, aristocracy and the increasingly influential middling
sort. It has, in the past, been assumed that the educated levels of society
were slowly but surely ascribing to natural philosophy and 'rational'
religion. As is now established though, the bulk of orthodox Anglican
intellectual opinion did not reject the concept of witchcraft—just that
witches ceased to exist in enlightened Britain. As the opinions of such
esteemed thinkers of the second half of the eighteenth century as
Samuel Johnson (1709–84) and William Blackstone (1723–80) demonstrate, the literal biblical instruction on witchcraft had to be upheld,
and the weight of historical evidence was thought to be incontrovert-
ible. Eminent judges and theologians of the sixteenth and seventeenth
centuries could not have been wrong in their judgement. Nevertheless,
witchcraft had ceased to exist by the early eighteenth century, and only
groundless gossip and credulity about witches continued. The evidence
of the Moredike affair proved as much.

A rare window into the private world of witchcraft belief amongst
the middling sort and ruling elite in the years running up to 1736 is
provided by the career of the deaf and dumb seer Duncan Campbell
(d. 1730). Duncan claimed he was born in Lapland to a native woman
and a Scottish seaman. The truth of the Lapp connection is difficult to
disprove, but it was quite likely a fabrication constructed because of the
reputation Lapland had as a land of great seers and wizards. He moved
to London from Scotland in the 1690s where his predictions attracted
the attention of some in London's fashionable circles. Over the next few
years he suffered various financial setbacks and it was only during the

---

[27] Thomas Gordon, *The Humorist. Essays upon Several Subjects* (London, 1725), II, pp.
70, 74.
[28] Jonathan Barry, 'Public Infidelity and Private Belief? The Discourse of Spirits in
Enlightenment Bristol', in *Beyond the Witch Trials*, (see Davies and de Blécourt above),
ch. 7.

second decade of the eighteenth century that his fame spread widely. He was evidently friends with the journalist William Bond, though they later fell out, and with the celebrated actress and novelist Eliza Haywood. Both of them wrote promotional literature for Campbell.[29] He was no stranger to aristocratic circles either. In 1720 he was introduced to the King and presented him with a copy of *The History of his Life and Adventures*.[30] When his *Secret Memoirs* were published a dozen years later, amongst the respectable subscribers were several influential Scottish aristocratic politicians, all Hanoverian supporters by 1720, such as the Earl of Marchmont, Sir Archibald Grant, Lord John Gower, Archibald Campbell the Duke of Argyll (Lord Islay), who was Walpole's election manager for Scotland, and Argyll's friend Alexander Brodie.[31] Whether they ever met Campbell is another matter. He claimed that Lord Islay once offered to act as his second when he was challenged to a duel, and he records Islay as once stating in public "that Duncan Campbel, was his Relation, and as good a Gentlemen as any there."[32] There is also an independent account that a youthful William Wyndham, Earl of Egremont, consulted the fortune-teller. Passing through Charing Cross one day Wyndham's curiosity was aroused by a crowd gathered in the street. On asking why they were there, he was informed that they were waiting to consult Campbell. Wyndham decided to seek a consultation himself and was told by the fortune-teller that he should beware of a white horse, which friends interpreted as the symbol of the House of Hanover.[33]

Duncan Campbell strenuously sought to distance himself from fortune-tellers and conjurors, warning that "The Persons, who are most to be avoided, are your ordinary Fortune-telling Women and Men about this Town, whose Houses ought to be avoided as a Plague or a

---

[29] For details of his life, some of it dubious, see William Bond, *The History of the Life and Adventures of Mr Duncan Campbell* (London, 1720); Eliza Haywood, *A Spy on the Conjurer* (London, 1724). For a detailed consideration of these works see Rodney M. Baine, *Daniel Defoe and the Supernatural* (Athens, Georgia: University of Georgia Press, 1968), ch. 7; Felicity A. Nussbaum, 'Speechless: Haywood's Deaf and Dumb Projector', in *The Passionate Fictions of Eliza Haywood*, ed. by Rebecca Bocchicchio and Kirsten T. Saxton (Lexington: University Press of Kentucky, 2000), pp. 194–217.

[30] Baine, *Daniel Defoe*, p. 144.

[31] Duncan Campbell, *Secret Memoirs of the late Mr. Duncan Campbel, the Famous Deaf and Dumb Gentleman* (London, 1732).

[32] Campbell, *Secret Memoirs*, p. 35.

[33] Thomas Newton, *The Works of the Right Reverend Thomas Newton*, 2nd edn (London, 1787), I, pp. 87–88.

Pestilence, either because they are Cheats and Impostors, or because
they deal with the Black Arts". To this end he mentioned several of
the worst offenders, including an astrologer in Moorfields who used
to be a tailor, and a woman who lived close to the Old Bailey who
pretended "to give Charms written upon Paper with odd Scrawls,
which she calls Figures".[34] Nevertheless, Campbell's business was little
different to that of cunning-folk. He made predictions, detected stolen
property, dispensed medicine and most significantly cured witchcraft.
Part of Duncan's practice, detecting stolen property, was a criminal
offence under the 1604 Witchcraft Act and more generally under the
vagrancy laws, and as he recalled in his biography, an enemy once, as
an act of revenge, "employ'd with Lawyers to indict me in the Crown
Office, on the Statute against Gypsies, Fortune-tellers, Witches, &c."
However, Campbell's friend Justice Botelar sent the lawyers packing
when he came to bargain with Campbell.[35]

In his posthumously published *Secret Memoirs* of 1732, Campbell
included a chapter defending the reality of witchcraft and grumbled
that the crime was, "now looked on as such an old Wife's Tale, that
if any Person is apprehended for it, a Justice of the Peace is afraid to
sign a Commitment, tho' on the most plain Proofs, for Fear of being
laugh'd at by those, Wise in their own Conceit, Gentlemen, who will
have it no more than Imagination."[36] If he is to be believed, and there
is no reason to suggest otherwise, Campbell dealt with many bewitched
clients from London and its environs. "I should be too tedious", he said,
"in attempting to relate the twentieth Part of the Number of Children
to whom I have been serviceable, even though they were reduced so
low by the Force of an ill Tongue."[37] The few examples he gives were
not concerned with labourers, but with merchants and the families of
gentlemen. He recounted, for example, the case of the three-year-old
child of a Mr Tiveston, who had an estate in Berkshire. The child was
playing before the door one day, a slice of cake in hand, when an old
woman came and asked for a piece. The reluctance of the child annoyed
the woman, who rapped her stick on the ground three times and cried
"Meeli! Mali! Meeli!" before running off with the swiftness of a young
woman. Shortly after, the child began to mew like a cat, foamed at

[34] Bond, *The History of the Life and Adventures*, pp. xvii, xviii.
[35] Campbell, *Secret Memoirs*, pp. 35–36.
[36] Ibid., p. 38.
[37] Ibid., p. 43.

the mouth and spat at people. The local doctors could do nothing, so a friend advised Mr Tiveston to take his daughter to Campbell. His Second Sight enabled him to draw a picture of the old woman who had laid the spell. He gave Tiveston a sealed written charm, which he was instructed to bury half in the ground on the spot where the old witch had stood. The servants were ordered to watch night and day. Lo and behold, on the third night the old woman returned to the spot, and the next day she begged to see the child and after muttering some words the child recovered.[38]

Another success, in the year 1713, concerned the bewitchment of a tobacco and wine merchant named Richard Coates, who lived in Fenchurch Street. In *The History of the Life and Adventures*, William Bond described how Coates had spent hundreds of pounds trying to get a cure for the "violent distemper" from which he suffered. Campbell achieved what all the eminent physicians consulted by Coates could not, for the reason that Campbell detected a witch at work and recommended a cure that consisted, in part, of boiling his urine in the manner of the sympathetic magical practice of witch bottles.[39] Campbell's *Secret Memoirs* further included a transcript of an affidavit provided by Coates and purportedly signed in January 1725 in the presence of Robert Raymond, who a couple of months later would become Lord Chief Justice of King's Bench. We know nothing of Raymond's personal views on witchcraft, though it is noteworthy that he acted as a junior counsel for the Crown in the prosecution of Richard Hathaway in 1702.[40] In his testimonial, Coates stated that "most people" judged his distemper "to be the Effect of Witchcraft". He had been treated for four years by Dr Ratcliffe and Dr Cade, and sent to Bath for a water cure. The statement concluded that since consulting Campbell he had for the last ten years "been blessed with a very good State of Health, and been totally freed from the said Distemper."[41]

The fact that Campbell believed in and cured witchcraft as part of his occupation does not, of course, mean that his aristocratic sympathisers subscribed to all his claims. It is telling that in Eliza

---

[38] Ibid., pp. 43–45.

[39] On witch bottles see Ralph Merrifield, *The Archaeology of Ritual and Magic* (London: Guild Publishing, 1987), pp. 163–75.

[40] *New DNB*.

[41] Bond, *History of the Life and Adventures*, pp. 281–82; Campbell, *Secret Memoirs*, pp. 39–40.

Haywood's supportive "collection of surprising and diverting stories" concerning Campbell, which was addressed to Lord Rutland, she stated: "As to his Cure of Witchcraft, I shall forbear expressing so much of my Sentiments on that Head as I would do, if I did not know your Lordship's positive Disbelief, that there is such a Thing in the World, would render all I could say of no effect".[42] The support he attracted in Scots aristocratic circles—if true—can, in part, be put down to clan support for a Campbell, and also because of his claim to possess Second Sight. While there was a definite intellectual shift away from the reality of supernatural interventionism during the late seventeenth and early eighteenth centuries, the notion of Second Sight continued to quiz the minds of those who rejected the possibility of spirit conjuration and the continued existence of witches.[43] Even Defoe, who rubbished the claims of those who said they possessed powers of foresight and magic, accepted the possibility of Second Sight, though not when claimed by the dubious likes of Campbell.[44]

Campbell died in his lodgings in Buckingham Court, near Charing Cross, on the 29 March 1730, but his reputation lived long in the public memory. Some thirty years later a waxwork of "Campbell, the dumb Fortune-Teller" was still on display at Mrs Salmon's Wax-Works in Fleet Street, a lasting testament to the private and public discourse on witchcraft in the capital.[45]

The Passing of the 1736 Act

We know that John Crosse, John Conduitt and George Heathcote were the sponsors of the bill to repeal the laws against witchcraft, presented to the Commons and the Lords in the 1735/6 session, but their motivation for doing so at that particular moment is difficult to pin down; as Bostridge commented, the bill "seems to emerge from nowhere".[46] Their backgrounds provide some indication. Heathcote was the nephew of the influential merchant and politician Sir Gilbert

---

[42] Haywood, *Spy on the Conjurer*, p. 27.
[43] See *The Occult Laboratory: Magic, Science and Second Sight in Late Seventeenth-century Scotland*, ed. by Michael Hunter (Woodbridge: Boydell & Brewer, 2001).
[44] See Baine, *Daniel Defoe*, pp. 157–59.
[45] J. Morgan, *The New Political State of Great Britain* (London, 1730), I, pp. 203–04; handbill entitled *At Mrs. Salmon's Royal Wax-Work* ([n.p.], *c.* 1763).
[46] Bostridge, *Witchcraft*, p. 182.

Heathcote (1652–1733), and the family had Nonconformist sympathies
and several Quaker relatives.[47] By 1736 George had been appointed an
Alderman and in 1742 he would become Lord Mayor of London. He
was a frequent speaker in the House and his family's religious sympathies are evident from the fact that he supported the repeal of the Test
Act. Conduitt (1688–1737) was married to the niece of his idol Isaac
Newton, whose biography he resolved to write but never did. By the
1730s he was a prominent supporter of Walpole's government and an
influential parliamentary speaker.[48] Less is known of Crosse, though
he was a friend of Walpole's brother and chaired the committee that
oversaw the final reading of the bill.[49]

Conduitt's admiration for Newtonian thought suggests an obvious
rationalist motive for his interest in repealing the witchcraft laws, but
apart from all three men being Whigs, there is little to connect the
other two men to such a scientifically-inspired project. Furthermore
the three men, though aligned to the same party, were by no means
of the same hue on all political and religious matters. Bostridge has
convincingly speculated, however, that one issue they may have had in
common, and which was the prime inspiration behind their bill, was
less philosophical and more a matter of restricting ecclesiastical political influence. The main reason for suggesting as much concerns the
Quaker's Tithes Bill, which was debated in the Commons the same
year as the Witchcraft Act gained Royal assent, and agitation by some
Whigs in the same parliamentary session for the repeal of the Test and
Corporation Acts. With the relaxation of the restrictions on Nonconformists and Catholics proving too contentious, the pushing through
of the Witchcraft Act could have been intended as a less provocative
statement of Whig intent regarding the secularisation of the state. In
this context it is intriguing that the repeal of the 1563 Scottish Act was
only added as an amendment by the House of Lords while Ireland was
excluded altogether. Was this merely a sign of the "insensitivity" of the
Commons towards Scottish and Irish affairs, as Bostridge suggests, or
was there something more to it?

While applauding Bostridge's skilful dissection of the political origins
behind the Witchcraft Bill, the final Act should not be seen purely as a

---

[47] *New DNB.*
[48] *New DNB.*
[49] Bostridge, *Witchcraft*, p. 183.

political pawn in the party manoeuvring over the relationship between
state and Church. As the Bill went through Parliament a fourth section
was added for the "more effectual preventing and punishing" of those
pretending to possess the power of "Witchcraft, Sorcery, Inchantment,
or Conjuration". The politicians clearly had other preoccupations
regarding magical practice than the mere repeal of a redundant law.
The 1542, 1563 and 1604 Acts against Conjuration and Witchcraft
were inspired as much by concerns over the diabolical activities of
cunning-folk and conjurors as of *maleficium*, and so it is not surprising
that the eighteenth-century legislature also viewed witchcraft, however
defined, as part of a broader problem.

Although the witchcraft debate subsided during the early eighteenth
century, vigorous attacks against cunning-folk and fortune-tellers continued. In 1707 the author of the *Black Art Detected and Expos'd* fulminated
over the "Hellish impiety" of such people. Daniel Defoe rounded on
them in his *A Compleat System of Magick* (1727). *The Genuine Life and Confession of Richard Walton, a Reputed Conjuror*, published in 1733 and again in
1744, was an autobiographical *mea culpa* exposing the fraudulent basis of
much of their business. The Whig poet Ambrose Philips complained that
"Indigent Cunning Men know very well, that they may tax the People
as they please, so long as they can contrive to feed their Curiosity".[50]
An essay in the *London Magazine* (August 1737) observed that:

> In our Times Conjuring has been in such high Reputation, that Men
> in several Professions, have endeavoured to impose themselves upon the
> World for Conjurers [...] nay, the most ignorant have made Pretences this
> Way. Coblers and Tinkers have call'd themselves Astrologers and Fortune-
> tellers. Every Fellow with a brazen Face, and nothing in his Head, has
> attempted to impose upon Mankind, by pretending to be a Conjurer.[51]

As Malcolm Gaskill has observed, furthermore, in the two decades
leading up to 1736 Act the term 'witchcraft' was increasingly redefined
in publications to denote the fraudulent activities of conjurors, fortune
tellers, jugglers and other 'pretenders', rather than the diabolic activities
of witches.[52] Thus the anti-Newtonian philosopher John Hutchinson
wrote in 1736: "though the extraordinary Power of the Devil be ceas'd,

---

[50] Ambrose Philip, *The Free-Thinker* (London, 1733), I, p. 16. This was a collection
of essays from his periodical *The Free-Thinker*, which ran from 1718 to 1721.
[51] *The London Magazine* (London, 1736–46), VI, p. 436.
[52] Gaskill, *Crime and Mentalities*, pp. 109, 114–15.

yet as they act upon his Motives, if there by any Statutes in force against those Impostors who have been called Witches, they ought to be prosecuted upon those Statutes for pretending to such Powers."[53] The Rev. Clement Ellis, one-time rector of Kirkby, Nottinghamshire, warned in 1738 of the evils of "consulting devils, or asking help of any who hold communication with them", but referred to "witches, or sorcerers, magicians, called now wise men or women, and such as do wonders by whispering and muttering certain words, called commonly charmers [...] wizards, or cunning men".[54]

The 1736 Act's inclusion of measures against those who "undertake to tell Fortunes" also reflected broader, increasing concerns over vagrancy and its threat to social order and private property. In 1713 various laws relating to vagrancy were coalesced into one statute commanding that "Constables or other Inhabitants are to apprehend Vagrants, and carry them before a Justice of the Peace". The lengthy list of such offenders delineated in the Act included, "Jugglers, Gypsies, or Persons wandering in their Habit and Form, Pretenders to Physiognomy, Fortune-Tellers, Users of subtle Craft or unlawful Games". In other words, people like the vagrant Agnes Clark and her family, who had been arrested for telling fortunes in Bishop Burton in 1723 and were examined at the East Riding Quarter Sessions. She claimed they had no legal settlement because her husband had been born at sea.[55] In 1744 the law was further revised and the section on diviners expanded to "all persons pretending to be gypsies, or wandering in the habit or form of Egyptians, or pretending to have skill in physiognomy, palmistry, or like craft science, or pretending to tell fortunes, or using any subtil craft to deceive and impose on any of His Majesty's subjects".[56]

Gypsies were a particular focus of intellectual denunciation and authoritarian concern in the years before and after 1736. Addison, for instance, denounced them as "idle profligate people".[57] More to the point, they were frequently maligned as fortune-tellers. In his biography

---

[53] John Hutchinson, *The Religion of Satan, or Antichrist, Delineated* (London, 1736), p. 10.

[54] Clement Ellis, *The Scripture Catechist: or, the Whole Religion of a Christian* (London, 1738), p. 201.

[55] East Riding, QSF/60/D/8.

[56] Joseph Shaw, *Parish Law: or, a guide to Justice of the Peace*, 2nd edn (London, 1734), p. 362; Dudley and Ward, *The Law of a Justice of Peace*, p. 991.

[57] *The Spectator*, 130 (1713), p. 174.

Duncan Campbell highlighted this prejudice when he tried to deflect criticism by warning his readers of "being impos'd upon in your Pockets by Cheats, Gypsies and common Fortune-tellers".[58] In a commentary on the false prophets mentioned in chapter eight of Ezekiel, Samuel Smith's *Christian's Guide* (1738) referred to the flatteries and deceptions of "these Gypsies or Fortune-tellers".[59] The Vagrancy Acts singled out gypsies as a specific nuisance, and it is surely significant that the edition of William Nelson's *The Office and Authority of a Justice of Peace*, published in 1736, stated that the new Witchcraft Act was "chiefly pointed at a Set of idle People called Gypsies, who travel the Countries to deceive the Innocent."[60] People like the thirteen members of the Lovell family, well-known gypsies, who were brought before the Cornish Quarter Sessions in 1738/39 as "idle wandering persons and some of them pretending to be fortune tellers". They were ordered back to their last legal place of settlement, Murshall in Kent.[61]

Just as the definition of witchcraft shifted, so the terminology of magic and divination was also increasingly used as a metaphor for petty theft, reflecting broader concerns at the time regarding the perceived culture of thievery that vagrancy fostered. Addison, in one of his accounts of Sir Roger, told how after benignly giving succour to a beggar he found his pocket had been picked, leading Addison to remark that it was "a kind of Palmistry at which this race of vermin are very dextrous."[62] A 1727 pamphlet on provision for the poor described "idle and disorderly" pilferers as "the Practicers in the black Arts". Another referred to "those black arts of defamation, lying, slandering, backbiting, &c."[63] The author of an essay in the *Middlesex Journal* in 1737, welcomed the fact that "a good many of those idle fears concerning witches, spirits, and the like" had been banished, but bemoaned the fact that fortune-telling was as prevalent as ever. He referred to the "comfortable livelihood" of "those retailers in divination, who otherwise would probably be, literally speaking, picking their neighbours pockets, or infesting the highways, to

---

[58] Bond, *The History of the Life and Adventures*, p. v.

[59] Samuel Smith, *The Christian's Guide; or, the Holy Bible* (London, 1738), p. 706.

[60] William Nelson, *The Office and Authority of a Justice of Peace* (London, 1736), I, p. 335.

[61] Cornwall Record Office, QS/1/1/37–44.

[62] *The Spectator*, 130, p. 79.

[63] Philo Devonian, *A Devonshire Hospital: being a treatise, shewing how the poor of the county of Devon may be maintained and provided for* (Exeter, 1727), p. 14; Charles Owen, *Religious Gratitude: Being Seven Practical Discourses* (London, 1731), p. 205.

the great terror of his majesty's subjects."[64] Duncan Campbell's name was unsurprisingly dragged into the discourse of denunciation. An account of the notorious thief and thief-taker Jonathan Wild, published in 1725, claimed that Campbell had boasted he had taught Wild the 'Black Arts' to help him in his trade. The pamphleteer denounced the fortune-teller as "one of the greatest Impostor's that ever was born, and doth as much Harm amongst the simple and honest Maidens, as ever Jonathan did good among the Thieves".[65]

Responses to the Act

The 1736 edition of Nelson's, *The Office and Authority of a Justice of Peace*, referring to the recently passed Witchcraft Act, commented that, "The Notion of Witchcraft seems to have taken a new Turn, and is pretty much exploded in this Kingdom".[66] As we shall see, this was far from true, but the Act certainly engendered greater confidence to denounce the supposed sagacity of the eminent judges and theologians of the past without attracting a barrage of accusations of deism and atheism. This new freedom is well demonstrated by an essay published in 1744 attacking the view that "antient Laws" be held in unquestioned reverence. Witchcraft was used as a fresh, relevant example: "Surely it will not be said, that our Ancestors never made an unjust or ridiculous Law. But a few Sessions ago, we repealed a Part of our antient Law, which was both unjust and ridiculous; I mean the Laws against Witchcraft".[67] A generation on from the last conviction for witchcraft, the weight of history argument for the reality of witchcraft could begin to be removed from the scales of justice. As the later opinions of Johnson and Blackstone show, though, this may not have been a mainstream position. It is noticeable, nevertheless, that the outspoken, anti-clerical polemicists of the 1720s were joined by a broader, less religiously or politically motivated chorus of disapproval. Thus in August 1737 an Essayist writing in the *London Magazine* marvelled at the "Ignorance and Superstition of our Ancestors, in enacting penal Laws against Witches

---

[64] *Middlesex Journal*, 19 November 1737; reprinted in *Essays on Various Subjects* (London, 1738), p. 20.
[65] *The History of the Lives and Actions of Jonathan Wild* (London, 1725), p. 29.
[66] Nelson, *The Office and Authority of a Justice*, p. 334.
[67] *The London Magazine* (November 1744), p. 521.

and Wizards". "It is true, the Law was in a great Measure become obsolete;' but, he continued, 'for which we may thank the Wisdom, or, perhaps, the Infidelity of the Age; but while it continu'd unrepeal'd, it might still have been in the Power of any malicious Person to have prosecuted his Neighbour for being a wiser Man than himself."[68]

It is telling that in the lengthy account of the trials of Moredike and Hathaway, provided in his *Tryals for High Treason, and Other Crimes* (1720–31), the historian Thomas Salmon (1679–1767) avoided making any adverse remarks. Yet, in an abridged edition of 1737, he was outspoken in his criticism of those members of authority instrumental in pursuing Moredike. "It is impossible to read Hathaway's Trials," he commented, "without blushing for the Credulity and Superstition of our Country-men". In reference to the "credulous" London magistrate Thomas Lane, who had Mordike stripped and searched for witch's teats, Salmon went on to hope that "in our Days, I presume, the Government takes Care to exclude all such weak and credulous Creatures from the Magistracy".[69] Several years later Salmon launched a similar attack on the 'learned' men involved in the more recent Wenham trial:

> If I have advanced Opinions contrary to those of the Worshipful Sir Henry Chauncy, whose great age may excuse the Commitment of the Person that occasions this Dissertation, and cannot join with the Reverend Clergymen, whose Depositions were thought of weight enough by the Jury…it is to be presumed I shall not be though to fall under the Statute of Defamation, or be denied the Benefit of Clergy.[70]

Just as the Witchcraft Act freed restraints on outspoken scepticism regarding witchcraft, it made the public defence of witch belief all the more socially unacceptable in educated circles. The defenders stood out like a sore thumb, just as the deists had a couple of decades before. The most obvious public opponent of the Witchcraft Act was James Erskine, Lord Grange, who had delivered his Maiden Speech against the Bill as it passed through the Lords. While his stance was derided at the time, giving him a reputation as an eccentric, Bostridge is right to see Erskine's speech not as that of a lone, naive voice, but as that "of a Scottish member, concerned for Scottish particularity in govern-

---

[68] *The London Magazine* (August 1737), pp. 436–37.
[69] Thomas Salmon, *A new abridgment and critical view of the state trials* (Dublin, 1737), II, pp. 765–66.
[70] Thomas Salmon, *A Collection of Proceedings and Trials against State Prisoners* (London, 1741), p. 424.

ment and religion".[71] After all, Erskine, had been on good terms with the likes of Islay during their student days, but having been thwarted in his political career, he had come to oppose bitterly Walpole and his Scottish supporters. It is impossible to prove, but Erskine would presumably not have been so outspoken if he had not felt he had significant private support for his views from some of his peers. The history of Duncan Campbell suggests that it may have been forthcoming. Perhaps the initial exclusion of Scotland from the Witchcraft Bill was not, then, an act of insensitive dismissal of Scottish affairs but rather a cautious acknowledgement of Scottish political sensitivities.

The most vocal and widespread criticism was, however, more religious than political in inspiration, and broader than it has usually been portrayed. Nonconformists were seen, with some justification, as the most ardent opponents of repeal. Thomas Salmon stated there were "a Set of People amongst us, especially the Sectaries, that seem determined never to be undeceived; that look upon every Piece of pretended Witchcraft, as a strong Proof of their Religion and another World, and call all Men Atheists and Infidels that won't believe them."[72] This view was given powerful credence decades later by the well-known denunciations of the legislation by the likes of John Wesley and the Calvinist Independent Minister Edmund Jones (1702–93).[73] As we have seen, however, Nonconformist sympathisers proposed the Witchcraft Bill and so some caution is required. While most eighteenth-century Wesleyans probably shared their spiritual leader's profound regret at the repeal of the laws against witchcraft, other Dissenting groups would presumably have had no objections to the Act. The Unitarians, for instance, rejected outright the idea that Satan had any influence on human affairs. One group of religious anti-repealers we can confidently generalise about were the Seceders from the Church of Scotland, who saw the passing of the Act as further confirmation that the Church of Scotland's Calvinist purity had become diluted and tainted by rationalism. In 1737 the Associate Presbytery complained that "the penal statutes against Witches have been repeal'd, contrary to the express Letter of the Law of God". They saw this as a grave error at a time when they perceived the abominable growth of "Popish Errors and Delusions" across the country. They

---

[71] Bostridge, *Witchcraft*, p. 190.
[72] Salmon, *A new abridgment*, p. 765.
[73] Edmund Jones, *A Relation of Apparitions of Spirits, in the Principality of Wales* (Trevecca, 1780), p. 12.

publicly reiterated the complaint again in 1744 and finally in 1762–63.[74] Peter Maxwell-Stuart has quite rightly noted, though, that the Seceders were motivated as much by ecclesiastical politics as theology.[75]

It is difficult to generalise about the Catholic response to the Witch-craft Act for obvious reasons. One of the few Catholics to air an opinion on the subject was the priest Simon Berington (1680–1755), whose views were influenced by his widely-shared abhorrence of Deists, freethink-ers and other such "modern infidels". In a discourse upholding spirit intervention in human affairs, he observed:

> Tis pity but our prudent Legislature had consulted some learned natu-ralists, when they forbid all Prosecutions for Witchcraft; by which the Generality of the World may think that they deny all Operations of evil Spirits. Some of our Right Reverend Bishops might have informed them, that they cannot believe the Bible, if they deny all Operations of Spirits, both good and bad.[76]

More influential was a hardcore strain of High Anglican clergymen, primarily Tory but also some Whigs, who were no doubt privately and occasionally publicly unhappy about the repeal. Malcolm Gaskill has observed that some Anglican intellectuals, who subscribed to the campaign against popular 'superstition', as embodied in the clause to prosecute 'pretended' witchcraft, were nevertheless "ambivalent about the repeal because of the religious battle to be fought with Free Think-ers, deists and nonconformists."[77] The Somerset rector and staunch Whig Arthur Bedford (d. 1745) was one such character who, from his published criticisms of Newtonianism and denunciations of the language of diabolism promoted by the theatre, would probably have privately had reservations about repeal. Bedford may have rejected the power of the Devil to directly intervene in human affairs, but he feared that the playful mockery of witchcraft on stage could actually promote a pernicious familiarity with the Devil, and consequently weaken popular

---

[74] *Act, Declaration and Testimony for the Doctrine, Worship, Discipline and Government of the Church of Scotland* (Edinburgh, 1737), p. 86; *Acts of the Associate Presbytery* (Edinburgh, 1744), p. 109; *Acts of the Associate Presbytery* (Glasgow, 1762–63), p. 34.

[75] Peter Maxwell-Stuart, 'Witchcraft and Magic in Eighteenth-Century Scotland', p. 92.

[76] Simon Berington, *Dissertations in the Mosaical Creation* (London: published by the author, 1750), p. 217.

[77] Gaskill, *Crime and Mentalities*, p. 117.

resistance to his inspiration.[78] Bedford was by no means a maverick and it is worth pointing out that, in the year of the Witchcraft Act, a Church of England catechism was still emphasising the dangers of satanic influence. In response to the question "How are you to renounce the Devil in Person?" the catechist was to answer:

> I am to live in a State of War, Defiance, and Opposition against him, and all his real, or pretended Confederates and Adherents, as Witches, Conjurers, Sorcerers, Diviners, Soothsayers, Augurs, Necromancers, Prognosticators, and Fortune-tellers; so as never to consult with, or encourage them, but punish and suppress them to the utmost of my Power.[79]

After 1736, though, few Anglican clergymen could express themselves as freely as Francis Bragge had done in 1712 in defending the conviction of Jane Wenham.[80] Once the secular authorities had labelled witchcraft a mere pretence, Anglican clerical disquiet on the subject was effectively consigned to private or anonymous discourse. It is telling that in a flurry of publications debating the reality of possession that appeared in 1737 the debate was kept strictly in a Biblical context.[81]

One of the few outlets for Anglican venting of witchcraft belief, albeit from the point of view that witchcraft had existed but had now ceased, were the periodic debates over the relaxation of restrictions against Catholics and Dissenters.[82] The link was explicitly made by the chaplain Philip Withers in his attack on a parliamentary motion to repeal the Test and Corporation Acts in 1790. "Let the law be abrogated, and Popery encouraged," he warned, "and I pledge my life that witches and wizards will again abound in every Town and Village in the kingdom. Popery is the parent of superstition. The Miracles and Legends of the Saints have a direct tendency to prepare the minds of the multitude for witchcraft, fortune-telling, and every absurdity under Heaven." If this were to happen, then the repeal of the Witchcraft Act

---

[78] See Jonathan Barry, 'Hell upon Earth or the Language of the Playhouse' in *Languages of Witchcraft: Narrative, Ideology and Meaning in Early Modern Culture*, ed. by Stuart Clark (Basingstoke: Macmillan 2001), pp. 139–59. See also the *New DNB* entry for Bedford.

[79] Thomas Bishop, *A Plain and Practical Exposition of the Catechism of the Church of England* (London, 1736), p. 36.

[80] My thanks to Simon Walker for pointing out the common confusion between the Rev. Francis Bragge and his son of the same name.

[81] See, for example, Thomas Church, *An essay towards vindicating the literal sense of the demoniacks* (London, 1737); Leonard Twells, *An answer to the enquiry into the meaning of Demoniacks in the New Testament* (London, 1737).

[82] See Bostridge, *Witchcraft*, pp. 183, 195–96.

would be regretted. Although he admitted there may "be no present pretenders to sorcery, or the black art…The time may arrive when it [the Act] may be again useful. And this reasoning is decisive against the abrogation of all ancient penal statutes".[83] A similar view was expressed anonymously in a pamphlet denouncing the belated repeal of Elizabethan Irish Statute against witchcraft in 1821.[84]

In the secular, social sphere the only definable group to be identified as opponents of the Witchcraft Act were the provincial squire-Justices—at least that is how they were portrayed by satirists and novelists. Addison had poked fun of the 'superstitious' Tory squirearchy in his *Spectator* stories of Sir Roger de Coverley and his quandary over a local witch, and others painted similar, though less affectionate portraits of the rustic gentry. The humorous playwright Thomas Baker characterised the backwardness of the magistracy in term of their witch belief. One of the characters in his *Tunbridge-Walks*, referring to the fate of another's daughter, remarks, "I warrant you'd match her to a Country Justice, that like some of our modern Commissioners, has no more Sense than to commit Old Women for Witchcraft, or some blockedly Mayor of a Corporation."[85] Written later in the century, John Trusler's novel, *Modern Times*, contains a dialogue between a parish clerk whose wife is bewitched by a local 'hag' and a country squire-Justice. The Justice bemoans his inability to help, complaining: "If our wiseacres in London had not repealed the act against witchcraft, I could have made an example of her; but, as it is, we can do nothing."[86] The scholar Richard Bentley, in an influential defence of the Church and critique of the work of the freethinking deist Anthony Collins, which was first published in 1713 and had reached its seventh edition in 1737, concurred that witchcraft had ceased, but could not help observing that "fewer of the Clergy give in to particular Stories of that kind, than of the Commonalty or Gentry."[87] To what extent the stereotype was justified

---

[83] Philip Withers, *Theodosius; Or a Solemn Admonition to Protestant Dissenters, on the Proposed repeal of the Test and Corporation Acts* (London, 1790), p. 63.

[84] *Antipas: a solemn appeal to the Archbishops and Bishops with reference to several Bills* (London, 1821).

[85] Thomas Baker, *Tunbridge-Walks: or, the Yeoman of Kent* (London, [1703] 1736), p. 27.

[86] John Trusler, *Modern Times, or, the Adventures of Gabriel Outcast* (London, 1785), III, pp. 149–50.

[87] Richard Bentley, *Remarks upon a late Discourse of Free-Thinking* (London, 1713), p. 33.

is, of course, difficult to assess, though the point has already been made that the last of the indictments for witchcraft could not have occurred without the sympathies of the magistracy. Despite being the author of the respected *Historical Antiquities of Hertfordshire*, Henry Chauncy, the magistrate in the Wenham affair, was, perhaps, an enduring inspiration for the satirical stereotype. The Worcestershire justice John Goodere was, though, far more of an embarrassment to the reputation of the country justice. Not only did he attend the swimming of a witch in 1716 but afterwards he stripped naked, swam around the ducking pool, and on getting out made obscene invitations to the women present.[88]

The Impact of the Act

Samuel Johnson famously asserted that witchcraft had ceased, "and therefore an act of parliament was passed to prevent persecution for what was not witchcraft. Why it ceased, we cannot tell".[89] These words, spoken at a dinner party in 1773, were in response to comments made by the lawyer and Scottish antiquary Andrew Crosbie (1736–85). Crosbie rejected the possibility that evil spirits had any power over natural forces, for God would not allow it. To believe that witches could perform the evils attributed to them was, therefore, blasphemy. Thankfully, he remarked, "an act of parliament put an end to witchcraft." Crosbie's perception that the Witchcraft Act actually helped dispel the belief in witchcraft was also shared by Peter Annet (1693–1769), one of the most outspoken critics of Christian supernaturalism in eighteenth-century England. In 1747 he observed: "How many People have been punished and put to Death for Witchcraft? And when there was a Law against it, people believed it; but now that Law is annulled, there is no Witchcraft to be found".[90] For Annet, then, witchcraft was merely a chimera generated by legislation, and therefore once the concept was finally rejected by the legislature people would see there was no justification for their belief, and so it would quickly dwindle. This was also pretty much the view of Walter Scott, writing with greater hindsight:

---

[88] Norma Landau, *The Justices of the Peace, 1679–1760* (Berkeley: University of California Press, 1984), p. 91.

[89] James Boswell, *The Journal of a Tour to the Hebrides* (London, 1785), p. 40.

[90] Reprinted in Peter Annet, *A Collection of the Tracts of a Certain Free Thinker* (London, *c.* 1750), p. 138.

"Since that period witchcraft has been little heard of in England", he confidently asserted, as "the rabble have been deprived of all pretext to awaken it by their own riotous proceedings."[91]

They were all wrong of course. Their confidence in the trickle-down effect of the Enlightenment, and their lack of understanding of popular beliefs—something not usually said of Walter Scott—blinkered them to the pervasive fear of witches amongst the poor and humble in society. Only months after the repeal Joseph Juxon, vicar of Twyford, Leicestershire, publicly reproved his parishioners for swimming a suspected witch, and numerous other violent expressions of communal and individual witch belief occurred over the next two centuries.[92] One of the pioneering historians of English witchcraft, Wallace Notestein, thought that the Witchcraft Act led to an increase in illegal popular justice enacted against witches, but there is no evidence to suggest that such incidents increased *because* of the decriminalisation of witchcraft.[93] After all, the courts had never been the main way of dealing with suspected witches. Both before and after 1736 counter magic, whether employed by cunning-folk or otherwise, provided the usual means of identifying, proving and punishing supposed witches.

As to the efficacy of section four of the Witchcraft Act, largely for the reason just mentioned, it was a complete failure. Christina Larner noted that it was hardly, if ever, implemented in Scotland during the eighteenth century, partly because the Scottish penal system was not equipped to carry out the required punishments for "pretenders to witchcraft". There were no proper institutions to imprison convicts for the length of a year, no pillories and no quarter days.[94] One of the first records of its enactment in Scotland was the prosecution of the cunning-woman Jean Maxwell in 1805.[95] In 1822 a cow and horse doctress

---

[91] Walter Scott, *Letters on Demonology and Witchcraft* (London: Routledge, [1830] 1884), p. 221.

[92] Joseph Juxon, *A Sermon Upon Witchcraft. Occasion'd by a Late Illegal Attempt to Discover Witches* (London, 1736). For numerous examples of violence against suspected witches see Davies, *Witchcraft, magic and culture*, chs 2 and 4; Davies, *A People Bewitched*, ch. 5.

[93] Wallace Notestein, *A History of Witchcraft in England* (New York: Russell & Russell, [1911] 1965), p. 315.

[94] Larner, *Enemies of God*, p. 78.

[95] *Remarkable Trial of Jean Maxwell, the Galloway Sorceress* (Kirkcudbright, 1805). The detailed indictment is reprinted in John Maxwell Wood, *Witchcraft and Superstitious Record in the South-Western District of Scotland* (Wakefield: EP Publishing, [1911] 1975), pp. 99–110. A summary can be found in Cowan and Henderson, 'The Last of the Witches?', pp. 212–13.

named Isabella Whitefield, of Invergordon, was similarly prosecuted.[96] Prosecutions in England were hardly frequent during the eighteenth century, but searches through newspapers and quarter sessions records are beginning to reveal a pattern of sporadic indictments under the Act. A fortune-teller named Elizabeth Fowl was prosecuted under the Act at the Devon Assizes in 1739, and in 1787 one Robert Barrett, of Sculcoates, was prosecuted before the East Riding Quarter Sessions for pretending to detect the whereabouts of stolen goods.[97] It would seem, though, that the Vagrancy Act was more frequently invoked, perhaps because there was a degree of judicial sensitivity about dealing with 'witchcraft' even if it was only 'pretence'. Anyone hoping that the Witchcraft Act would lead swiftly to the widespread suppression of cunning-folk and fortune-tellers was to be disappointed. Nine years after the passing of the Act an essayist complained: "I am assur'd that there are Persons at this Day, who, in defiance of the Laws, assume the Characters of Conjurers, or Cunning-Men; and that many or so weak, especially among the Fair Sex, as to consult and pay them".[98] Court records and ethnographic sources show that the same still held true a century and more later.[99]

As is well known, the last person to be prosecuted under the Act was the medium Helen Duncan in 1944.[100] A few years later, the concept of 'witchcraft' was finally expunged from the statute books with the passing of the Fraudulent Mediums Act of 1951. The last legal link with the era of the witch trials was broken. The 1736 Act had remained law for 215 years but had become an anachronism and an embarrassment. The punishment of the pillory, as laid out in section four of the Act, had been abolished back in 1837. Social legislation and the rise of the welfare state had diminished authoritarian concerns regarding vagrancy. By the Second World War cunning-folk, who the 1736 Act had redefined as 'pretend' witches, had disappeared as misfortune ceased to be explained in terms of witchcraft. With spiritualism receiving support from sections of both the middle and working classes, and with

---

[96] National Archives of Scotland AD14/22/71.

[97] Owen Davies, 'Newspapers and the Popular Belief in Witchcraft and Magic in the Modern Period', *Journal of British Studies*, 37 (1998), p. 142; East Riding QSF/316/B/1, QSF/319/F/3. For other examples see Davies, *Cunning-Folk*, pp. 22–23.

[98] *The London Magazine* (January 1745), p. 36.

[99] See Davies, *Cunning-Folk*.

[100] See Malcolm Gaskill, *Hellish Nell: Last of Britain's Witches* (London: Fourth Estate, 2001).

fortune-telling being absorbed into modern mass culture in the form of
newspaper horoscopes, the patrician concerns that had shaped section
four of the 1736 Act were thoroughly undermined. Consequently the
question of 'pretence' became all the more difficult to determine—as
the subsequent redundancy of the Fraudulent Mediums Act proved. The
1604 Act was repealed when the majority of the population continued
to fear witches. The 1736 Act was repealed when witches, however
defined, ceased to worry the popular consciousness.

APPENDIX I

THE WITCHCRAFT ACT OF 1563 (5 ELIZ I, C. 16.)[1]

St.33 H.VIII.
c.8. against
Witchcraft,
repealed by the
Operation of
Stat 1 E.VI.
c.12.

An Act agaynst Conjuracions[2] Inchantmentes and Witche-craftes.[3]

WHERE at this present, there ys no ordinarye ne condigne Punishement provided agaynst the Practisers of the wicked Offences of Conjuracions and Invocacions of evill Spirites, and of Sorceries Enchauntmentes Charmes and Witchecraftes, the wch Offences by force of a Statute made in the xxxiij yere of the Reigne of the late King Henry the Eyghthe were made to bee Felonye, and so continued untill the sayd Statute was repealed by Thacte[4] and Statute of Repeale made in the first yere of the Reigne of the late King Edwarde the vj^th; sythens the Repeale wherof many fantasticall and devilishe persons have devised and practised Invocacions and Conjuracions of evill and wicked Spirites, and have used and practised Wytchecraftes Enchantementes Charms and Sorceries, to the Destruccioon of the Persons and Goodes of their Neighebours and other Subjectes of this Realme, and for other lewde Intentes and Purposes contrarye to the Lawes of Almighty God, to the Perill of theyr owne Soules, and to the great Infamye and Disquietnes

---

[1] From *Statutes of the Realm* (London, 1819), IV, Part 1, p. 446. The earlier Henrician Act of 1542 (33 Hen. VIII, c. 8) can be found in *Statutes of the Realm* (London, 1819), III, p. 837, and is also given in *Witch Hunting and Witch Trials*, ed. by C. L'Estrange Ewen (London: Kegan Paul, Trench, Turner & Co., 1929), p. 13; *Witchcraft in England 1558–1618*, ed. by Barbara Rosen (Amherst: University of Massachusetts Press, 1991), pp. 53–54; and *Witchcraft and Society in England and America 1550–1750*, ed. by Marion Gibson (London: Continuum, 2003), pp. 1–2. It was repealed by 1 Edw. VI, c. 12 in 1547.

[2] Contractions have been given in full, as it is impossible to reproduce the old-fashioned contraction marks using modern computer typesetting, and it does not seem desirable to reproduce words such as person as "pson" without clearly indicating, as the original does, that this is a contraction.

[3] In these transcriptions all long "s"s have been modernised to a capital or lower case "s" as best seems to fit the sense. Original punctuation is maintained.

[4] Contracted form of "the act".

Persons using
any Invocations
of Spirits what-
ever, or practis-
ing Witchcraft,
&c. whereby
Death shall
ensue, declared
Felons without
clergy.

of this Realme: For REFORMACION wherof bee it enacted by
the Quenes Matie wth thassent[5] of the Lordes Spirituall and Temporall and the Commons in this presente Parliament assembled,
and by thaucthoritee[6] of the same, That yf any person or persons
after the first daye of June nexte comming, use practise or exercise
any Invocacions or Conjuracions of evill and wicked Spirites, to
or for any Intent or Purpose; or els if any person or persons after
the said first daye of June shall use practise or exercise any Witchecrafte Enchantment Charme or Sorcerie, wherby any person
shall happen to bee killed or destroyed, that then aswell every
suche Offendo^{r} or Offendo^{rs} in Invocacions and Conjuracions
as ys aforesayd, their Concello^{rs} & Aidours, as also every suche
Offendo^{r} or Offendo^{rs} in Witchecrafte Enchantement Charme or
Sorcerie whereby the Deathe of anny person dothe ensue, their
Aidours and Concello^{rs}, being of either of the said Offences laufully convicted and attainted, shall suffer paynes of Deathe as
a Felon or Felons, and shall lose the Priviledg and Benefite of
Sanctuarie & Clergie: Saving to the Wief of such persone her
Title of Dower, and also to the Heyre and Successour of suche
person his or theyr Tytles of Inheritaunce Succession and other
Rightes, as thoughe nu suche Attayndour of the Auncestour or
Predecessour had been hadd or made.

Penalty on
practising
Witchcraft, &c,
to the Bodily
Harm of any
one; First
Offence, One
Year's Impri-
sionment and
Pillory; Second
Offence, Felony
with Clergy.

II. And further bee yt enacted by thaucthoritee aforesayd, That if
any person or persons, after the saide first daye of June nexte com-
myng, shall use practise or exercyse any Wytchecrafte Enchaunte-
ment Charme or Sorcerie, wherby any person[7] shall happen to
bee wasted consumed or lamed in his or her Bodye or Member, or
wherby any Goodes or Cattelles of any person shalbee destroyed
wasted or impayred, then every suche Offendour or Offendours
their Councelloures and Aydoures, being therof laufully convicted,
shall for his or their first Offence or Offences, suffer Imprisment
by the Space of one whole Yere, w^{th}out Bayle or Mayneprise,[8]

---

[5] Contracted form of "the assent".
[6] Contracted form of "the authority".
[7] Note in this case contracted as "pon" as opposed to usual "pson".
[8] Neil Corre and David Wolchover in *Bail in Criminal Proceedings*, 3rd edn
(Oxford: Oxford University Press, 2004) note that bail and mainprise came to
be used interchangeably, as appears to be the case here, although Matthew Hale
noted technical differences between the two, see *Pleas of the Crown*, 2 vols (London,

and once in every Quarter of the said Yere, shall in some Market Towne, upon the Market Daye or at such tyme as any Fayer shalbee kepte there, stande openly upon the Pillorie by the Space of Syxe Houres, and there shall openly confesse his or her Erroure and Offence; and for the Seconde Offence, being as ys aforesayd laufully convicted or attaynted shall suffer Deathe as a Felon, and shall lose the Privilege of Clergie and Sanctuarye: Saving to the Wief of suche person her Title of Dower, and also to theire[9] & Sucesso[r] of suche person, his or their Titles of Inheritance Succession and other Rightes, as thoughe no suche Attandor of Thancesto[r] or Predecesso[r] had beene hadde or made.

Peers shall be tried by Peers.

II.[10] Provided alwaies, That yf the Offendour, in any of the Cases aforesayd for whiche the paynes of Deathe shall ensue, shall happen to bee a Peere of this Realme, then his Triall thereyn to be hadd by hys Peeres, as yt ys used in cases of Felonye or Treason and not otherwyse.

Penalty on practising Witchcraft, &c. to discover Treasure, or to provoke unlawful Love, &c. First Offence, One Year's Imprisonment and Pillory: Second Offence, Forfeiture of Goods and Imprisonment for Life.

III. And further to thintent that all maner of practise use or exercise of Witchecrafte Enchantement Charme or Sorcerye shoulde bee from hensforthe utterly avoyded abolished and taken away; Bee it enacted by thaucthoritee of this presente[11] Parliament. That yf any person or persons shall from and after the sayd first daye of June nexte coming, take upon him or them, by Witchecrafte Enchantement Charme or Sorcerie, to tell or declare in what Place any Treasure of Golde or Sylver shoulde or might bee founde or had in the Earthe or other secret Places, or where Goodes or Thinges lost or stollen should bee founde or becume, or shall use or practise anye Sorcerye Enchantement Charme or Witchcrafte, to thintent to provoke any person to unlaufull love, or to hurte or destroye any person in his or her Body, Member or Goodes; that then every suche person or persons so offending, and being therof laufully convicted, shall for the said offence suffer Imprysonement by the space of One whole yere w[th]out Bayle or Mayneprise, and

---

1736), II, p. 140. James Stephen described the differences as "very obscure", see *A History of the Criminal Law of England*, 3 vols (London, 1883), I, p. 241.

[9] Contracted form of "the heir".
[10] Continued.
[11] Note in this case contracted as "pnte".

once in every Quarter of the said yere, shall in some Market Towne, upon the Marcket Daye or at such tyme as any Fayer shall bee kepte there, stande openly upon the Pillorie by the space of Six Houres, and there shall openly confesse his or her Error and Offence; And yf anye person or persons, beyng once convicted of the same Offences as ys aforesayd, doo eftesones perpetrate and committ the lyke Offence, that then every suche Offendour beyng thereof the seconde tyme convicted as ys aforesaid, shall forfaitee unto the Quenes Majestie her heires and successoures, all his Goodes and Cattelles and suffer Imprysonement during Lyef.

N. B. The 1580 *Act against seditious words and rumours uttered against the Queen's most excellent Majesty* prohibited enquiring about the date of Queen Elizabeth I's death by astrology, prophecy, witchcraft, conjuration, or any like means.[12]

---

[12] See 23. Eliz., c. 2. in *Statutes of the Realm*, IV, Part 1, p. 659. The relevant part of the text is also given in *Witchcraft in England*, pp. 56–57, and *Witch Hunting and Witch Trials*, p. 18.

APPENDIX II

THE WITCHCRAFT ACT OF 1604 (1 JAS. I, C. 12.)[1]

A new Act dealing with witchcraft entered the House of Lords on 2 March 1604 and was referred to a committee on 29 March, which met at 2 pm on the following Saturday in the Outward Chamber.[2] On 2 April it was noted that "The Bill, intituled An Act concerning Conjuration, Witchcraft and dealing with Evil and Wicked Spirits, having been considered of by the committees, and the same by them found to be imperfect, the said Committees thought meet to frame a new Bill instead thereof, bearing the same Title, which new Bill (together with the former) was brought into the House by the Earl of Northumberland".[3] On 9 May it was "returned to the House [...] with certain Ammendments thought meet to be added; which Ammendments were presently Twice read, and thereupon the Bill appointed to be ingressed".[4] It was read in the House of Commons for the first time on 11 May.[5] It was passed by the Commons and returned to the Lords a month later.

---

[1] The text is taken from *The Lawes against Witches, and Conivration* (London, 1645), pp. 2–3, except in two places where we have followed the text given in *The Statutes of the Realm* (London, 1819), VI, Part 2, pp. 1028–29. In the instances where the latter is followed, the differences are noted. Given the very minor differences between the two sources, *The Lawes against Witches* is preferred as although it is not a legal source book there are no major discrepancies with the legal text (the differences appear to be two missing letter in *Lawes*), it is of an earlier date than *The Statutes of the Realm* and the spelling and punctuation are closer to those we currently use. The headings and marginalia are taken from *The Statutes of the Realm*. *The Lawes against Witches* heads it as "Anno primo Iacobi Regis, Cap.12.// The penalty for practising of Invocations, or Conjurations, & c." *Statutes at Large*, ed. by Danby Pickering (Cambridge, 1765), VII, p. 89, only gives a brief description of the act as it had been repealed at that time.

[2] *The Journal of the House of Lords*, II, p. 269, col. 1. The committee consisted of the Earls of Northumberland, Shewsbury, Worcester, Hartford, and Northampton; The Bishops of London, Durham, Winchester, Rochester, Lincoln, Worcester, St Davies, Chester, Carlisle, Ely, Peterborough and Hereford; and Lords Zouche, Mountegle, Sheffield, Cronwell, Evre, Effingham, Chandos, Burghley, Norris, Sydney, Knollys, Wotton, Russell, Gray, Petre, and Spencer. Also present in attendance to the Lords were the Lord Chief Justice of the Common Pleas, Lord Chief Baron, Mr Justice Yelverton, Mr Justice Williams, Mr Sergeant Crooke, Mr Attorney General, and Sir John Tyndall.

[3] Ibid., II, p. 270, col. 1.

[4] Ibid., II, p. 293. col. 1.

[5] *The Journal of the House of Commons*, I, p. 207, col. 2.

AN ACTE against Conjuration Witchcrafte and dealinge with evill and wicked Spirits.

5 Eliz. c. 16. repealed.

BE it enacted by the King our Soveraigne Lord; the Lords Spirituall and Temporall, and the Commons in this present Parliament assembled, and by the authority of the same, that the Statute made in the fifth yeare of the Reigne of our late Soveraigne Lady of most Famous and Happy memory, Queen *Elizabeth*, Entituled, *An Acte againste Conjurations, Inchantments and Witchcraftes*; be from the Feast of Saint *Michael* the Archangel next comming, for and concerning all offences to bee committed after the same Feaste, utterly repealed.

II. Invoking or consulting with Evil Spirits, taking up Dead Bodies, & c. for the purposes of Witchcraft, & c. or practising Witchcraft, & c. to the Harm of others, declared Felony without Clergy.

And for the better restraining of said offences, and more severe punishing the same, be it further Enacted by the Authority aforesaid; That if any person or persons, after the said Feast of St. *Michael* the Archangell next comming, shall use, practise, or exercise any invocation or conjuration of any[6] evil and wicked spirit: or shall consult, covenant with, entertaine, imploy, feed, or reward any evil and wicked spirit, to or for any intent or pupose; or take up any dead man, woman, or child, out of his, her, or their grave, or any other place where the dead body resteth; or the skin, bone, or any other part of any dead person, to be imployed, or used in any manner of *Witchcraft, Sorcery, Charme*, or *Inchantment*, or shall use, practise, or exercise, any *Witchcraft, Incantment, Charme* or *Sorcery*, whereby any person shall be Killed, Destroyed, Wasted, Consumed, Pined, or Lamed, in His or Her body, or any part therof; that then every such Offender, or Offenders, their Ayders, Abettors, and Counsellors, being of the said offences duly and lawfully Convicted and Attainted, shall suffer paines of death as a Felon or Felons, and shall lose the priviledge and benefit of Clergy and Sanctuary.

---

[6] Following *The Statutes of the Realm*, given as "an" in *The Lawes against Witches*, p. 2.

III. Penalty
on declaring
by Witchcraft
where Treasure,
& c. is hid-
den; procuring
unlawful Love;
or attempting
to hurt Cattle
or Persons: 1st
Offence Impris-
onment; 2^d
felony without
Clergy.

And further, to the intent that all manner of practise, use or exercise of *Witchcraft, Inchantment, Charme*, or *Sorcery*, should be from henceforth utterly avoided, abolished, and taken away: Be it Enacted by the Authority of this present Parliament, that if any person or persons, shall from and after the said Feaste of Saint *Michaell* the Archangell next comming, take upon him or them, by *Witchcraft, Inchantment, Charme*, or *Sorcery*, to tell or declare in what place any Treasure of Golde or Silver should or might be found or had in the earth, or other secret places; or where goods, or things lost, or stolne, should be found or become, or to the intent to provoke any person to unlawfull love, or whereby any Cattell, or Goods of any person shall be destroyed, wasted, or impaired; or to hurt or destroy any person in his or her body, although the same be not effected and done, that then all and every such person or persons so offending, and being therof lawfully convicted, shall for the said offence suffer imprisonment by the space of one whole year, without baile or maineprise;[7] and once in every quarter of the said year, shall in some Market-Town, upon the Market day, or at such time as any faire shall be kept there, stand openly upon the Pillory by the space of 6. hours, and there shall openly confesse his or her errour and offence.

Saving of Dower,
Inheritance,
& c.

And if any person or persons, being once convicted of the same offences as is aforesaid, do eftsoones perpetrate and commit the like offence, that then every such offender, being of any the said offences the second time lawfully, and duly convicted, and attainted as is aforesaid, shall suffer paines of death as a Felon, or Felons, and shall lose the benefit and priviledge of Clergy, and Sanctuary, saving to the wife of such person as shall offend in any thing contrary to this Act, her title of Dower, and also to the Heire and Successor of every such person, his, or their titles of inheritance, succession, and other rights, as though no such attainder of the Ancestor or Predecessor had been made: provided alwayes, that if the offender in any the cases aforesaid, shall happen to be a Peer of this Realm, then his tryall therein, to be had by his Peers, as it is used in cases of Felony or Treason, and not otherwise.

Peers shall be
trued by Peers

---

[7] See note 8.

APPENDIX III

CANON 72 OF THE CHURCH OF ENGLAND (1604)[1]

Ministri publicaieiunia, prophetias appellatas,[2] & exorcismos priuato ausu[3] celebrare prohibiti.[4]

NVllus Minister aut Ministri nisi mandatum & licentiam Episcopi Diœcesani priùs impetrauerint, ipsius manu & sigillo cōmunitam, solennia vlla ieiunia siue publicè, siue in priuatis ædibus indicent, aut celebrabunt, vel etiam eisdē scienter intererunt (exceptis ijs, quæ aut iam legibus instituta sunt, aut publica authoritate in posterum instituentur) sub pœna suspensionis pro delicto primo, excommunicationis pro secundo, & depositionis pro tertio. Nec quisquam Minister præsumet, absque licentia (vt dictum est) impetratâ, cōdicere, aut celebrare vlos conuentus pro concionibus, quæ vulgò Exercita, aut Propetiæ à nonnullis nuncupantur, in oppidis mercatorijs, aut alio quouis loco sub pœnis supradictis; nec sine simili licenctia tentabit sub quo libet prætextu siue possessionis, sive obses-

Ministers not to appoint publike or priuate Fasts, or Prophesies, or to exorcize, but by authority.

No Minister or Ministers shall without the Licence and direction of the Bishop of the Diocese first obtained and had vnder his and and Seale, appoint or keep any solemne Fasts, either publikely or in any priuate houses, other then such as by Law are, or by publike authoritie shall be appointed, nor shall be wittingly present at any of them, vnder paine of Suspension for the first fault, of Excommunication for the second, and of Deposition from the Ministry for the third. Neither shal any Minister not licensed, as is aforesaid, presume to appoint or hold any meetings for Sermons, commonly tearmed by some, Prophesies or Exercises, in Market townes or other places, vnder the sayd paines: Nor without Such License to attempt vpon any pretence whatsoeuer, either of Possession or

---

[1] Latin text transcribed from *Constitvtiones Sive Conones Ecclesiasticii* (London, 1604), sig. K ff. The vernacular is taken from the English equivalent *Constivtions and Canons Ecclesiasticall* (London, 1604), sig. M4 ff.

[2] Should properly be 'appellata'. Thanks to Dr Guido Giglioni for his invaluable assistance with the Latin text of the Act. The English translation which follows in the notes is his.

[3] Should properly be 'usu'.

[4] For comparison a modern translation from the Latin is given here: 72 Ministers are prohibited from celebrating public fasts, called prophesyings, and private exorcisms. With the exception of those fasts that have already been established by law or will be established by public authority in the future, no minister or ministers shall call or celebrate or even privy to any solemn fasts, regardless of whether they are held

sionis,[5] per ieiunium & precationes, dæmonia seu spiritus malos eijcere, atq; expellere, sub pœna imposturæ imputandæ, & depositionis a Ministerio sacro.

Obsession, by fasting any prayer to cast out any deuill or deuills, vnder paine of the imputation of Imposture, or Cousenage, and Deposition from the Ministerie.

---

in public or in private houses, under penalty of suspension with respect to the first offence, excommunication with respect to the second and deposition from office with respect to the third, unless they have first obtained the mandate and the permission of the diocesan bishop, validated by his signature and seal. Nor shall any minister, without having obtained a permission (as already said), dare to call or celebrate in market towns or in any other place any meeting for preaching, which are commonly called by some people 'exercises' or 'prophesyings', under the penalty already stated. Nor without any similar permission, under whatsoever pretext of either possession or obsession, shall he try to eject and expel demons or evil spirits by means of fast and prayer, under penalty of being charged with imposture and deposition from the office of holy ministry.

    [5] The concept of obsession, as distinct from possession, was probably introduced by John Deacon and John Walker in their reply to John Darrell *Dialogicall Discourse of Spirits and Divels* (London, 1601), and is certainly discussed there at some length.

APPENDIX IV

THE WITCHCRAFT ACT OF 1736 (9 GEO. II, C. 5.)[1]

An act to repeal the statute made in the first year of the reign of King *James* the First, intituled, *An act against conjuration, witchcraft, and dealing with evil and wicked spirits*, except so much thereof as repeals an act of the fifth year of the reign of Queen *Elizabeth, Against conjurations, inchantments, and witchcrafts*, and to repeal an act passed in the parliament of *Scotland* in the ninth parliament of Queen *Mary*, intituled, *Anentis witchcrafts*, and for punishing such persons as pretend to exercise or use any kind of witchcraft, sorcery, inchantment, or conjuration.

BE it enacted by the King's most excellent majesty, by and with the advice and consent of the lords spiritual and temporal, and commons, in this present parliament assembled, and by the authority of the same, That the statute made in the first year of the reign of King *James* the First, intituled, *An act against conjuration, witchcraft, and dealing with evil and wicked spirits*, shall, from the twenty fourth day of *June* next, be repealed and utterly void, and of none effect [set text in margin]except a clause repealing 5 Eliz. c. 16. [end margin text] (except so much thereof as repeals the statute made in the fifth year of the reign of Queen *Elizabeth*, intituled, *An act against conjurations, inchantments, and witchcrafts*.)

[margin: 1 James I. c. 12. repealed]

II. And be it further enacted by the authority aforesaid, That from and after the said twenty fourth day of *June*, the act passed in the parliament of *Scotland* in the ninth parliament of Queen *Mary*, intituled, *Anentis witchcrafts*, shall be and is hereby repealed.

[margin: The act in Scotland 9 Mariæ also repealed.]

---

[1] Taken from *The Statutes at Large*, XVII, pp. 3–4. At the time it was put onto the books, the act was published by John Baskett in London in 1736. However, no copy of this could be traced in England, despite a search by staff at the British Library.

After 24 June, 1736, no person to be prosecuted for witchcraft, & c.

III. And be it further enacted, That from and after the said twenty fourth Day of *June*, no prosecution, suit, or proceeding, shall be commenced or carried on against any person or persons for witchcraft, sorcery, inchantment, or conjuration, or for charging another with any such offence, in any court whatsoever in *Great Britain*.

Persons pretending to exercise witchcraft, tell fortunes, or by crafty science discover stolen goods...to be imprisioned for a year...be pillory'd,...and bound for good behaviour.

IV. And for the more effectual preventing and punishing of any pretences to such arts or powers as are before-mentioned, whereby ignorant persons are frequently deluded and defrauded; be it further enacted by the authority aforesaid, That if any person shall, from and after the twenty fourth day of *June*, pretend to exercise or use any kind of witchcraft, sorcery, inchantment, or conjuration, or undertake to tell fortunes, or pretend from his or her skill or knowledge in any occult or crafty science to discover where or in what manner any goods or chattles, supposed to have been stolen or lost, may be found; every person so offending, being thereof lawfully convicted on indictment or information in that part of *Great Britain* called *England*, or on indictment or libel in that part of *Great Britain* called *Scotland*, shall for every such offence, suffer imprisonment by the space of one whole year without bail or mainprize,[2] and once in every quarter of the said year in some market town of the proper county upon the market day there stand openly on the pillory by the space of one hour, and also shall (if the court by which such judgement shall be given shall think fit) be obliged to give sureties for his or her good behaviour, in such sum, and for such time, as the said court shall judge proper according to the circumstances of the offence, and in such case shall be further imprisoned until such sureties be given.

---

[2] See note 8.

INDEX